PENANCE AND THE ANOINTING OF THE SICK

THE HERDER HISTORY OF DOGMA

PENANCE
AND THE ANOINTING
OF THE SICK

BERNHARD POSCHMANN

Translated and revised
by Francis Courtney, S.J.

HERDER AND HERDER

1964

HERDER AND HERDER NEW YORK

232 Madison Avenue, New York 16, N. Y.

Original edition: "Buße und Letzte Ölung",

(Handbuch der Dogmengeschichte, vol. IV, part 3).

Herder, Freiburg im Breisgau.

Editors of the Handbuch der Dogmengeschichte:

Professor Michael Schmaus

Professor Aloys Grillmeier S. J.

  64 - 2137

De licentia superiorum ordinis

Nihil Obstat: Joannes M. T. Barton, S. T. D., L. S. S. Censor deputatus

Imprimatur: †Georgius L. Craven, Epus. Sebastopolis Vic. Cap.

Westmonasterii, die 16ª Julii, 1963

Library of Congress Catalog Card Number: 64-11976

First published in West Germany © 1964 Herder KG

Printed in West Germany by Herder

TRANSLATOR'S NOTE

THE AUTHOR of this book, Mgr. Bernard Poschmann (1878—1955), was a distinguished German theologian who taught at Braunsberg, 1910—1928, Breslau, 1928—1945, Münster, 1946—1948, and Königstein, from 1949. He had an international reputation as an historian of the sacrament of penance. On the occasion of his seventieth birthday in 1948 he was honoured by a bio-bibliographical notice in the *Theologische Revue,* 44 (1948) col. 109—111. Subsequently he published *Der Ablaß im Licht der Bußgeschichte* (1948), *Katholische Frömmigkeit* (1949) and *Buße und Letzte Ölung* (1951). The present volume is a translation of the last-mentioned work. For this English edition I have revised and enlarged the bibliographies with a view to incorporating the most important studies which have appeared since the publication of the original German edition. I have, however, left substantially intact the literature mentioned by Prof. Poschmann, as it is constantly referred to in the course of the book. Some footnotes have been added, and one or two slight additions made to the text. These are enclosed in square brackets and marked Tr. Chapters one and two and chapter five of the present work are a masterly summary of the much fuller treatment of the same subjects which is to be found in his three great works on the history of penance, mentioned below in the list of general literature, and in his *Der Ablaß im Licht der Bußgeschichte.* The value and influence of the present work, which has been out of print for some years in the original German edition, are well known to students. It is both an exact history of the administration and theology of penance, indulgences and the anointing of the sick, and a consistent interpretation of the historical development. The immediate effect, or *res et sacramentum,* of sacramental reconciliation or absolution is seen as reconciliation with the Church, which in turn is the sign and the pledge of reconciliation with God. This interpretation is undoubtedly in line with much recent general sacramental theology. A fuller treatment of this theory is to be found in an important article which Prof. Poschmann contributed to the *Münchener Theologische Zeitschrift,* 1 (1950) 12—30, entitled "Die innere Struktur des Bußsakramentes". Similarly in the treatment of indulgences the author does more than present an accurate account of the historical and theological development. He utilizes his profound knowledge of the sources to propose what he calls a first attempt at a positive advance in the doctrine of indulgences, one which he considers will dispel the doubts of those who are not attracted by a one-sided juridical presentation of the subject.

Heythrop College.

F. COURTNEY S. J.

CONTENTS

Penance

The Anointing of the Sick

ABBREVIATIONS

ACW   *Ancient Christian Writers*, ed. Quasten-Plumpe, Westminster (Md.); London 1946 ff.

AkK   *Archiv für katholisches Kirchenrecht* (Innsbruck) Mainz.

AL   O. Bardenhewer, *Geschichte der altkirchlichen Literatur*, 5 vols. Freiburg 1902—1932.

Ant   *Antonianum*, Rome.

BJRL   *Bulletin of the John Rylands Library*, Manchester.

BKV   *Bibliothek der Kirchenväter*, Kempten.

BLE   *Bulletin de littérature ecclésiastique*, Toulouse.

BM   *Benediktinische Monatschrift*, Beuron.

BZ   *Biblische Zeitschrift*, Paderborn.

CIC   *Codex Iuris Canonici.*

CC   *Corpus Christianorum*, series latina, Turnhout 1953 ff.

CR   *Clergy Review*, London.

CSEL   *Corpus scriptorum ecclesiasticorum latinorum*, Vienna.

DAFC   *Dictionnaire apologétique de la foi catholique*, Paris.

DBS   *Dictionnaire de la Bible*, Supplément, Paris 1928 ff.

Denz   Denzinger, *Enchiridion Symbolorum*, ed. 28, Freiburg im Br. 1952.

DTC   *Dictionnaire de théologie catholique*, Paris.

DTh   *Divus Thomas*, Fribourg.

DThP   *Divus Thomas*, Piacenza.

EThL   *Ephemerides Theologicae Lovanienses*, Louvain.

ErJb   *Eranos Jahrbuch*, Zürich.

GChS   *Die griechischen christlichen Schriftsteller*, Berlin.

Gr   *Gregorianum*, Rome.

HJ   *Historisches Jahrbuch der Goerresgesellschaft*, Munich.

IKZ   *Internationale kirchliche Zeitung*, Bern.

ITQ   *Irish Theological Quarterly*, Maynooth.

JLW   *Jahrbuch für Liturgiewissenschaft*, Münster.

JPhTh   *Jahrbuch für Philosophie u. spekulative Theologie*, Paderborn.

JTS   *Journal of Theological Studies*, London.

LThK   *Lexikon für Theologie u. Kirche*, ed. 2, Freiburg 1957 ff.

LZ   *Liturgische Zeitschrift*, Regensburg.

MSR   *Mélanges de science religieuse*, Lille.

MThZ   *Münchener theologische Zeitschrift*, Munich.

NRT   *Nouvelle revue théologique*, Tournai.

ABBREVIATIONS

PG   Migne, *Patrologia series graeca.*
PL   Migne, *Patrologia series latina.*
RACh   *Reallexikon für Antike u. Christentum,* Stuttgart 1950 ff.
RB   *Revue biblique,* Paris.
RCE   *Revue Catholique des Églises,* Paris.
RechSR *Recherches de science religieuse,* Paris.
REPTh   *Realenzyklopädie für protestantische Theologie,* Leipzig.
RGG   *Die Religion in Geschichte u. Gegenwart,* ed. 3, Tübingen 1956 ff.
RHE   *Revue d'histoire ecclésiastique,* Louvain.
RHLR   *Revue d'histoire et de littérature religieuse,* Paris.
RHR   *Revue d'histoire des religions,* Paris.
RQ   *Römische Quartalschrift,* Freiburg.
RSR   *Revue des sciences religieuses,* Strasbourg.
SB   H. L. Strack and P. Billerbeck, *Kommentar zum Neuen Testament* I—IV, Munich 1922—28; repr. 1956; V ibid. 1956; VI ibid. 1961.
Sch   *Scholastik,* Freiburg im Br.
SC   *Sources chrétiennes,* Paris 1947 ff.
ThG   *Theologie u. Glaube,* Paderborn.
ThQ   *Theologische Quartalschrift,* Stuttgart.
ThR   *Theologische Revue,* Münster.
ThW   *Theologisches Wörterbuch zum Neuen Testament,* ed. G. Kittel — G. Friedrich, Stuttgart 1933 ff.
TS   *Theological Studies,* Woodstock (Md.).
TU   *Texte u. Untersuchungen zur Geschichte der altchristlichen Literatur,* Leipzig-Berlin 1882 ff.
TZ   *Theologische Zeitschrift,* Basle.
VD   *Verbum Domini,* Rome.
VigChr *Vigiliae Christianae,* Amsterdam.
ZKG   *Zeitschrift für Kirchengeschichte,* Stuttgart.
ZkTh   *Zeitschrift für katholische Theologie* (Innsbruck) Vienna.
ZNW   *Zeitschrift für die neutestamentliche Wissenschaft,* Berlin.

Penance

GENERAL LITERATURE: J. Sirmond, *Historia paenitentiae publicae* (1659). D. Petavius, *De paenitentiae vetere in Ecclesia ratione* (1622). J. Morinus, *Commentarius historicus de disciplina in administratione sacramenti paenitentiae* (1651). H. Ch. Lea, *A History of Auricular Confession and Indulgences in the Latin Church,* 3 vols. (Philadelphia 1896). O. D. Watkins, *A History of Penance,* 2 vols. (London 1920; repr. New York 1960). P. Galtier, *De paenitentia : tractatus dogmatico-historicus* (Ed. noviss. Rome 1956). P. Anciaux, *Le sacrement de la pénitence* (Louvain 1957; Eng. tr., *The Sacrament of Penance* [London 1962]). E. Doronzo, *De paenitentia,* 4 vols. (Milwaukee 1949—1953). P. F. Palmer, *Sacraments and Forgiveness* (Westminster [Md.] 1959, London 1960). Z. Alzeghy, *De paenitentia Christiana* (Rome 1961). K. Rahner, "Buß-disziplin" and "Bußsakrament" in *LThK* (ed. 2, vol. 2, 1958). J. A. Jungmann, *Die lateinischen Bußriten in ihrer geschichtlichen Entwicklung* (Innsbruck 1932). Id., *The Early Liturgy to the Time of Gregory the Great* (London 1960). W. Telfer, *The Forgiveness of Sins* (London 1959). B. Poschmann, *Paenitentia secunda* (Bonn 1940 [Poschmann I]). Id., *Die abendländische Kirchenbuße im Ausgang des christlichen Altertums* (Munich 1928 [Poschmann II]). Id., *Die abendländische Kirchenbuße im frühen Mittelalter* (Breslau 1930 [Poschmann III]). M. Righetti, *Manuale di storia liturgica* IV : I sacramenti, I sacramentali (Milan 1959). *DTC* XII: "Pénitence", I, "Absolution", III, "Confession", XIV, "Satisfaction". *DAFC* III, "Pénitence". P. Meinhold, *Bußwesen in der christlichen Kirche* (*RGG* ed. 3 vol. 1). H. Edmonds — B. Poschmann, "Buße" etc. (*RACh* vol. 2).

AMONG HISTORIES OF DOGMA: J. Tixéront, *History of Dogmas* (Eng. tr. from 5th Fr. ed. 1923—1930); A. v. Harnack, *Outlines of the History of Dogma* (London 1960, 6th Germ. ed. 1922); R. Seeberg, *Grundriß der Dogmengeschichte* (ed. 7 1936, Eng. tr. from 5th Germ. ed. Grand Rapids 1952); F. Loofs, *Leitfaden zum Studium der Dogmengeschichte* (5th ed. K. Aland, 2 vols., 1950—1953). Much useful material also in B. Altaner, *Patrology* (Freiburg, Edinburgh, New York 1960, tr. from 5th Germ. ed. of *Patrologie,* 1958); J. Quasten, *Patrology* (Utrecht, to date 3 vols., 1950—1960). The most important specialist literature is indicated at the head of chapters and sections.

1

THE SACRAMENT of penance, in which personal penitence is combined with an ecclesiastical judicial process, is an institution of a very complex character. In addition to repentance, which as a basic Christian disposition is also indispensable for baptism, the sacrament of penance requires an external manifestation of repentance by an expiation corresponding to guilt. At this point it is the function of the Church to determine the measure of expiation by a judicial decision, and to absolve a sincerely repentant sinner. What is required, therefore, is the combined effect of very different factors. According as one or other of these factors is stressed, or, conversely, allowed to be relegated into the background, the structure of the whole is exposed to the possibility of a radical transformation. Penance presents different aspects according as attention is focussed on personal penance or on the rôle of the Church; and so does personal penance, according as attention is paid to interior repentance, to works of penance or to confession of sins.

In the nature of things penitential requirements are dependent on the customs, and on national and juridical traditions, as well as on the strength of faith at a given epoch. So, too, the way in which the Church organizes the judicial procedure for dealing with penitents is conditioned to a large extent by the age. It is, therefore, quite intelligible if the sacrament of penance in its administration and outward form has, even more than the other sacraments, undergone extensive development. What has been said of the practice applies also to the doctrine of penance. Corresponding to the manifold changes of form in the external administration of penance, there is a mass of theoretical problems. These are dependent on the various factors which in combination operate in the sacrament. For example, what degree of causality belongs to the individual factors in regard to the forgiveness of sins? What is the efficacy of contrition, of satisfaction, of confession? Above all, what is the relation of personal penitential effort to ecclesiastical forgiveness? How is the sacrament affected if one or other factor is defective? These problems were first posed systematically and in exact conceptual form by the schoolmen. In their essentials, however, they are in fact at the root of the early-Christian disputes over penance. These had as their immediate causes not theory but practice. The development of doctrine through dogmatic decisions of the Church has secured a settlement of the most important questions which affect practice, but there are others which still await a solution.

The starting-point for an historical account of the dogmatic development is the New Testament, for the sacrament of penance is specifically Christian in origin. A major difficulty in the way of a history of the dogma of penance is the sparseness and obscurity of the earliest source material. This explains why there are conflicting interpretations on the nature of penance precisely in reference to the first centuries. But even for the early medieval period, during which a fundamental transformation was completed in the procedure of penance, the sources leave much to be desired in respect of clarity.

A word about method. In the chronological exposition of the development our purpose is, in so far as the source material permits, to emphasize the features which are specially characteristic of the particular periods, and so to make possible a general appreciation of individual pieces of evidence. Reflection on the history enables us to distinguish in it four periods: 1. Christian antiquity (the first six centuries): the period of public penance. 2. The early middle ages: the gradual transition to private penance. 3. The early scholastic period to the Reformation: the formation of a theoretical doctrine of penance. 4. The period from the Council of Trent to the present day: problems still remaining after the doctrinal decisions of the Council. The exposition will be divided according to these periods. By way of an additional chapter, indulgences, which arose out of the medieval penitential procedure, will then be considered in their origin and development.

Chapter One

EARLY CHRISTIAN PENANCE

I. THE NEW TESTAMENT

LITERATURE: Introductions to the N. T.: *A. Robert and A. Feuillet, *Introduction à la Bible,* 2 vols. (Tournai 1959). *A. Robert and A. Tricot, *Initiation biblique* (ed. 3, Tournai 1954; Eng. tr., *Guide to the Bible,* vol. 1, ed. 2, New York 1960; vol. 2, 1955). P. Feine and J. Behm, *Einleitung in das Neue Testament* (ed. 9, Heidelberg 1950). M. Goguel, *Introduction au Nouveau Testament,* 4 vols. (Paris 1922—1927). K. Lake and S. Lake, *An Introduction to the New Testament,* (New York 1937). A. H. McNeile, *An Introduction to the Study of the New Testament* (ed. 2, rev. by C. S. C. Williams, Oxford 1953). *M. Meinertz, *Einleitung in das Neue Testament* (ed. 5, Paderborn 1950). W. Michaelis, *Einleitung in das Neue Testament* (ed. 2, Bern 1954). *A. Wikenhauser, *New Testament Introduction* (New York, Freiburg, Edinburgh 1959; Eng. tr. of *Einleitung in das Neue Testament* [ed. 2, 1956]).

COMMENTARIES: *A Catholic Commentary on Holy Scripture,* ed. B. Orchard and E. F. Sutcliffe (London 1953 — *CCHS*). *Etudes bibliques* (Paris from 1907 — *EB*). *Bible de Jérusalem* (Paris 1948—54, ed. 2 from 1957, single vol. ed. 1956 — *BJ*). *Black's New Testament Commentaries* (London from 1957 — *BNTC*). *Cambridge Greek Testament Commentary* (Gen. ed. C. F. D. Moule, London from 1955 — *CGTC*). *Commentaire du Nouveau Testament,* ed. P. Bonnard, O. Cullmann and others (Neuchâtel and Paris from 1949 — *CNT*). *Handbuch zum Neuen Testament,* ed. H. Lietzmann and now by G. Bornkamm (Tübingen from 1906 — *HNT*). *Herders theologischer Kommentar zum Neuen Testament* (Freiburg from 1953 — *HThK*). *Kritisch-exegetischer Kommentar über das Neue Testament* (Göttingen, 16 vols. often revised — Meyer). *Regensburger Neues Testament,* ed. A. Wikenhauser and O. Kuss (Regensburg, new editions of the 10 vols. in recent years — *RNT*). *Verbum salutis* (Paris, ed. J. Huby, new edition in progress ed. S. Lyonnet — *VS*).

BIBLICAL THEOLOGY: J. Guillet, *Thèmes bibliques* (ed. 2, Paris 1954). P. Feine, *Theologie des Neuen Testaments* (ed. 8, Berlin 1950). O. Kuss, *Die Theologie des Neuen Testa-*

---

* Introductions to the N. T., and N. T. commentaries by Catholic authors.

5

ments : Eine Einführung (ed. 2, Regensburg 1937). M. Meinertz, *Theologie des Neuen Testaments* (Bonn 1950). A. Richardson, *Introduction to the Theology of the New Testament* (London 1958). E. Stauffer, *New Testament Theology* (London 1955). C. R. Smith, *The Bible Doctrine of Sin* (London 1953).

SPECIAL STUDIES ON PENANCE IN N.T.: E. Roche, "Pénitence et conversion dans l'Evangile et la vie chrétienne" in *NRT* 74 (1957) 113—144. S. Lyonnet, "De natura peccati quid doceat N.T." in *VD* 35 (1957) 271 ff., 332 ff. K. Adam, "Zum außerkanonischen und kanonischen Sprachgebrauch von Binden und Lösen" in *ThQ* 96 (1914) 49—64; 161—197, (and in *Gesammelte Aufsätze* [Augsburg 1936] 17—52). G. Fitzer, "Die Sünde wider den Heiligen Geist" in *TZ* 13 (1957) 161—182. B. Collins, "Tentatur nova interpretatio Hebr. 5: 11 — 6: 8" in *VD* 26 (1948) 144—151. J. de la Potterie, "Le Péché, c'est l'iniquité" in *NRT* 78 (1956) 785—797. A. H. Dirksen, *The New Testament Concept of Metanoia* (Washington 1932). P. Galtier, "Le chrétien impeccable" in *MSR* 4 (1947) 127—154. Id., "La réconciliation des pécheurs dans la première épître à Timothée" in *RechSR* 39 (1951) 317—20. *Lumière et Vie* No. 47 (1960): "Conversion" (Studies in O.T. and N.T. theology by M-F. Lacan, Jacques Dupont, M.-E. Boismard, N. D. Mollat). A. Lefèvre, "Péché et Pénitence dans la Bible" in *La Maison-Dieu* 55 (1958) 7—22. A. E. Ruthy, "Buße und Bußlehre im N.T." in *IKZ* 44 (1954) 34—36. Id., "Zur neutestamentlichen Begründung des Bußsakramentes" ibid. 218—234. J. Schmitt, "Simples remarques sur le fragment Jo. XX 22—23" in *Mélanges Andrieu* (Strasbourg 1956) 415—423. F. Courtney, "Preliminary Considerations on the Sacrament of Penance" in *CR* 40 (1955) 513—519. B. Xiberta, *Clavis Ecclesiae* (Rome 1922). H. Windisch, *Taufe und Sünde im ältesten Christentum bis auf Origenes* (1908).

1. The Gospels

Penance and the forgiveness of sins are at the very centre of the preaching of Jesus. He entered on his messianic work with the appeal "repent and believe the Gospel" (Mk 1: 15) and he took leave of his disciples with the charge that "penance and the remission of sins should be preached in his name to all nations" (Lk 24: 47). The divine willingness to forgive the repentant knows no bounds (Lk 15:20 ff.). Faith and baptism do away with all sins (Mk 16: 16). All this is universally acknowledged as the clear teaching of the Gospel.

Not even those who fall away by sinning afresh after baptism are excluded from pardon. Jesus does indeed insist on a whole-hearted, irrevocable renunciation of evil on the part of sinners. They are now confronted with a sole alternative: either with

Christ or against him (Lk 9:62; 14:25). A merely passing conversion is of no avail (Mt 13:3ff.). The state of the recidivist is far worse than it was before his conversion (Mt 12:43ff.). Yet all this leaves untouched the possibility of a new conversion; for such is the weakness of man that a relapse can always occur, even where at first the will was most determined. Forgiveness is excluded only when a sinner impenitently hardens his heart against God, thus committing "the sin against the Holy Ghost" (Mt 12:31f. and par.). The idea, very prevalent among Protestant theologians, that Jesus did not envisage the possibility of a further repentance after baptism is untenable.[1] Against it is the immensity of the divine mercy on which Jesus laid such emphasis in his preaching, and also his attitude to the sinfulness with which he had to reckon everywhere, even among his closest followers (Mt 6:12; 7:11). Not even the infidelity and apostasy of his disciples were in his sight an impediment to their restoration to grace and to their vocation to leadership in the kingdom of God. Moreover, if the Father in heaven will forgive our sins in the same measure as we are ready to grant repeated forgiveness to our brethren (Mt 18:22, 35), then repeated acts of divine forgiveness are obviously presupposed.

Forgiveness, however, is not a matter which is concluded simply between God and man: it comes through the mediation of the Church, of which a Christian has become a member by baptism, and which by his sin he has dishonoured and defiled. Jesus expressly grants to the Church disciplinary power over believers who fall into sin (Mt 18:15—17). After a fruitless private admonition "in the sight of four eyes", or before two witnesses, the sinner is to be denounced to the Church, and, if he will not listen to this highest tribunal, he is to be treated "as the heathen and the publican". This means that in accordance

---

[1] Cf. the various manuals of the history of dogmas. H. Windisch's work, listed above, is a typical attempt to substantiate the so-called "theory of sinlessness" or "baptism theory".

7

with Jewish usage (cf. Jn 9: 22; 12: 42; 16: 1) he is to be excommunicated. Then, in confirmation of this ecclesiastical authority, the word of power is directed to the disciples in their capacity as the authoritative representatives of the Church: "Amen I say to you, whatsoever ye shall bind upon earth shall be bound in heaven; and whatsoever ye shall loose upon earth shall be loosed in heaven" (Mt 18: 18).[2] "Binding" and "loosing" are rabbinical expressions; they signify in the first place "to forbid" and "to permit", but they also have the secondary meaning "to impose the ban" and "to lift the ban". As our text is dealing with a case of punishment only this second meaning comes into question.[3] When, therefore, the disciples "bind", they exclude the guilty not only from the fellowship of the earthly Church, but also from the Kingdom of Heaven. "Loosing", on the other hand, has indirectly the sense of "forgiveness of sins", inasmuch as by the lifting or non-imposition of the penalty sin has no further consequences for men.

In non-metaphorical language forgiveness of sins is announced as an apostolic power in Jn 20: 21—23. Here the risen Saviour passes on to his disciples the mission which he himself has received from the Father. The structure of the sentence is very similar to that in the Matthaean passage. "Forgive" and "retain" are parallel to "bind" and "loose". In both places no limits are assigned to the plenitude of power which is conveyed: no sins are excluded from its scope.[4] In both texts the objective efficacy for the hereafter of the act of forgiveness is vividly expressed by the use of perfect passive verbal forms. We may leave on one side the question whether the disciples, as fully empowered by God, thereby grant pardon directly in his name; or whether, in

---

[2] On the authenticity of the passage see K. L. Schmidt, G. Kittel, *ThW* III (1938) 522 ff.

[3] *SB* (1922) 738 f. Further literature in Poschmann I 6, n. 1.

[4] It is for this reason that the Fathers have correctly applied the Johannine text both to the baptismal power of the Church (Cyprian, *Ep.* 69,11; 73,7) and also to the power of forgiving sins in penance (Origen, *De or.* 28,9; Ambrose, *De paen.* 1, 2, 6; *De Spir. S.* 3,18,137).

the first place, as the representatives of the Church, they only grant forgiveness on her part, which then has forgiveness from God as its certain result.[5] The biblical texts allow both interpretations. In any case Jesus has given power to the disciples to forgive sins with effect for the hereafter.

2. St. Paul

Penance plays an important part in the epistles of St. Paul, even though he only occasionally uses the word μετάνοια.[6] Like Jesus he insists on a thoroughgoing conversion (1 Cor 5:7f.; Rom 6: 2—12; 8: 5—13; Gal 2:19 f.). Yet for him sin remains a frightening power, even in the lives of the baptized. Confronted by it neither he nor the faithful can feel secure (1 Cor 4:4; 9:27; Phil 2:12). Constantly and insistently he warns them against it (Rom 6:12f.; 13:14; 1 Cor 6: 18f.; Col 3: 10; Eph 4: 24 etc.). And it is not only with the danger of sinning that he has to reckon. His catalogues of sins (Gal 5:19ff.; 1 Cor 6:9f.; Eph 5:3ff.; Col 3:5) are manifestly conditioned by actual moral failings of believers.[7] On a number of occasions he expressly reproves concrete lapses in the communities, such as dissensions, uncharitableness (1 Cor 3:3ff.; 11:18ff.), idleness (2 Thess 3:6ff.), and other "impure adulterous and wanton living" (2 Cor 12:21). Yet not even such backsliding Christians are lost. "For the grief that is according to God worketh repentance without regret,

---

[5] Thus first Fr. B. Xiberta in *Clavis Ecclesiae* 12. [Xiberta's conception has been adopted by Poschmann. Cf. esp. "Die innere Struktur des Bußsakramentes" in *MThZ* 1 (1950) 12—30. Reconciliation with the Church is considered as the *res et sacramentum* of penance. Similarly K. Rahner, *e.g.* in *Zur Theologie der Buße bei Tertullian,* Festschr. K. Adam, Düsseldorf 1952 (129—167). See also by the same author **Zur Theologie des Symbols* in *Schriften zur Theologie,* vol. IV (1960). For an account of the state of research on this question shortly after the appearance of the first edition of this book, see H. Weisweiler, "Ein Umschwung in der Erforschung der frühchristlichen Bußgeschichte" in *Scholastik* 28 (1953) 241—46. Tr.'s note.]

[6] 2 Cor 7:9f.; 12:21; Rom 2:4; 2 Tim 2:25.

[7] Cf. S. Wibbing, "Die Tugend- und Lasterkataloge im Neuen Testament" in Beih. z. *ZNW* 25 (1959). [Tr.'s note.]

unto salvation" (2 Cor 7:10). Christ, seated at the right hand of God and pleading for us, gives us assurance of forgiveness (Rom 8:34). For this reason all the Apostle's warnings to sinning believers are aimed at moving them to repentance. The theory of sinlessness finds no support in St. Paul. In addition to sincere conversion, penance also includes expiation. Judgement awaits sin, and judgement can only be averted if the sinner is chastised here on earth either by his own hand or by God (1 Cor 11:31f.). The "destruction of the flesh" is the way by which the "spirit may find salvation in the day of the Lord" (1 Cor 5:5). Penance is "sorrow that is according to God"; its fruits are goodness of will, holy fear, expiation, obedience (2 Cor 7:10f.; cf. 2:9). Fundamentally sin, and consequently penance, is something which concerns the Church too. She is responsible for the holiness of her members. Fraternal charity imposes the duty of admonishing one who errs (Gal 6:1f.; 2 Tim 4:2; 2:25), but where there is gross immorality severe proceedings must be taken against the offenders. The classical example is provided by the case of the incestuous man. Faced with this appalling crime, the community should have at once broken off all intercourse with the evildoer in obedience to an earlier instruction of the Apostle. This they had negligently omitted to do, and Paul now does it himself. Conscious of his union with them in spirit, he pronounces judgement along with them in the name of Jesus "to deliver up such a one to Satan for the destruction of the flesh, that his spirit may be saved in the day of the Lord" (5:3—5). The "delivering up to Satan", as the context indicates, as also does the traditional meaning of the term attested as early as Tertullian,[8] is nothing else than excommunication. It implies, however, that the person excommunicated is subjected to Satan's dominion more completely than before, and is punished by him with bodily and spiritual afflictions.[9] In 1 Tim 1:20, Paul

[8] *De pud.* 13.
[9] For other interpretations, ancient and modern (purely spiritual influence of Satan, possession, bodily death) see Poschmann I 27f.

makes use of the same formula in excommunicating Hymenaeus and Alexander who have made shipwreck of their faith, "in order that they may be taught not to blaspheme". The same procedure is attested without the use of the formula in 2 Thess 3:6, 14—16, except that in this less serious case the curative purpose and the maintenance of love are more emphasized. "And do not regard him as an enemy, but admonish him as a brother." Excommunication, or severance of relations with an evildoer, is simply the severest form of admonition. In Tit 3:10 the charge "give a heretic one warning, then a second, and after that avoid his company" corresponds perfectly with the directions in St. Matthew's gospel, 18:15—17.

From what has been said it follows that the exclusion of the sinner does not imply his final condemnation; its chief purpose is to promote his salvation. The question then arises, whether his pardon is something to be hoped for only from God in "the day of the Lord", or whether the Church too grants her pardon and reconciliation. The traditional view, supported by all the Fathers (except Tertullian in his Montanist period), by the medieval theologians, and until recently by more modern exegetes, finds this question settled in 2 Cor 2:5—11. In this text it sees attested the restoration of the incestuous man of 1 Cor 5. Contemporary opinion is rather more inclined to take the line that in 2 Cor there is question of an altogether different case, one involving a personal affront of the Apostle. Even so, the text retains its importance as evidence for ecclesiastical forgiveness. Paul, desirous of maintaining his authority, has required the community to assert itself against the offender. Now that satisfaction has been made him, he finds that "this punishment inflicted on him by so many" is sufficient, and that it is time "to pardon and comfort him" and to "assure him of love", "lest he be overwhelmed by excess of grief" (2:7—8). This can only mean that the faithful have broken off intercourse with him. The punishment has now served its purpose, which was to make him see reason and bring him to repentance. A prolongation of the

11

excommunication could only have harmful effects on his state of soul, with the result that he would be "overreached by Satan" (2: 11). For this reason the penitent must be restored to grace. To use a later terminology, reconciliation must follow excommunication. The procedure employed here as a matter of course, so to speak, is also obviously applicable to other similar cases (1 Cor 5: 5; 2 Thess 3: 14ff.; 1 Tim 1: 20). It is also presupposed in 2 Cor 12: 21, where the Apostle expresses the hope that on his next visit he will not have "to mourn" over those guilty of unchastity who have not yet done their penance. He expects, therefore, that by that time these sinners will once more have set right their relationship to the community.[10]

Ecclesiastical forgiveness is, therefore, attested by Paul. However, he provides no direct answer to the final and most important problem of the relationship of ecclesiastical to divine forgiveness. Nevertheless, he makes it quite clear that he attaches supratemporal consequences to the Church's measures in regard to a sinner. The excommunication of the incestuous man is a judgement which the community pronounces over him "in the name of Jesus" (1 Cor 5: 4). The effect of the judgement, "handing over to Satan", essentially exceeds the power of any human sentence. The same, then, must also hold good for the act of reconciliation with or reincorporation into the Church. If the Church is not just an external association, but, as the Apostle teaches, the body of Christ, the living instrument of his grace, the indispensably necessary society of salvation,[11] then it follows that expulsion from the Church, if deserved, and, conversely,

---

[10] See Poschmann I 35. [More exactly, St. Paul fears that they will not yet have put their relationship to the community in order. Cf. W. V.: "For I fear... when I come again... lest I should mourn over many that were in sin before, and have not repented of the uncleanness and impurity and licentiousness which they practised." Tr.'s note.]

[11] See vol. I, 4 of this series [as also A. Wikenhauser, *Pauline Mysticism* (New York, Edinburgh 1960); L. Cerfaux, *The Church in the Theology of St. Paul* (New York, Edinburgh 1959). For periodical literature, see B. M. Metzger, *Index to Periodical Literature on the Apostle Paul* (Grand Rapids 1960) 144f. Tr.'s note.]

readmission to it are of decisive significance. This conclusion is further justified by the fact that it is in harmony with the Gospel proclamation (Mt 18:18; Jn 20:23), and also with the claims of the Church which will soon be unmistakably manifest.

3. The Epistle to the Hebrews

This epistle only calls for special consideration in so far as a few texts in it have been made to serve as the principal proof for the "baptism theory". It is supposed that they absolutely exclude the possibility of penance to those who have lapsed from the faith. In fact, however, this interpretation is untenable.

In Heb 6:4—6 we read: "For it is impossible to renew again unto repentance those who have once been enlightened, and have tasted the heavenly gift... and then have fallen away; since they crucify again for themselves the Son of God, and make him a mockery." A careful exegesis, which takes account of the context, makes it clear that the author has no intention of rejecting as useless any eventual repentance on the part of an apostate. What he does say is that those people who have thrown away the blessings of salvation, and who make a mockery of the grace of the redemption, are impossible to convert once more. It is a question of the possibility of conversion, and not of whether the penance of the apostate is still of any profit to him if he is converted. It is a bad misunderstanding to confuse these two questions. All the text says is that those who have apostatized with full deliberation are in a state of obduracy, and normally indisposed for penance.[12]

No less mistaken is the exposition of another passage, 10:26 ff., in a sense which excludes the possibility of penance for Christians. "For if we sin willingly after having received knowledge of the truth, there remaineth no further sacrifice for sin; but only

---

[12] For further detail and the relevant literature see Poschmann I 39—43. [Also C. Spicq, *L' épître aux Hébreux* II 167—178 (*EB,* Paris 1953). Tr.].

a terrible expectation of judgement...." Almost always the phrase οὐκέτι περὶ ἁμαρτιῶν ἀπολείπεται θυσία is understood to mean that for "deliberate sinners" there is no question of a new sacrifice of Christ, which would make possible a renewal of forgiveness. In reality what we have is an allusion to the Old Testament law (Num 15:22—31), according to which unpremeditated offences are to be expiated by sin-offerings, whereas anyone who sins deliberately "with upraised hand" is a "blasphemer against the Lord", and must be ruthlessly exterminated. Now the author of the Epistle finds the condition of such a "deliberate sin" verified, if anywhere at all, in the apostate Christian who has "trodden under foot the Son of God... and has insulted the Spirit of grace" (10:29). Such a one is inevitably liable to judgement; but this is not because the sacrifice of Christ can be of no avail to him a second time, but by reason of his state of soul which is closed against the operation of grace. No "sin-offering" can help him. Judgement is the unavoidable consequence of fully deliberate separation from Christ. The problem of the dogmatic possibility of a renewed reception into grace, which was raised by the Novatianists and by modern historians of dogma, is very far from the mind of the author of the Epistle.[13] Chapter 12, v. 17 expresses the same idea as 10:26 f., but makes use of a different scriptural argument. For those who are tempted to fall away the terrifying example is adduced of Esau, who sold his birthright for a single dish and then "afterwards, when he wished to inherit the blessing, he was rejected: μετανοίας γὰρ τόπον οὐχ εὗρεν, καίπερ μετὰ δακρύων ἐκζητήσας αὐτήν". This text can indeed be lined up in favour of the theory of a single baptismal repentance if τόπος μετανοίας is understood in its obvious sense of the possibility of doing penance. However, that cannot be the meaning of the expression here. There is not a word in Scripture of any fervent striving after penance in the sense of conversion on Esau's part. What it does relate is simply

[13] Poschmann ibid. 44—48.

14

his attempt to secure the reversal of what had been done. Consequently μετάνοια must also be here understood in this sense, and translated with more recent authors: "found no possibility of reversing what had been done".[14] This text, also, then, is not concerned with the dogmatic possibility of penance.

From all this it follows that the sin which the Epistle to the Hebrews declares unforgivable is none other than deliberate renunciation of Christ, that is the sin against the Holy Ghost. By reason of the sacrifice of our High Priest which is forever efficacious, a Christian finds forgiveness for all other sins in the measure that he strives after it by repentance. He "who has been tried in every way, like ourselves" has "compassion on our infirmities", and so, we can "go, therefore, with confidence to the throne of grace, that we may obtain mercy, and find grace" (4:15, 16; cf. 5:2; 7:24f.).

4. The Catholic Epistles and the Apocalypse

In general we find confirmed in the writings of the original Apostles the conclusions we have drawn from Paul. Indeed, James and John provide a valuable supplement to them. The campaign against the sins of Christians is very wide in its scope. The tension between the ideal of sinlessness and the reality of life is very clearly revealed. Christians are "begotten by God through the word of truth" (Jas 1:18). Their business is to be "perfect and entire, failing in nothing" (1:4). Even more pointedly, John says "Whosoever is born of God committeth not sin: for his seed abideth in him, and he cannot sin, because he is born of God . . ." (1 Jn 3:9f.; cf. 2:8—11 etc.). In contrast to these texts, there is not merely the complaint that many Christians are unfaithful to their obligations, but the fact of a general sinfulness is established. James recognizes that "in many

---

[14] Thus B. F. Westcott, E. Riggenbach and O. Michel. Further details in Poschmann I 48—52.

things we all offend" (3:2). He campaigns against a sham Christianity that consists of words instead of deeds (1:22f.; 2:14f.). For John, in his war with heretical teachers, who do not admit Christ to be the Son of God, and who therefore deny sin and the need of forgiveness, the recognition of the universality of sin is an essential point of the faith. "If we say that we have no sin, we deceive ourselves, and the truth is not in us" (1 Jn 1:8).[15]

Thus sin is universal, but divine forgiveness is also universal if there is sincere repentance. Even the gravest sinner can count on forgiveness (Jas 1:21; 5:19f.). The deferment of the *Parousia* is only to be explained by the patience of the Lord who is "not willing that any should perish, but that all should return to penance" (2 Pet 3:9). John gives the reason for the mercy which is denied to none: "But if any man sin, we have an advocate with the Father, Jesus Christ the just. And he is the propitiation for our sins, and not for ours only, but also for those of the whole world" (1 Jn 2:1f.). The universality of forgiveness is not prejudiced by the distinction, so important for the later history of penance, between the "sin unto death" and the "sin not unto death", of which pair only the latter can be the object of efficacious prayer (1 Jn 5:16). The distinction does not signify the opposition between mortal sins and venial sins in the sense of later theology, according to which mortal sin destroys the life of grace, and venial sin does not. John concedes that "life" is also lost through the "sin not unto death", just as, according to him, it is restored through intercessory prayer. He has another kind of opposition in mind: the "sin unto death" has for its consequence final death, the "second death" (Apoc 2:11) or "eternal death" (*Barn.* 20, 1). Its distinctive sign is not the special gravity of the offence, but the fundamental falling away from

---

[15] The text refers indeed to all sins, even to those erased by baptism. That it also includes the sins of those already baptized is clearly shown by 2:1f. As the polemical reference of 1 Jn 1:8 was overlooked, the text has, since Augustine, been restricted to venial, unavoidable sins and interpreted to signify the same as Jas 3:2. Thus, also, contemporary dogmatic theologians generally.

16

Christ that is manifested in it, which makes men "children of the devil" (1 Jn 3:10). In other words, like the "unforgivable sin" of the Epistle to the Hebrews, it coincides with the "sin against the Holy Ghost" (Mt 12:31).[16]

If intercessory prayer is recommended as a means for securing forgiveness, this is because, in accordance with Pauline teaching, the sin of an individual affects the whole community. The sinner's own penitential zeal is obviously presupposed along with the intercessory prayer. In any case John promises that the prayer will certainly be heard (1 Jn 5:14f.). Even more explicitly James does the same in the classical text on the anointing of the sick (5:14—16) when he ends the directive for the presbyters with the charge: "Confess, therefore, your sins one to another, and pray for one another, that you may be saved. For the continual prayer of a just man availeth much." Prayer is the connatural way in which penance and the assistance given in it by others first manifests itself. As a further way of doing penance James recommends mercy (2:13) and the conversion of a sinner (5:19f.).

In contrast to Paul the emphasis on confession is new, both in James and also in 1 Jn 1:9. In the context of the Johannine text the "confession of sins" is contrasted with the false self-righteousness of the heretical teachers who say that they "have no sin" (1:8). Confession is, therefore, a contrite consciousness of guilt, linked to a desire and prayer for forgiveness. It cannot be deduced from the text whether, in addition to interior confession to God, John also has in mind an external acknowledgement before others, such as the rulers of the church or the community, particularly in the form of a detailed confession of individual sins. Comparison with Jas 5:16 seems to indicate some kind of public confession. It is evident from the *Didache* (ch. 14) that some form of outward confession of sins was practised by the early

---

[16] Thus Augustine, *De corr. et gr.* 12,35; among modern authors W. Vrede, Fr. Hauck, W. Grundmann, O. Bauernfeind; R. Seeberg has a different view. Further details in Poschmann I 71—80.

Christians. However, when John, in 1 Jn 1: 9, makes confession a prerequisite for the remission of sins, he certainly does not envisage the outward form as the essential element of this confession.[17]

The Apocalypse provides an instructive supplement to the apostolic teaching on penance. In the introductory letters the moral condition of the Church is depicted in a few bold strokes. Those who have been censured are required in the plainest terms to do penance. For less serious failings, even for those which of their nature lead to spiritual ruin, such as negligence and tepidity, all that is required is repentance and emendation (2: 5; 3: 1—5, 15—19). But the bishops must not tolerate grave sins, such as idolatry and unchastity, in their churches. They will be severely judged if they do not take action against these offenders, *i.e.* if they do not expel them from the community (2:2; 2:14—16; 2:20). However, even the worst evildoers, such as the woman Jezebel, are not thereby delivered up to final perdition. On the contrary, God subjects them to affliction in order even now to induce them to repent, and to give them an opportunity of salvation, notwithstanding their obduracy hitherto. Here we have a practical commentary on the concept of "the sin unto death".

If we now summarize the results of our examination of the apostolic writings it is evident that much is lacking for a complete picture of primitive penitential doctrine and practice. Nevertheless, the main outlines have become clear. Every sin calls for penance; but no sin, not even the gravest, is excluded from forgiveness, provided that sincere penance is performed. Prayer and works of mercy are means for obtaining the remission of

---

[17] The use made on the Catholic side since the end of the 17th century of 1 Jn 1:9 as a scriptural proof for sacramental confession is unwarranted. More recent dogmatic theologians (*e.g.* Diekamp, Bartmann, Gierens, Schmaus) have abandoned this interpretation, or at least do not regard it as imposed. On the Protestant side, R. Seeberg (Festschrift für Ihmels [1928] 19—31) has attempted rather artificially to find support for the theory that "confession" in 1 Jn is to be understood as an ecclesiastical act parallel to the "confession" at baptism.

sins. Personal prayer receives efficacious support from the intercession of the faithful as its counterpart. Joined to prayer is confession of sins. Where the sins are grave, the rulers of the Church are obliged to admonish the guilty, and, if this proves fruitless, to exclude them from the community. If the excommunicated person is converted the Church grants him her forgiveness, and this is a guarantee of "forgiveness in heaven" also, in accordance with the promise of the Lord.

II. The Post-Apostolic Age

LITERATURE: P. Batiffol, *Etudes d'hist. et de théol. positive* (1920). A. d'Alès, *L'Edit de Calliste* (1914). J. Hoh, *Die kirchliche Buße im 2. Jahrh.* (1932). A. v. Harnack, *Die Lehre der zwölf Apostel* (1884). Id., *Einführung in die Alte Kirchengeschichte* (1929). W. Bauer, *Die Briefe des Ignatius u. des Polykarp,* Handbuch z. N. T. Ergänzungsband (1920). C. Schmidt, *Gespräche Jesu mit seinen Jüngern,* Texte u. Unters. 43 (1919). M. A. Lelong, *Le Pasteur d'Hermas* (1912) 173 ff. H. Koch, *Die Bußschrift des Pastor Hermae,* Festg. f. A. v. Harnack (1921) 173 ff. M. Dibelius, *Der Hirt des Hermas* (1923). R. van Deemter, *Der Hirt des Hermas : Apokalypse oder Allegorie?* (Delft 1929). A. v. Ström, *Der Hirt des Hermas : Allegorie oder Wirklichkeit?* (Uppsala 1936). Poschmann I 85—205. J. Grotz, *Die Entwicklung des Bußstufenwesens in der vornicänischen Kirche* (Freiburg 1955). K. Rahner, "Die Bußlehre im Hirten des Hermas" in *ZkTh* 77 (1955) 385—431. J. B. Lightfoot, *The Apostolic Fathers,* rev. texts with Eng. tr. ed. J. R. Harmer (London 1907). M. Whittaker ed., "Der Hirt des Hermas" in *GChS* 48 (1956). R. Joly ed., "Hermas Le Pasteur" in *SC* 53 (1958). Id., "La doctrine pénitentielle du Pasteur d'Hermas" in *RHR* (1955) 422—28. P. Galtier, *Aux origines du sacrement de pénitence* (Rome 1951). H. v. Campenhausen, *Kirchliches Amt. u. geistliche Vollmacht in den ersten drei Jahrhunderten* (Tübingen 1953). J. A. Kleist ed., *The Epistles of St. Clement of Rome and St. Ignatius of Antioch* (Eng. tr. *ACW* 1 [1946]). Id., *The Didache,* ibid. 6 (1948). Edgar J. Goodspeed, *The Apostolic Fathers : an American Translation* (New York 1950; London 1962).

1. General Evidence for Penance

The writings of the post-Apostolic age (up to the second half of the second century) likewise provide only scanty material for a knowledge of the nature of penance. Hermas treats *ex professo* of penance, but only from the point of view of its necessity. Apart

19

from him all we have are occasional observations which throw light on this or that point. They are, however, amply sufficient to confirm the basic conclusions which we have derived from the New Testament. But they leave us in the dark in regard to the detailed administration of the penitential procedure. There was as yet no uniformity in practice. It was left to the bishop to determine the form in which the Gospel principles should be carried out, and to hold a just balance between severity in the imposition of penance and the divine readiness to grant forgiveness. It was only gradually that forms of administration became fixed. Common problems contributed to the process of unification; thus the rise of heresies like Montanism and Novatianism, or mass apostasy during persecutions, called for a uniform regulation of penance sanctioned by conciliar decisions.

Witnesses from the earliest period are in agreement first of all that even for baptized Christians penance is still available. The modern theory of a sole baptismal penance has no advocate among them. They all lay emphasis on the absolute character of the baptismal obligation, and make profession of the Christian ideal of holiness.[18] Yet, in extolling this ideal, none of them closes his eyes to the fact that sin is to be found even among Christians, and not merely in the form of minor failings, but gross crimes also such as unchastity, adultery, hatred and abominable arrogance.[19] The so-called *Second Epistle of Clement* (14, 1), the oldest surviving Christian homily, does not shrink from applying the prophetical image of the "den of thieves" (Jer 1:11; Mt 21:13) to the Church on earth, in reference to its sinful members. Nevertheless, it is consistently taught that, thanks to the precious blood of Christ, there remains a possibility of penance

---

[18] Cf. Ignatius, *Eph.* 4, 2; 8, 2; *Barn.* 6, 11—13; 4, 1 f.; 11, 11; 16, 7 f; 2 *Clem.* 6, 9; 7, 6. 1 *Clem.* 1 and 2 gives a picture of the realization of the ideal, as also Justin, *Apol.* I 14, 61; *Dial.* 114, 4; Aristides, 15; Theophilus, *Ad Autol.* III 9—15; Minucius Felix, *Octav.* 35.
[19] Cf. Ignatius, *Eph.* 10, 3; *Philad.* 7, 2; 8, 1; *Trall.* 8, 2; 1 *Clem.* 30, 1.

and salvation for all.[20] Just as a potter can refashion a vessel that breaks in his hands while being shaped, as long as he has not thrown it into the furnace, so a man who is still living and has time for repentance is capable of being refashioned by God (2 *Clem.* 8, 1—3). The apocryphal *Epistola Apostolorum* provides an illustration of the same truth in an exposition of the parable of the wise and foolish virgins.[21] All its instructions are more or less direct admonitions to do penance while there is yet time.

Turning to the content of penance, we find that, as we would expect, its first requirement is conversion, or a break with sin, and obedience to the law of God (1 *Clem.* 56, 1; 2 *Clem.* 8, 4 etc.). In addition, the sinner must also seek to appease God by special penitential exercises. First among these comes prayer. According to the *Didache* (8, 2f.) Christians say the Our Father three times daily, and in the fifth petition implore forgiveness for their sins. The *First Epistle of Clement* (ch. 40) and St. Justin (*Dial.* 90, 141) speak of weeping and prostrations at prayer. Having regard to later penitential practice as evidenced by Tertullian, we take these to be not just a metaphorical expression but real actions connected with prayer and deriving from Jewish tradition. Fasting and almsdeeds are joined to prayer. Almsgiving is a "ransom for sins" (*Did.* 4, 6; *Barn.* 19, 10). In the *Didache* (7, 1) and Justin (*Apol.* 1, 61), fasting is required before baptism and for this reason it will also have its place in penance. For an appreciation of it, *Second Clement* 16, 14 is instructive: "Almsgiving is good as penance for sin; fasting is better than prayer, and almsgiving better than both. 'But charity covereth a multitude of sins' (1 Pet 4:8), and prayer from a good

---

[20] Ignatius, *Philad.* 3, 2; 8, 1; *Smyrn.* 9, 1; 1 *Clem.* 7, 4—5.
[21] C. Schmidt, *Gespräche Jesu mit seinen Jüngern* (1919), Ae (Ethiopic text) 136, 4 ff., (Ko [Coptic text] XXXIV 5 ff.). It is altogether unjustified and against the point of the parable, when Schmidt (ibid. 380 f.) interprets the passage in the sense of the "baptismal theory", asserting the fundamental impossibility of a penance for Christians. Similarly J. Hoh 66—68 f. Further details in Poschmann I 105 ff.

21

conscience purifies from death." But the penitential works are by no means a material equivalent of guilt. Rather it is "repentance from an upright heart which is true compensation" (ἀντιμισθία [ibid. 9:7f.]). Great importance is attached to confession of sins. As in John, this is to be understood first of all as confession to God, inasmuch as the sinner, instead of remaining obdurate in his own perverted will, humbly acknowledges his guilt and professes his readiness to do penance (1 *Clem.* 51, 3). Thus "confession" is just the same thing as doing penance, and corresponds to the term ἐξομολόγησις which is found later in Tertullian.[22] On the other hand, it also approximates to the meaning of "praise", which it has in Scripture, and which is still prevalent in early-Christian literature.[23] Penance is indeed true praise of God, not with the lips, but in mind and deed (2 *Clem.* 3, 4). Inasmuch as it is manifested externally, confession before God becomes also confession before men. But besides this indirect mode, formal, external confession was also practised. The evidence for this is clear from two passages of the *Didache* : "In the assembly (ἐν ἐκκλησίᾳ) confess your sins and go not to the prayer with an evil conscience" (4, 17),[24] and similarly 14, 1: "But on the Lord's Day come together, break bread and give thanks, after you have first confessed your sins, that thereby your sacrifices may be pure." On the question of the interpretation of this confession, it is to be observed that in both texts it serves as a preparation for the prayer.[25] It is required as a condition of God's propitious acceptance of the prayer, and is, so to speak, an essential element in it.[26] In accordance with 1 Cor 11:28 it is clearly most appropriate before the celebration of the eucharist,

---

[22] 2 *Clem.* 2, 3 ἐξομολογήσασθαι ἢ μετανοεῖν.
[23] In 1 *Clem.* apart from 51, 3 it always has this meaning. Cf. 26, 3; 48, 2; 52, 1; 61, 3.
[24] Similarly *Barn.* 19, 12.
[25] Cf. Ecclus 18:23; 1 Tim 2:8.
[26] Cf. Hermas, *Vis.* I 1, 3: "I began to pray to the Lord and to confess my sins." Similarly *Vis.* III 1, 5; *Sim.* IX 23, 4.

because communal liturgical prayer also calls for a preliminary purification of conscience. It is a public self-accusation before God couched in a general form, without mention of particular sins, a general prayer for forgiveness in the style of the later *Confiteor*. The designation of this kind of general self-accusation as a "confession of sins" was customary both in Judaism (cf. Lev 16:21) and throughout Christian antiquity. Detailed confession by all the assembled faithful in the course of the liturgy would hardly have been practicable, even in a community of only moderate size. Most decisive, however, is the consideration that the idea of a Sunday confession of this kind, which supposedly would suffice to allow access to the eucharist to everyone, including those guilty of mortal sin, lies altogether beyond the horizon of early-Christian penitential procedure, as known from other sources. On the other hand, a confession in the sense of a contrite prayer for forgiveness, such as is found for example in the Our Father, is in perfect harmony with early Church practice.[27]

The ecclesiastical aspect of penance appears first in the concern common to all for the salvation of sinners (cf. 1 *Clem.* 2, 4, 6). Fraternal correction, no less than its counterpart, intercession, is an elementary obligation of charity (*Did.* 15, 3; Ignatius, *Eph.* 10, 1; 1 *Clem.* 56, 2; 2 *Clem.* 15, 2; 17, 2; *Ep. Apost.* Ae 148, 1 ff.; 150, 4). In principle this obligation is incumbent on all, yet first of all it devolves upon the rulers of the Church, who in virtue of

---

[27] Against the unsuccessful attempts to make the prescription in the *Didache* a testimony for sacramental confession, the view that it represents a general confession is today accepted more and more by Catholic authors. Cf. the list in A. Weiss, *ThQ* 1915, 125 ff., and J. Hoh 107. See also E. Amann in *DTC* XII 757 f. On the Protestant side R. Seeberg, *Festschr. f. Ihmels* (1928) 26, has included *Did.* 14 in support of his theory of an "order of confession" in the apostolic age. R. Knopf, *Die Lehre der zwölf Apostel* (1920) 36, has also decided for a brief confession of particular sins, but only as a means of atonement for minor offences, whereas "the grave sins were submitted to ecclesiastical discipline".

their office are responsible for ecclesiastical discipline. Excommunication of obstinate sinners is required, and imposed as a normal procedure (*Did.* 4, 3; 15, 3; Ignatius, *Smyrn.* 4, 1; 7, 2; *Eph.* 7, 1; Polycarp, *Phil.* 6, 11; 11, 2; *Barn.* 19, 4; 2 *Clem.* 17, 3, 5). Its effect is that all intercourse is broken off with the offender "until he does penance" (*Did.* 15, 3). There is no irrevocable exclusion of sinners. Conformably with 2 Thess 3:15 they are not to be treated as enemies but rather to be recalled as *passibilia membra* (Polycarp, *Phil.* 11, 4). Prayer is offered for them even during the period of their exclusion (Ignatius, *Smyrn.* 4, 1).

Naturally resort was had to the penal measures only where the sins were grave. Venial or "indeliberate" sins were healed by contrite confession and prayer (1 *Clem.* 2, 3; *Did.* 4, 14; 14, 1). Mortal sin, on the other hand, has to be expiated by appropriate penance. For this reason, a sinner, even when prepared to do penance, continued to be excluded from the eucharist until he had made full satisfaction. This principle, for which there is clear evidence later, was also applied in the early-Christian period, as is shown by the solemn invitation at the end of the eucharistic prayer in the *Didache:* " Εἴ τις ἅγιός ἐστιν, ἐρχέσθω· εἴ τις οὐχ ἔστι, μετανοείτω" (10, 6). He who is holy, that is, free from sin, so that the offering is not defiled (14, 1) or profaned (14, 2) by him, may draw near; he who is not so should do penance. The word μετανοείτω cannot refer to the confession of sins before the breaking of bread, which was mentioned in 14, 1—3. For that confession is made by all without exception, and, besides, it has already been made before the celebration of the eucharist. On the other hand, the word is quite naturally explained as a warning against an unworthy communion, and is thus in harmony with the Pauline directive and with what was soon to become general practice. Even without ecclesiastical condemnation the sinner must "judge" himself (1 Cor 11:31), and, accepting the disgrace which it involved, separate himself from the communal Christian celebration until he has "purged"

24

his sin.[28] Whether the cooperation of the Church was also en-
listed in a penance of this kind which had been undertaken on
one's own initiative cannot be clearly established from the text,
but from the nature of the case it is likely. The need to seek
counsel on the amount of penance that was requisite and to
obtain a share in the intercessory prayers of the community on
which such great store was set, would of themselves have induced a sincerely penitent Christian to confess his sin. In addition, his protracted abstention from the eucharist would be bound
to give the Church authorities an occasion for addressing and
admonishing him. At the very least we can say that the prescriptions of the *Didache* leave plenty of room for a sacramental procedure envisaged in the sense of Mt 18:18.

The act of ecclesiastical forgiveness coincides with readmission to communion with the Church. Once the sinner has done
the required penance, the Church, as has been shown, refrains
from further punishment and thereby assures him of forgiveness.
Pardon, just as punishment, belongs to the judicial office of the
rulers of the Church. That is why Polycarp warns the presbyters
to be impartial, mild in judgement and ready to "forgive", as
"they also hoped to receive forgiveness from the Lord" (*Phil.*
6, 1f.). The forgiveness here envisaged is, as indeed constantly
in other authors too, in the first place simply an ecclesiastical
forgiveness. Nevertheless we find confirmation of our conclusion from Paul. Given the universal recognition of the significance of the Church as the community of salvation, readmission
into the Church is also a guarantee of God's forgiveness. Thus
Ignatius, *Philad.* 3, 2: "All who are of God and of Jesus Christ
are with the bishop; and all who do penance and come into the

---

[28] H. Lietzmann in *Messe und Herrenmah* (1926) 236 f. (Eng. tr. *Mass and the
Lord's Supper*, Leiden [1955] 192 f.) particularly has argued in favour of this interpretation of the *Didache* text. He sees in it simply "another formulation of the
phrase which occurs before the Communion" (τὰ ἅγια τοῖς ἁγίοις). For further
details and bibliographical references to special questions see Poschmann I 92 ff.

unity of the Church, these also will be of God"; similarly, 1 *Clem.* 57, 2: "It is better to be a little one and to be found inside Christ's flock, than to be held in high repute, but to be excluded from its hope."[29]

2. The Penitential Doctrine of Hermas

Hermas demands separate treatment. In addition to being the first writer to make penance the object of special and thorough study, he is particularly important for his connexion with one of the most controversial problems in the history of penance. The opinion that it was he who first broke with the strict theory of a single post-baptismal penance is prevalent to this day. According to this opinion, relying on a revelation made to him, he proclaimed an extraordinary opportunity for penance, after the fashion of a Jubilee, which would be allowed once only to sinful Christians.[30] Others, on the other hand, see him simply as a preacher of penance whose message does not add anything essential to previous penitential practice[31] while yet others adopt an intermediate view.[32] Various responses have also been given to the question as to whether Hermas allowed for an ecclesiastical forgiveness in connexion with God's forgiveness.[33] The ex-

---

[29] See 2 *Clem.* 14, 1—4 for the doctrine of the spiritual, pre-existent Church, which was manifested in the flesh of Christ, and which must be "preserved in the flesh" by us if we wish to obtain "participation in the Spirit". Cf. Poschmann I 131 f.

[30] Thus F. X. Funk, P. Batiffol, A. v. Harnack, Fr. Loofs, R. Seeberg, H. Windisch, E. Preuschen, E. Schwartz, H. Koch, M. Dibelius, H. Weinel, A. Puech, K. Bihlmeyer.

[31] J. Stufler, A. d'Alès, O. Bardenhewer, Fr. Hünermann, P. Galtier, J. Tixéront (in the later editions of his *History of Dogmas*), B. Altaner, B. Poschmann.

[32] G. Rauschen, K. Adam, J. Hoh, E. Amann, A. Ehrhard.

[33] The importance attached to the witness of Hermas is clear from R. Seeberg's judgement: "This controversy over penance, the first in the experience of the Church, is of enormous historic importance" (*Dogmengesch.* I[2] [1908] 126). In reality, this "controversy over penance" is a mere product of theory.

planation of these conflicting interpretations is to be sought principally in the peculiar character of Hermas' book. It is the work of a simple and upright man of a pious disposition and limited outlook who, as the result of visionary experiences, feels himself called to prophetic proclamation. With the aim of imparting a more practical and urgent form to the heavenly message, he develops it quite substantially by his own literary composition, making use of very elaborate imagery and allegory. The resultant obscurity and ambiguity are made even worse by lack of literary skill, so that from the outset we have to reckon with errors and inconsistencies.[34] Erroneous conclusions will certainly be drawn if account is not taken of the unscientific character of the author, and if his utterances are measured by a standard which applies to a writer with a theological training.

In reality, the theory that Hermas, in virtue of a new revelation, was the first to teach the possibility of penance for Christians is altogether mistaken. On the contrary, the saving power of penance and its practice appear already from the outset in *Visio* I as something which is taken for granted, and the alleged revelation is first mentioned in *Visio* II (*Vis.* I 1, 9; 3, 2; 4, 3). Moreover, in *Mandatum* IV the existence of a penitential procedure is presupposed. There the principle is laid down that a sinner who does penance is to be received back.[35] The sin in question is adultery. What Hermas in *Visio* II announces as a new revelation is not the basic possibility of penance but its limitation. From now on, it will only be available for those sins which have been committed up to this day and not for any future sins (*Vis.* II 2, 5). The psychological explanation of the "revelation" is to be found in Hermas' conviction that the end of the world was imminent. He who does not do penance now is irrevocably lost. This obsessive idea of his was embodied in

---

[34] On problems of literary criticism and the person of Hermas see especially R. van Deemter, op. cit. and the special studies there indicated.
[35] IV 1: δεῖ παραδεχθῆναι τὸν ἡμαρτηκότα καὶ μετανοοῦντα.

the vision in which God Himself proclaims a term to the availability of penance. Those who are so far unconverted will not miss the final chance still offered to them of obtaining forgiveness; of this he is certain (*Vis.* II 2, 3—4). It is, therefore, the proclamation not of the first, but of the last possibility of penance. By this means Hermas aims at arousing sinful Christians to an immediate and mass conversion.

The most controversial passage is *Mandatum* IV 3, 1—7. Hermas has heard from some teachers that there is no other penance than that of baptism. The "Shepherd" who is instructing him, endorses the statement as correct, seeing that a baptized person "should sin no more". However, he feels that the occasion is one for him to enlarge on, but in such a way that what he says will not provide the newly baptized and the catechumens with an "incitement" to commit sin. These, therefore, being excepted, the Lord in his mercy has instituted for the rest of the faithful another penance which will be accorded once only. This conversation between Hermas and the Shepherd has been produced as direct evidence of the contrast between the ancient ideal of holiness and the new practice of penance. Closer examination shows that this interpretation is groundless. The Shepherd sees no contradiction at all between the teaching of the "certain teachers" — τινὲς διδάσκαλοι — and the concession of another penance; on the contrary, both meet with the same approval. Moreover, penance is not something first announced by Hermas. It is God, we are told, who first made provision for it in advance, having regard to the weakness of human nature. The theory of the "Jubilee pardon" is, therefore, inadmissible. The way to the solution of the problem is indicated by the exceptional position of the newly baptized and the catechumens. No inducement to commit sin must be given them by the doctrine of a further possibility of penance. This means that the doctrine will be withheld from them. The reason is that "they do not have penance for sins, but remission of their previous sins". They do not need penance, because in the "remission" of sins granted in baptism, they have something more than penance,[36] and they must remain convinced that "he who has obtained remission of sins must sin no more". For pastoral and pedagogical reasons, therefore, the teaching on the forgiveness of sins was proposed in different ways according to the status of the hearers. Hermas had heard preachers who, desirous of impressing upon the newly baptized the inviolability of their baptismal obligations, laid stress on the fact that there could be for them no second remission of sins — ἄφεσις — similar to the one they had received. At the same time, they carefully avoided all reference to the possibility of doing penance in another manner. These are the τινὲς διδάσκαλοι who, however, in preaching to those baptized at an earlier period bade them do penance perhaps just as emphatically. This simple solution not merely fits smoothly into the text; it is positively demanded by it.[37]

The efficacy of penance extends, without restriction, to all sins, regardless of their gravity (*Sim.* VIII 11, 1). Not even offences such as apostasy from the faith and adultery, are excepted (*Vis.* II 2, 2—4; 3, 4; *Mand.* IV 1, 8). The only obstacle to forgiveness is lack of sincere repentance. This appears very clearly in *Similitudo* VIII at the examination of the willow rods which signify groups of penitents. The groups are not differentiated according to the objective gravity of the sinful act, but according to the degree of their attachment to evil and alienation from God. The problem, in so far as Hermas is concerned, is not for which sins forgiveness is available; it is, rather, which sinners are disposed to do penance.[38] Only in so far as certain sins of their nature presup-

---

[36] The contrast between μετάνοια and ἄφεσις is echoed throughout Christian antiquity. See Clement of Alexandria, *Strom.* 2, 55, 6.
[37] For a detailed analysis of the text see Poschmann I 159—168. A. d'Alès (op. cit. 67 ff.) was the first to propose this solution with solid proof but met with little approbation.
[38] In *Sim.* VIII 6,2 the Shepherd replies to Hermas' question why all have not done penance: "To those, whose heart He saw about to become pure... to them He gave repentance; but those whose craftiness and wickedness He saw, who

pose a state of mind in direct resistance to God, and, therefore, indisposed for penance, can it be said of them with a kind of moral certainty that they are unforgivable. An example of these is deliberate apostasy along with conscious blasphemy of God (*Sim.* VIII 6, 4; IX 19, 1; VIII 8, 2). The concept of "capital sins" which are unforgivable by reason of their objective gravity is quite foreign to Hermas.

Admittedly, the seer does make one reservation in his proclamation of the universal efficacy of penance. For Christians it is restricted to a single concession. That holds good not just in the sense that no penance will be possible after the time of the new revelation; it is laid down also as a matter of principle. The sinner who does penance must be received back, "yet not often, for there is but one repentance for the servants of God" — μὴ ἐπὶ πολὺ δὲ τοῖς γὰρ δούλοις τοῦ θεοῦ μετάνοιά ἐστιν μία (*Mand.* IV 1, 8). And again: If anyone, tempted by the devil, sins after baptism, he has a single penance; but if he goes on sinning and repents penance is unprofitable to such a man; he will attain to life with difficulty — μίαν μετάνοιαν ἔχει. ἐὰν δὲ ὑπὸ χεῖρα ἁμαρτάνῃ, ἀσύμφορόν ἐστι τῷ ἀνθρώπῳ τῷ τοιούτῳ· δυσκόλως γὰρ ζήσεται (*Mand.* IV 3, 6). However, as the last clause shows, the reason for the restriction is not to be sought in the denial of God's mercy to the recidivist. It is rather to be explained by the fact that the recidivist has made it evident by his repeated sinning — ὑπὸ χεῖρα ἁμαρτάνῃ — that he does not possess a sincere spirit of repentance, without which penance is "unprofitable". That is why it is "difficult" for him, and why little hope exists that he will attain to life.[39] The "impossibility", therefore, is

---

intend to repent in hypocrisy, to them He gave not repentance" (tr. J. B. Lightfoot, *The Apostolic Fathers* [London 1907], p. 457). God "gives repentance": this does not mean he grants the possibility of forgiveness but the power, the will to do penance.

[39] It is a falsification of the content of the text to take δυσκόλως in the sense of "impossible". Thus, *e.g.* M. Dibelius 510 and H. Koch, 176, n. 2. Against them A. d'Alès, 80, n. 1 has assembled all the texts in which this word is used by Hermas,

here also to be understood as a psychological and moral one, and implies no exclusion on dogmatic grounds. It is all in line with the same pastoral psychology when the prospect of another and repeated opportunities of penance is closed to sinful Christians, and any penance at all for Christians not spoken of to catechumens and neophytes.

In what concerns the nature of penance Hermas is in complete harmony with traditional conceptions. First of all, penance requires a sincere change of heart; in addition to this, it involves appropriate expiation (*Mand.* IV 2, 2). In contrast to normal Christian life, the time of penance must be taken up with acts of self-abasement and mortification. In the measure that expiation has been made, penance is considered complete or incomplete. This distinction has an important part to play in the visions of the Tower (cf. *Vis.* III 7, 6; *Sim.* VIII 2, 5; 8, 3). In practice penance is performed first of all by prayer, linked with confession of sins before God (*Vis.* I 1, 3; III 1, 5; *Sim.* IX 23, 4), then by fasting (*Vis.* III 10, 6; *Sim.* V 1, 3), almsdeeds (ibid. *Vis.* III 9, 4—6; *Mand.* VIII 10), and especially by humble acceptance of ecclesiastical punishment (*Vis.* I 3, 2; II 4, 3; III 9, 10). Where the offences are very grave, such as apostasy and adultery, the sinner is expelled from the community (*Mand.* IV 1, 9). Finally, very great weight is laid on the patient acceptance of trials imposed by God on sinners. Over these trials a special "angel of punishment" presides in the service of avenging Providence (*Sim.* VI—VII).

The efficacy of penance is placed on a level with that of baptism, both in regard to the forgiveness of sins and the restoration of life to the soul. Favourite terms for it in Hermas are "healing'- (*Vis.* I 19; *Mand.* IV 1, 11; 6, 2; *Sim.* V 6, 3, 4 etc.) or "purification" (*Vis.* III 2, 2; *Sim.* VII 2), or, even more directly, "for

---

and demonstrates that their view is mistaken. An exact counterpart to *Mand.* IV 3,6 is found in *Sim.* VIII 10,2.

giveness of sins" (*Vis.* II 4; *Mand.* IV 4, 4; *Sim.* VII 4; IX 33, 3).[40]
As sin brings death, so penance brings "life" or "salvation"
(*Mand.* XII 6, 3; *Sim.* VIII 6, 6; *Vis.* II 2, 5 etc.), and restores
the lost seal of baptism (*Sim.* VIII 2, 2, 4; 6, 3). This perfect restoration occurs when expiation proportionate to the guilt has
been made (*Sim.* IX 33, 3). However, even before the completion
of penance, conversion as such is of essential importance for
salvation. Those desirous of doing penance (θέλοντες μετανοῆσαι
[*Vis.* III 5, 5]) who have not yet finished their penance, are not
indeed admitted to the Tower which is a guarantee of salvation;
they are, however, within "the walls" (*Sim.* VIII 2, 5; 6, 6; 7,
3; 8, 3) in a more "humble place" (*Vis.* III 7, 6). Even though
salvation is not theirs directly, they are close to it, and have an
expectancy of it.[41]

This strongly emphasized distinction between complete and
incomplete penance heralds a problem which was an important
factor in the later development of the penitential procedure. The
fact that there is, in Hermas, no explicit information about the
ecclesiastical side of penance has led some to assert that for him
penance is a matter which is the sole concern of the sinner and
God.[42] In reality, however, the intervention of the Church can
be discerned through the whole work, and alone makes it intelligible. It is the idealized figure of the Church which com-
municates the revelation of penance to Hermas (*Vis.* I and II).
Similarly, it is the Church which is the goal of penance, since
readmission into the Tower which is the symbol of the Church
is the guarantee of the forgiveness of sins. He who remains

---

[40] If ἄφεσις in *Mand.* IV 3:3 is reserved for baptism then the word is to be
understood in the narrower sense of a purely gratuitous forgiveness in contrast to
that merited by penance (cf. above n. 36 and n. 37).
[41] Their fate in the next life remains obscure. A continuation of penitential punishment in the after life or an inferior degree of beatitude have been suggested.
However, these are mere guesses. For a more detailed discussion see Poschmann I
154 ff.; 172 ff.; 188 f.
[42] Thus Lelong LXXIII and H. Koch 178.

outside the Church is lost. Even if the Tower does not represent the visible Church with her sinful members, but the heavenly and spiritual Church, yet these two are connected with each other and cannot be separated. The empirical Church is simply the form in which the heavenly Church is to be reached. If, then, a sinner has to attain by penance, while still in this life, admittance to the Tower, which is the "holy Church", it must follow that after appropriate penance readmission to the visible Church is granted to him, in so far as he has been excluded from it on account of grave sin. There must be a reconciliation which corresponds to the excommunication.

Hermas also provides direct evidence that penitential discipline is under the control of the rulers of the Church, when he receives from the Church, which appears to him in the form of an old woman, the charge to read out the new revelation to the presbyters and the rulers (*Vis.* II 4, 3). This also is clear from the fact that on these the duty is imposed both by the old woman and by the Shepherd of instructing the elect of the Lord (παιδεύειν τοὺς ἐκλεκτοὺς κυρίου) and of seeking out the lost sheep (*Vis.* III 9, 7—10; *Sim.* IX 31, 5—6). That the "chastisement" for grave sins such as adultery and idolatry included the excommunication of the guilty party has already been established by reference to *Mand.* IV 1, 8—9. It is highly probable that the same text also provides evidence of reconciliation in the words: "One who has sinned and repented must be received" (δεῖ παραδεχθῆναι τὸν ἡμαρτηκότα καὶ μετανοοῦντα).[43] In favour of this interpretation there is the idea of a single penance taught by Hermas, which presupposes some kind of termination of penance. Only after this one penance is finished can there by any question of another penance. Finally, a very strong, indeed, decisive, extrinsic argument is the clear testimony of Tertullian who was not far removed in time from Hermas. He pours out the whole force of

---

[43] Against H. Koch 179, n. 4 and J. Hoh 18, who only see in it evidence of admission to penance.

his wrath on Hermas as the Shepherd of Adulterers *(Pastor moechorum)* because he had extended readmission to the Church even to adulterers *(De pud.* 10, 12; 20, 2).

Although we find the fact of reconciliation attested quite clearly in Hermas, we are left somewhat in the dark in regard to its significance for salvation. All that we can affirm is that Hermas does not regard it as the direct cause of divine forgiveness. Throughout his work on penance it is always God who forgives sins (cf. *Vis.* I 1, 9; 3, 1; *Mand.* XII 6, 2; *Sim.* VIII 11, 3) and who forgives them at his discretion because he "has power over all" *(Mand.* IV 1, 11; *Sim.* V 7, 3). He it is, too, who determines the measure of the expiation and the time for granting forgiveness. He "condones the past sins" of penitents when "he has seen that their penance is good and pure, and that they are constant in it" *(Sim.* IX 33, 3). In spite of this, reconciliation is not just a restoration of ecclesiastical rights which the Church concedes to a sinner as a logical consequence of his restoration to grace by God.[44] If it were only that, the salvific value of the Church, which Hermas himself proclaims so vigorously, would not be verified. This requires the existence of some kind of intrinsic causal relationship between the visible Church and the "Kingdom of God" which is the goal of penance. If readmission to the Church is not also a direct cause of the forgiveness of sins, it is at any rate a necessary presupposition for it. The Church forgives in order that God may forgive. Directly or formally, reconciliation has for its effect peace with the Church; indirectly it also secures peace with God.

Summarizing, then, the characteristic features of Hermas' position in the history of penance, we may say that, in regard to the basic questions of the possibility and conditions of the forgiveness of sins, his conceptions are much the same as those we encounter in other sources of that period. There is, however, one novelty in his proclamation of penance. This is the doctrine of a single

[44] Thus Lelong LXXIII.

penance — *paenitentia una* — which he was the first to formulate strictly, on pastoral and psychological grounds. It was afterwards taken over as a matter of principle, and was to be heavy with consequence for the later development of penance. For practical religious life Hermas has the incontestible merit of arousing consciences by his impressive proclamation, and especially that of reawakening confidence in the unlimited efficacy of penance.

III. The Development of the Doctrine of Penance and the Establishment of Penitential Practice in the Third Century

LITERATURE: P. de Labriolle, *La crise Montaniste* (Paris 1913). W. Schepelern, *Der Montanismus und die phrygischen Kulte* (1929). H. Kraft, "Die altchristliche Prophetie und die Entstehung des Montanismus" in *TZ* 11 (1955) 249—271. R. G. Smith, "Tertullian and Montanism" in *Theology* 46 (1943) 127—139. E. Benz, "Montanus Lehre vom Parakleten" in *ErJb* 25 (1956/57) 293—301. K. Aland, "Bemerkungen zum Montanismus und zur frühchristlichen Eschatologie" in *Kirchengeschichtliche Entwürfe* (Gütersloh 1960) 105—148.

1. The Montanist Movement

However meagre and inadequate on points of detail, the evidence so far considered justifies the conclusion that for the penance of sinful Christians substantially the same principles were valid everywhere. However, in the application of the principles, considerable scope was left to the discretion of ecclesiastical superiors. Such questions as, which sinners were worthy of admittance to penance, and whether the penance performed was sufficient for reconciliation, admitted of stricter or milder answers. On the one hand, pastoral needs, which with the growth of the churches were becoming increasingly urgent, pressed for a more lenient treatment of sinners; on the other, zeal for the Christian ideal of holiness and strict ecclesiastical discipline were in favour of a more severe procedure.

This situation explains the swift spread of Montanism, which may be considered as a protest against the laxity which had crept in, and also the influence exercised over a wide area by its teaching on penance. In the beginning it was regarded simply as a revivalist movement within the Church. Its penitential doctrine is contained in the "Oracle" of the Paraclete speaking in Montanus which has been preserved by Tertullian, *De pud.* 21, 7: "The Church can forgive sins, but I will not do so, lest others also commit sin" (*Potest ecclesia donare delicta, sed non faciam, ne et alii delinquant*). The utterance, which is probably an answer to the opponents of Montanus, admits in principle that the Church has the power to forgive sins, and is an indirect witness that up to that time she had exercised it. Henceforward, however, lest mildness should provide an inducement to commit sin, the Paraclete will no more grant forgiveness. This is a new rigorism which matches the other demands of the Phrygian movement. The revolutionary element in the doctrine lies in the undermining of the Catholic concept of the Church. It is no longer the bishops, but the "new prophets" who are the organs of the Paraclete, and thereby the authoritative agents of the Church, as Tertullian formally expressed it later on in his concept of the *Ecclesia Spiritus* (ibid.). Montanus himself, however, seems hardly to have been aware of the full implications of his claim, any more than the leaders of the great Church from whom his followers sought to obtain recognition.[45] He was nowhere, not even in polemical works, accused of such far-reaching opposition. All that was noticed at first in the movement were the harsh and rigoristic demands. These were, indeed, a cause of disquiet, but in stricter circles they were often sympathetically received. It is, therefore, no mere coincidence that from the time of the rise of Montanism history

[45] According to Tertullian's claim (*Adv. Prax.* 1) in the beginning they had already won over the Pope to their side. See de Labriolle 60; A. Ehrhard, *Die Kirche der Märtyrer* (1932) 236; Poschmann I 263f.

reveals numerous traces of rigoristic tendencies even within the Catholic Church.

Two letters, preserved by Eusebius, and written by Dionysius, bishop of Corinth, a contemporary of Pope Soter (c. 165—174) provide a first instance of this. They are directed against excessive demands in the matter of sexual abstinence, and against the refusal of forgiveness of sins. In one of the letters which is simultaneously addressed to the Church of Amastris in Bithynia and the churches in Pontus, Dionysius ruled that "all those who are converted from any fall, be it error or even heresy, should be received".[46] This was an assertion of the traditional practice against rigorism. We have direct evidence of the influence exercised by the Montanists even on distant churches from a letter of the churches of Vienne and Lyons to "the brethren in Asia and Phrygia" of the year 177/178 which also comes to us from Eusebius (*H. E.* V 1—4). From this letter it appears that ideas propagated by the "followers of Montanus" were a cause of grave concern to these churches. Irenaeus, at that time still a presbyter, was sent to Pope Eleutherius in Rome to obtain restoration of peace to the Church. No direct information can be gathered from the letter concerning the ecclesiastical administration of penance. However, it does contain an indirect criticism of the intolerable harshness of the Montanists towards the lapsed by the strong emphasis which it puts on the charity and mercy manifested by the martyrs of those regions in their treatment of those unfortunates.[47]

The Montanist movement attained its peak in Latin Africa when Tertullian took over its leadership, and with equal brilliance and fanaticism set himself to its defence. A remark of

---

[46] δεξιοῦσθαι προστάττει: Eusebius, *H. E.* IV 23, 6. Some writers, *e. g.* A. v. Harnack and H. Koch would see indicated in the phrase "should be received" only admittance to penance. But it must obviously mean that the sinner is to be forgiven, peace is to be granted him; and this only occurs at the moment of reconciliation which is the communication of "peace". Thus, de Labriolle, d'Alès, A. Ehrhard, J. Hoh. See Poschmann I 267.

[47] de Labriolle 230. The part played by the martyrs in penance is considered later.

St. Cyprian in *Ep.* 55, 21 is important for the history of the influence of Montanism on the Catholic Church in this region. It affirms that among his predecessors in the province of Africa some — *quidam* — were of the opinion that "they should not grant peace to adulterers, and that they had absolutely barred admittance to penance in cases of adultery", without, however, on this account separating themselves from the collegiate body of their fellow bishops and rupturing the unity of the Church. From this it is clear that reconciliation of adulterers was both ancient practice and still maintained by the majority of the African bishops, and that those faced with a contrary procedure did not see in it any reason for ecclesiastical schism.

2. Penance in the Age of Tertullian

LITERATURE: J. Döllinger, *Hippolytus und Kallistus* (1835). E. Rolffs, "Das Indulgenzedikt des röm. Bischofs Kallist" in *TU* 11 (1894). F. X. Funk, *Kirchengeschichtl. Abhandlungen u. Unters.* I (1897) 155—181; id., *ThQ* 1906, 541—568. P. Batiffol, *Etudes d'hist. et de théol. positive* (1902; 6 Aufl. 1920). G. Esser, "Die Bußschriften Tertullians u. das Indulgenzedikt des Papstes Kallistus" in *Bonner Universitätsprogramm* 1905. Id., "Nochmals das Indulgenzedikt" in *Katholik* 1907, II 194—204; 297—309; 1908, I 12—28; 93—113. Id., *Der Adressat der Schrift Tertullians "De pudicitia" und der Verfasser des röm. Bußedikts* (1914). J. B. Stufler, "Die Bußdisziplin der abendländischen Kirche bis Kallistus" in *ZkTh* (1907) 433—478. K. Adam, *Der Kirchenbegriff Tertullians* (1907). Id., *Das sog. Bußedikt des Papstes Kallist* (1917). A. d'Alès, *L'Edit de Calliste* (1914). H. Koch, *Kallist und Tertullian* (1920). P. de Labriolle, *La crise Montaniste* (1913). G. Bardy, "L'Edit d'Agrippinus" in *RSR* (1924) 1—24. P. Galtier, *L'Eglise et la rémission des péchés aux premiers siècles* (1932). Poschmann, I 283—367. J. Grotz, *Die Entwicklung des Bußstufenwesens in der vornicänischen Kirche* (Freiburg im Br. 1955). E. Langstadt, "Tertullian's Doctrine of Sin and the Power of Absolution in De pudicitia" in *Studia Patristica* II 251—257, *TU* 64 (1957). H. Karpp, *Schrift und Geist bei Tertullian* (Gütersloh 1956). W. P. Le Saint, *Tertullian. Treatises on Penance* Trans. and annotated (*ACW* 28 Westminster [Md.] London 1959). C. B. Daly, "The Sacrament of Penance in Tertullian" in *IER* 69 (1947) 693—707; 815—821; 70 (1948) 731—746, 832—848. C. Chartier, "L'Excommunication ecclésiastique d'après les écrits de Tertullian" in *Antonianum* 10 (1935) 301—344, 499—536. K. Rahner, "Zur Theologie der Buße bei Tertullian" in *Abhandlungen über Theologie und Kirche* (Festschrift für Karl Adam, Düsseldorf 1952) 139—167. H. Holstein, "L'Exhomologèse dans l'Adversus haereses de Saint Irénée" in *RSR* 25 (1948) 282—286.

a. The Controversy on Penance in Africa

The problem of the history of ancient Christian penance comes to a head in Tertullian. His testimony so dominates the scene that judgement of the practice and doctrine of penance of the earliest centuries depends on the interpretation that we give to it. Once again, opinions are sharply divided. Some find in him the forgiveness of sins clearly proclaimed as Catholic practice; for others he is a witness and advocate of the early-Christian ideal of holiness who protested violently against the violation of a principle which was being practised in his day for the first time. The difficulty derives primarily from the contradictory statements of Tertullian in the *De paenitentia* and the *De pudicitia,* both of which works are of particular importance for his teaching on penance. Of these, the first dates from his Catholic period and is of a purely paraenetic and ascetical character. It is an urgent call to penance which makes use of detailed scriptural arguments to assure all sinners without exception of the certainty of forgiveness, provided they do sincere penance. The *De pudicitia,* on the other hand, is a Montanist polemical work of his final period. It is a venomous tract against the Catholics, which flatly denies to the Church any power whatsoever in respect of the forgiveness of grave sins. Tertullian, therefore, is in opposition to Tertullian. The conciseness of the African's assertions and the obscurity of his style make the attainment of the truth even more difficult. We will first examine the controversy on penance and then describe the actual organization and the theory of penance.

The first question is, who was the adversary whom Tertullian time after time apostrophizes so passionately in the *De pudicitia* without mentioning his name? Right at the beginning he introduces him as the author of a "peremptory edict": *Pontifex scilicet Maximus quod est episcopus episcoporum, edicit : Ego moechiae et fornicationis delicta paenitentia functis dimitto (De pud.* 1,6).[48] Be-

---

[48] The *De pud.* and the *De paen.* are cited according to G. Rauschen, *Florileg. Patrist.* 10, the other writings of Tertullian according to Fr. Oehler.

cause of the title *Pontifex Maximus* the edict has been ascribed to a bishop of Rome since the time of Pamelius, Baronius and Morinus; and originally it was supposed that its author was Zephyrinus (198—217). However, after the discovery of the *Philosophumena* of Hippolytus in 1850 opinion was centred more and more on Callistus, the successor of Zephyrinus, with the result that Tertullian's "edict" was generally designated simply as "The Edict of Callistus".[49] That made Tertullian's adversary no less a person than the Pope. By the readmission of adulterers to the Church he took, in the judgement of Protestants, a step of incalculable consequence not only for the administration of penance but also for the whole concept of the Church. In recent decades, however, faith has been rudely shaken in this identification which had become an axiom of Church history, and in fact it can no longer be maintained.[50] Closer examination shows that there is nothing in favour, but much against the Roman origin of the edict. The title *Pontifex Maximus* is obviously used ironically of the claim to authority and can apply equally well either to the Bishop of Rome or to any other bishop. It would lead us too far afield if we were to mention all the proofs adduced in favour of our assertion.

It is enough to mention one simple fact. History has not left the slightest record of an edict so decisive for the life of the Church on the part of a pope. Hippolytus, who made a bitter attack on his enemy Callistus on the ground of his alleged laxity, makes no mention of it, nor does the *Liber Pontificalis* which under Callistus contains notices of a remission of fasting, of ordinations performed by him and of buildings which he erected (1, 141, ed. Duchesne). Most important of all, Tertullian himself makes no reference to Rome. One can imagine what capital he would have made out of an act of interference on the part of a

---

[49] For further detail see E. Rolffs, 1 ff.
[50] The chief contributors to this clarification have been G. Esser, K. Adam, and P. Galtier. H. Koch was the most emphatic defender of the old thesis against Esser and Adam. Further particulars in Poschmann I 349 f.

foreign bishop, and out of the pusillanimity of the African bishops in tamely submitting to it. The silence of history is, on the other hand, quite intelligible if the affair was only concerned with a controversy within the African church. In all probability, the "edict" has been maliciously distorted by Tertullian and is nothing more than a statement of his policy by an influential bishop of the region on the question of the reconciliation of adulterers.[51] Who this bishop was is of no special importance. It has been conjectured with good reason that he was Agrippinus of Carthage, who is mentioned by Cyprian as a man of gracious memory *(vir bonae memoriae)* who as president of a great synod, pronounced against heretical baptism *(Ep.* 71, 4; 73, 3). If regard is had to the statement of Cyprian already cited, that among his predecessors there were some African bishops who altogether excluded adulterers from admission to penance *(Ep.* 55, 21), it appears probable that, faced with these rigorists, the then primate of Africa clearly affirmed his own contrary practice and thereby provoked Tertullian to make his attack on this authoritative "edict". The chronology and date are very much in favour of identification of this bishop with Agrippinus.[52]

The reconciliation of adulterers which was the principal subject of controversy was in no way an innovation, as is evident from our description of earlier practice. In the *De paenitentia,* Tertullian himself had preached full forgiveness for the gravest sins and had represented readmission to the Church as the connatural fruit of penance: *conlocavit in vestibulo paenitentiam secundam, quae pulsantibus patefaciat* (7, 10). As the door of pardon — *ianua ignoscentiae*[53] — which was open to the candidate for baptism was closed to the sinning Christian, the purpose of the "second penance" is to open the door to the penitents who are

---

[51] Cf. E. Preuschen *ZNW* (1910) 142f.; Poschmann I 302.
[52] For further details see K. Adam, *Das sog. Bußedikt* (1917) 56 ff. and A. Ehrhard, *Die Kirche der Märtyrer* (1932) 363.
[53] "Pardon" in the sense of a gratuitous remission is, as in Hermas, reserved to baptism. See above p. 28 f.

standing in the vestibule and knocking at the door. The image of the door leading inside from the vestibule absolutely excludes every interpretation except that of admission to the Church. Later it was in very general use to designate penance with reconciliation.[54] Tertullian, then, in the *De pudicitia,* nowhere accuses the Catholics of innovating. On the contrary, right at the beginning he says in plain words that he himself formerly shared their view, and that he has no reason to be ashamed of his renunciation of an error (1, 10—13). In the face of this recantation, it is simply closing one's eyes to facts to charge Tertullian's opponents with innovating. His change of outlook is perfectly explicable by his conversion to Montanism. Similarly, it was only the application of the rigid *non faciam* of the Paraclete that made this fanatical writer invert the scriptural arguments which he had used in the *De paenitentia* in favour of the opposite opinion.[55]

Against the conclusion that the Catholics both before and afterwards were committed to the principle of readmission of all kinds of sinners to the Church there is an objection of some weight which is the chief argument in support of the contrary opinion. It is seen in the charge of inconsistency which Tertullian constantly levels against his opponents in the *De pudicitia.* They are, he objects, very ready to grant forgiveness to those guilty of unchastity, yet they refuse it to apostates and murderers. This objection is the chief prop of Tertullian's polemic. He makes his point categorically and decisively: *Hinc est quod neque idololatriae neque sanguini pax ab ecclesiis redditur* (12, 1). There must have been some sort of foundation in the penitential practice of Catholics for this assertion. Uttered as it was in the heat of controversy, it need not be taken as strictly true, yet one cannot suppose that he was so stupid as to put himself in contradiction with known facts. It is hardly possible to give a clear and certain solution of

[54] Cf. A. d'Alès, 400 ff. (Appendix II: *Limen cclesiae*).
[55] *De paen.* 8, 2 and *De pud.* 2, 3; *De paen.* 10, 6 and *pud.* 19, 25; *paen.* 8, 4—9 and *pud.* 7—9; *paen.* 8, 1—2 and *pud.* 9, 9.

the difficulty. Tertullian's assertion is not in any case objectively correct if the words *ab ecclesiis* are taken to refer to the universal Church, as was clearly his intention. For Rome, this is already ruled out by the evidence adduced from Hermas (the *Pastor moechorum*), for Corinth by Dionysius,[56] and by Clement (*Quis div. salvetur*, 24) for Alexandria. A certain amount of scepticism is, therefore, permissible in regard to the absolute veracity of Tertullian's assertion in regard to Africa. One may hazard the conjecture that the Montanist movement had also given impetus to rigorism in Africa. If certain bishops, according to the testimony of Cyprian (*Ep.* 55,21), adopted a policy of perpetual exclusion of sinners guilty of unchastity, it is only to be expected that the judgement of the still graver sins of apostasy and murder will have been even more severe. However, in contrast to sinners against chastity, no apostates or murderers would have been found in the vast majority of the churches. There would, therefore, have been no tradition in existence in regard to the manner of dealing with them, as the question simply did not arise. In that situation, Tertullian could venture on his assertion without being given the lie by the known facts. Moreover, the inconsiderate character of his polemic shows that he would have felt no particular scruple even if one or other of the bishops still granted reconciliation to an apostate or a murderer.[57] Another eyplanation, which Esser in particular has expounded, is that in the majority of cases reconciliation was granted by Catholics to idolaters and murderers, but only on their deathbed. Because this procedure did not carry with it any actual and visible reunion with the Church, Tertullian has simply treated it as if it were equivalent to a denial of pace, which was the practice here and there.[58] Whatever we may think of it, Tertullian's assertion cannot do away with the fact that in opposition to him the

[56] See above 37.
[57] See Poschmann I 328 f.
[58] See also d'Alès 204. F. X. Funk (*ThQ* [1906] 543) and G. Koch 45 have also admitted that this is a possible explanation.

Catholics defended the universality of forgiveness most emphatically, nor with the fact, which he himself admitted, that formerly he too had shared that view.

b. The Organization and Theory of Penance

The importance of Tertullian for the early Christian doctrine of penance consists first in the evidence which he provides for Catholic penitential procedure, and secondly in the influence which he himself exercised on the development of the doctrine of penance. His witness is the first we have which provides a graphic picture of the conduct of penance, and one in which the fundamental elements, attested since the Apostolic age, have taken on a fixed form. Penance, which is necessary for "satisfaction", for "propitiation", and for "reconciliation" with God (*De paen.* 7,14; 8,9; 9,2; 11,3) demands an *operosa probatio*. This is accompanied not merely interiorly, but also by means of an outward act, the exomologesis (ἐξομολόγησις [9,1—2]). This includes confession, not so much by word as by deed, consisting of various acts of humiliation and mortification, and in a "mode of life that calls down mercy" (9,3). Part of it is "prostration in sackcloth and ashes", neglect of cleanliness, severe fasts, protracted sighing, weeping and prayer, beseeching on bended knee the assistance of the presbyters, of "God's beloved" (in the first place are meant the martyrs and confessors) and of all the brethren (9,4). Hardest of all, however, and this causes most to shrink from exomologesis, is the self-accusation — *publicatio sui* — before the congregation. This public act is, however, necessary in order to obtain forgiveness through the intercession of the faithful: *An melius est damnatum latere quam palam absolvi?* (16,8). It is accomplished in two stages: at first in front of the Church door — *in vestibulo* (7:10), or *pro foribus ecclesiae* (*De pud.* 3,5; 5,14) — later inside the Church (*De pud.* 13,7) and ends with reconciliation which, like excommunication, rests with the bishop. For the baptized there can be only one concession of penance: *sed iam semel, quia iam secundo ; sed amplius numquam, quia proxime frustra* (*De paen.* 7,10). Clearly, the restriction is based on Hermas, whose influence is seen elsewhere in the *De paenitentia*. The difference between them is that what was impossible for psychological reasons has now become so on dogmatic grounds.[59] Tertullian's influence on penitential teaching was primarily indirect, in that by his denials he compelled his opponents, the *diversa pars,* to set out the theoretical foundations of their practice and particularly to support them by biblical arguments. Already in the *De pudicitia* he is aware of a firm Catholic penitential doctrine reacting against his attack. However, he did also contribute some positive elements towards the further development.

The essential difference of the Montanist penitential doctrine of Tertullian from that of his Catholic period lies in its division of sins into remissible and irremissible sins *(peccata remissibilia* and *irremissibilia* [*De pud.* 2,12—15 etc.]). The latter were designated as *capitalia* (9,20; 21,14), *mortalia* (3,3; 19,28; 21,2), *maiora* (18:18), *graviora et exitiosa, quae veniam non capiunt* (19:25); the former as *modica* (1, 19), *mediocria* (7, 20), *leviora* (18, 18). Compensation for remissible sins will be made by *castigatio ;* for the irremissible sins by *damnatio.* Even a mortal sin is only excluded from ecclesiastical forgiveness; it does not render penance fruitless even in the sight of God: *de venia Deo reservamus* (19,6). A sinner of this kind may do penance on the fringe of the Church knowing that: *"si pacem hic non metit, apud Dominum seminat"* (3,5). Only unnatural sexual sins constitute an exception. These are not sins, but perversions, *non delicta, sed monstra,* and are altogether excluded from ecclesiastical penance. The division into remissible and irremissible sins is new and unheard of up to that time. A distinction had, of course, always been made between venial and grave sin and only the latter had been punished by expulsion from the Church. In his Catholic period Tertullian, too, was unaware of

---

[59] See above 31.

any unforgivable crimes,[60] and the new attitude in the *De pudicitia* forces him into manifest self-contradiction. He is only able to defend the impossibility of ecclesiastical forgiveness by making use of arguments which also exclude divine forgiveness,[61] in spite of the fact that he holds out to the penitents the prospect of "forgiveness by God". Similarly, the outward form of penance, which included the appearance of the penitents at the Church door and their efforts to secure the tears and compassion of the brethren (*De paen*. 3,5), is only intelligible in Catholic practice. Among the Montanists, the Church remains irrevocably closed against those guilty of mortal sin. The intercession of the congregation on their behalf is fruitless:[62] its practice has lost its significance, and even where it is retained it is only under the pressure of tradition. It is this force of tradition, so fundamentally opposed to the principles of Montanism, which does not allow ecclesiastical forgiveness to disappear altogether. Tertullian withdraws mortal sins from its scope, but expressly admits its validity for lesser sins, "*leviora*". In regard to these, ecclesiastical penance still remains in force, both in regard to the preliminary exclusion from the Church — *ob tale quid extra gregem datus est* (*De pud*. 7,16) and to the forgiveness granted by the bishop — *venia ab episcopo* (18, 18). In proposing this doctrine, the African stands alone. There is not the slightest support for it either before his time, or afterwards. It was produced as a way out of a predicament, and even in Montanist practice will have played hardly any part.[63]

On the question as to which sins were "mortal", Tertullian is in agreement with the Catholics. He does not provide an exhaustive list. Besides idolatry, murder and adultery, he mentions fraud, false witness and other crimes.[64] For Tertullian the Montanist

---

[60] H. Koch's attempt (24 ff.) to prove the contrary is vitiated throughout by exaggerated conclusions. See Poschmann I 293—300.
[61] Cf. *De pud*. 17, 8 and supra, n. 55.
[62] *De pud*. 9, 15 in conjunction with *De paen*. 10, 6.
[63] For a detailed proof see Poschmann I 317 ff.
[64] Cf. from his Catholic period *De bapt*. 4; *Apol*. 2, 11; *De spect*. 3, 20; from his

all of these are unforgivable. It is, therefore, an error, which has its origin in the strange reasoning of the *De pudicitia,* when recent histories of dogma speak of "three capital sins" to which the primitive Church, according to Tertullian, is supposed to have refused forgiveness. Idolatry, murder and adultery occupy a primary, but not an exclusive place among capital sins. Their grouping together as a triad, along with the artificial reasoning by which this is justified from the Decalogue and the Acts of the Apostles (*De pud.* 5 and 12) are simply to be attributed to the exigencies of Tertullian's polemic.[65] However — and this shows how wide his influence extended — even in the fourth and fifth centuries the triad was of profound significance for the organization of penance in a number of churches, where it was regarded as the sole subject matter for ecclesiastical penance.[66] The same sort of thing happened to the concept of the "sin against God", which was introduced into the doctrine of penance by Tertullian and used by him as a polemical weapon. At first he contrasts it with a sin against one's fellow men, but then goes on to lay down that it is unforgivable, on the grounds that the Lord only promised forgiveness to a sin committed against a brother (Mt 18:22), while those committed against God would obtain forgiveness from God alone (*De pud.* 2, 10; 21, 15). Accordingly, sins against God are all *peccata capitalia,* sins against men are the *delicta leviora.* The arbitrary and illogical equivalence here involved is put up with in order that the restriction of the Church's power of forgiveness to lesser sins might be bolstered up more firmly by an appeal to the authority of Christ. Although Tertullian's interpretation of it was rejected by the Catholics, this vague and in practice unusable concept did gain admittance to the theology

---

Montanist period *Adv. Marc.* 4, 9; *De pud.* 19, 25. On the same question, see Cyprian, *De bono pat.* 14; Origen, *De or.* 2, 28.
[65] Cf. A. Ehrhard, *Die Kirche der Märtyrer* (1932) 365.
[66] Cf. Pacianus, *Paraen. ad paen.* 4; Augustine, *Specul. de Script. sacr.* 29: *nonnulli putant tria tantum crimina esse mortifera.*

of penance, which thus became burdened with an unnecessary problem.[67]

In regard to the part played by the Church in penance Tertullian the Montanist is in agreement with his Catholic opponents except for his restriction of it to lesser sins, *delicta leviora*. It consists, first of all, in the assistance given to the penitent by the intercession of the congregation. He teaches in the *De paenitentia* (10, 6), and takes for granted in the *De pudicitia,* that the prayer of the Church is the prayer of Christ, who pleads before the Father — *exorator Patris* — and pronounces forgiveness. By thus identifying it with Christ's prayer Tertullian attributes to the prayer of the Church which formed part of the exomologesis a kind of sacramental efficacy. He is thus the first writer to provide a dogmatic basis for the procedure of public penance. This was a valuable contribution to the future development of the doctrine of penance. Precisely because Christ's prayer never goes unheard (*De paen.* 10, 7) the Church can on her side grant forgiveness to a sinner. The only difference is that later as a Montanist he restricts both the bishop's pardon *(venia ab episcopo)* and the Church's intercession to lesser sins, and makes an attack on the forgiveness of grave sins.

At that time, the Catholics appealed for the first time to Mt 16:18f. for the power to forgive sins (*De pud.* 21, 9).[68] They claimed that the power of binding and loosing conferred on Peter has been transmitted to every Church deriving from Peter — *ad omnem ecclesiam Petri propinquam ;* in practice that meant to its bishop. Tertullian's unrestrained and passionate retort is again full of inconsistency which at once reveals the weakness of his position. At first he claims that the power is personal to Peter, and is not given to the Church: *dabo tibi claves, non ecclesiae* (*De pud.* 21, 10). But then he goes on to attribute it once again to the Church, but only to the "Church of the Spirit",

---

[67] See Poschmann I 336f.
[68] At any rate Tertullian is the first to cite the text, already in *Scorp.* 10.

not to the "Church of the bishops": *Ecclesia quidem delicta donabit, sed ecclesia spiritus, non ecclesia numerus episcoporum ; domini enim, non famuli est ius et arbitrium ; Dei ipsius, non sacerdotis* (21, 17). Although he thus basically denies to the bishops any power whatsoever of forgiveness, this does not prevent him, by means of an impossible exegesis of Mt 18:22, from leaving to them the forgiveness of venial sins. It is hard to imagine a more crass contradiction.[69] It can hardly be explained except by supposing that, owing to the fanaticism of his polemic in establishing the theoretical basis of his new attitude, he took no account whatsoever of any desire to retain elements of the ancient practice. Tertullian's position, therefore, in the controversy on penance, shows clearly that the motive which inspired his tragic evolution from the position of a most determined advocate of the Church to that of her most vehement opponent was much less dogmatic conviction than a blind fanaticism which disregarded all that was fundamental in tradition.

c. The Evidence from outside Africa

The picture of Catholic penitential procedure which has been obtained from Tertullian is confirmed by contemporary testimony from other regions. Postponing for the time being our consideration of the doctrine of Clement of Alexandria, we may point in the first place to Dionysius of Corinth, who was insistent that readmission to the Church should be granted to repentant heretics.[70] The position of St. Irenaeus also deserves consideration; in him Eastern and Western tradition were united. He, too, has been erroneously represented as an advocate of the ancient ideal of holiness which, it is claimed, never allowed full readmission to the Church to anyone who had fallen into grave

---

[69] Cf. de Labriolle 438; Poschmann I 314.
[70] Above 37.

sin.[71] The remark of the "presbyter" (*Haer.* IV 27), which serves as a proof of this claim, in reality merely states that, as against the Gnostic distinction between the vindictive God of the Old Testament and the merciful God of the New, Christians have to expect a much stricter judgement than those who were under the Old Covenant. Whether the punishment may still be avoided by the performance of penance is a question which is not given any consideration in the context; no firm conclusion concerning it can be derived from the text.[72] Elsewhere Irenaeus says explicitly that God grants peace and friendship to "those who do penance and are converted" (IV 40, 1), and that eternal fire is prepared for Satan and "all who are impenitently obstinate in heresy" (V 26, 2). There are also numerous references to the ecclesiastical aspect of penance. As leaders and judges of the people the presbyters have charge over moral discipline. They have to make use of *correptio* and where necessary pass sentence of excommunication (IV 26, 3—4; 27, 4). Penance is performed under the control of the Church. Exomologesis, as a designation of ecclesiastical penance, appears also in Irenaeus as an established term signifying a lengthy period of penance. It is thus used of the wife of a deacon in the story of the women who had been seduced by the Gnostics, and who afterwards came back to the Church: "she always continued to do penance" (τὸν πάντα χρόνον ἐξομολογουμένη διετέλεσεν [I 13, 5]). Of another group of similar unfortunates it is said that some of them "confessed their guilt openly" — εἰς φανερὸν ἐξομολογοῦνται — others, however, are wavering and "are neither out nor in" (13, 7). Cerdon, the Gnostic, also submitted to exomologesis from time to time (III 4, 3). It cannot be shown from Irenaeus that any reconciliation of penitents took place,[73] but there is not the slightest

---

[71] Thus H. Koch *ZNW* (1908) 45; H. Windisch, *Taufe u. Sünde* (1908) 404; G. H. Bonwetsch, *Die Theologie des Irenäus* (1925) 131 f. For the opposite view see especially J. Stufler *ZkTh* (1908) 488 ff.   [72] See Poschmann I 213—218.
[73] Against Stufler 447 ff.; Windisch 4, 10; Loofs, *Dogmengeschichte* ed. 4 (1906) 206, n. 11.

evidence to the contrary. His belief in the efficacy of penance, and the emphasis he lays on the necessity of the Church for salvation, taken together with the evidence from the practice of other churches make it highly probable that he, too, granted reconciliation.[74]

According to a view which has had much support up to recent times, it was at this time that the Roman church took a step of decisive importance for the establishment of the institution of penance. Now, however, that the "Edict of Callistus" has been shown to be an untenable historical construction, this pope no longer has the same position in the history of penance. We know nothing about him beyond what Hippolytus relates. This account, however, does not tell us anything about his attitude towards ecclesiastical penance in the proper sense which was open to the faithful. The burden of its complaint is simply that he receives former sectaries into the Church indiscriminately, and without imposing penance on them. However, the report of Hippolytus leaves no room for doubt that even in regard to ordinary ecclesiastical penance, Callistus certainly belonged to the milder school of thought, and shared the views of the opponents of Tertullian, even though he did not come into direct conflict with him.

As for Hippolytus himself, it is clear from his attitude to Callistus that the rigorist tendency made itself felt in Rome as elsewhere. We cannot be sure to what extent his rigorism was applied in the treatment of penitents. It is uncertain whether, like the African bishops already mentioned, he refused forgiveness to adulterers and, if so, to idolators also and murderers; or whether he was content to impose a greater, perhaps lifelong, penance. In any case his rejection of the teaching of Callistus, according to which the Church contains both saints and sinners (*Philosophum.* IX 12, 22 f.), is not incompatible with the re-admission of repentant sinners who have expiated their guilt.

[74] See Poschmann I 211—229.

There is positive evidence that Hippolytus admitted in principle forgiveness of sins through the Church in the *Egyptian Church Order* which is today almost universally ascribed to him.[75] In the prayer for the ordination of a bishop which is found in this work, the power of "loosing every bond" which was conferred on the Apostles is attributed to the bishop.[76] In transmitting this prayer the author of the *Apostolic Tradition* thereby indirectly testified to the exercise of the power of ecclesiastical forgiveness and at the same time to his own approval of the practice. Even more instructive is an account handed down by Eusebius, and by many attributed on good grounds to Hippolytus, of the penance of the confessor Natalis. It relates how after he had lapsed into the heresy of Theodotus he was brought in a miraculous manner to do penance, and then once again admitted to communion by Pope Zephyrinus.[77] Even if the story does not emanate from Hippolytus, it does show that, even for so serious a sin as heresy, a public penitential procedure which included reconciliation was customary in Rome, even as we find it attested by Tertullian as the Catholic practice in Africa.

3. Cyprian and the Question of Penance in the Decian Persecution

LITERATURE: J. Stufler, "Die Behandlung der Gefallenen zur Zeit der decischen Verfolgung" in *ZkTh* 14 (1907) 517—618. B. Poschmann, "Zur Bußfrage in der cyprianischen Zeit" ibid. 21 (1913) 25—54; 244—265. A. Vanbeck, "La pénitence dans S. Cyprien" in *RHLR* 10 (1913) 422ff. A. d'Alès, *L'Edit de Calliste*, (1914) 297ff.; Id., *La théologie de S. Cyprien* (1922). H. Koch, *Cyprianische Untersuchungen* (1926) 211—285. A. Ehrhard, *Die Kirche der Märtyrer* (1932) 369 ff. P. Char-

---

[75] [i. e. *The Apostolic Tradition of St. Hippolytus of Rome,* tr. and ed. Gregory Dix, London 1939. Tr.'s note.]
[76] [*Apostolic Tradition*, ed. Dix, p. 5 f. Tr.'s note.]
[77] Eusebius, *H. E.* V 28, 8—12; for the authorship of Hippolytus see O. Bardenhewer, *A. L.* II ed. 2 (1914) 514; A. d'Alès, *La théologie de S. Hippolyte* (1906) 109. Hesitation is felt by A. Puech, *Hist. de la litt. grecque chrét.* II (1928) 565.

tier, "La discipline pénitentielle d'après les écrits de S. Cyprien" in *Antonianum* 6 (1939) 17—42; 135—156. Poschmann I 370—424. K. Rahner, "Die Bußlehre des hl. Cyprian von Karthago" in *ZkTh* 74 (1952) 257—276; 381—438. J. H. Taylor, "St Cyprian and the Reconciliation of Apostates" in *TS* 3 (1942) 27—46. R. C. Mortimer, *The Origins of Private Penance in the Western Church* (Oxford 1939). M. Bévenot, "The Sacrament of Penance and St. Cyprian's De Lapsis" in *TS* 16 (1955) 175—213; Id., *St. Cyprian : The Lapsed ; The Unity of the Church*, Tr. and ed. M. Bévenot (London 1957 [*ACW* XXV]).

a. The Treatment of the Lapsed

Barely a generation after Tertullian the question of penance became more actual than ever owing to the great number of those who apostatized during the persecution of the Christians under Decius. When steps were being taken to bring back the lapsed to the Church, it was necessary to draw up a uniform policy governing the requirements of penance, which would hold the balance between disciplinary severity and practical needs. The writings of St. Cyprian, and particularly his correspondence with the Roman Church, provide a graphic picture of the problems and controversies that arose at this time. Along with the testimony of Tertullian, they are the most important source for the history of penance up to the time of St. Augustine. The decades of peace preceding the persecution had altered nothing in the situation concerning penance. Historical research, therefore, is faced with the same problem as it encountered in the confusion stirred up by Tertullian, and once again the same conflicting views confront one another. The opinion that Callistus was the first to open the doors of the Church to carnal sinners now maintains that St. Cyprian and his contemporary Pope Cornelius went a step further. It is supposed that under the pressure of circumstances, and fearing that otherwise the Church would be emptied of its members, for the first time they now granted reconciliation to those who had denied their faith. The opposite view, however, sees no innovation in this practice; it was nothing more than a clear and decisive application of a line of conduct for which there was earlier, even if not universal, precedent.[78]

The correctness of the second view is seen at once from the fact that at the very outset of the persecution the possibility of the readmission of the lapsed was regarded as a self-evident principle. This is attested by Cyprian in a whole series of letters which he sent from his place of retreat to Carthage and Rome, and also by some letters sent to him by the Roman church which at that time was without a bishop. When Cyprian, with great firmness, rejected the demands of the lapsed, who relied on the "letters of peace" which they had obtained from the martyrs and claimed reconciliation as theirs by right, it was not its concession as such to which he was opposed, but its overhasty concession, which took no account of the necessity of making expiation (*Ep.* 15, 2). The fruit must not be plucked before it is ripe (*crudo tempore* or *importuno adhuc tempore* [*Ep.* 16, 2; 17, 3], *ante expiata delicta, ante exomologesim factam criminis* [*De lapsis* 16]). The Romans and their spokesman, Novatian, are in agreement. To them, too, it is only the overhastily applied remedies of reconciliation (*properata nimis remedia communicationum* [*Ep.* 30, 3, 6; 31, 6; 36, 3]) that are objectionable because they are harmful. In itself, striving after reconciliation is not merely lawful; it is also enjoined (*Ep.* 30, 7). As the performance of appropriate penance was a preliminary condition for its concession, the problem of reconciliation was especially acute in the case of the sick who had not yet made any satisfaction. Yet even these are "to be succoured" by the concession of peace (*Ep.* 8, 3; 30, 8) and it is left to God to determine what he will do with such as these, and how he will moderate the weight of his judgement — *quid de talibus faciat et*

---

[78] The most thorough representative of the first view is H. Koch, who cites the following names in its favour: K. Müller, R. Geiger, A. v. Harnack, R. Seeberg, K. Holl, E. Schwartz, H. Achelis, F. X. Funk, P. Batiffol, G. Rauschen, K. Adam (for Africa, not Rome), P. de Labriolle, O. Watkins (H. Koch, *Cypr. Unters.* 211, n. 2). Against it are J. Stufler, A. Vanbeck, A. d'Alès, F. Hünermann, A. Ehrhard, B. Poschmann, who in his *Paenitentia Secunda* upholds his treatment of the subject in 1913 against Koch's objections.

qualiter iudicii sui examinet pondera, for harsh cruelty — *dura crudelitas* — is no less objectionable than easy compliance — *prona facilitas.* These are the impressive sentiments of Novatian, himself later a rigorist. St. Cyprian at first felt more uneasy about this kind of reconciliation than the Romans, and before allowing it required a letter of peace from a martyr (*Ep.* 18, 1; 19, 2; 20, 3.) What a different form the discussion on the problem as a whole would have taken if the readmission of an apostate had been a thing unheard of up to that time.

The decrees of the councils which after the persecution assembled in Carthage and Rome in the year 251 were in agreement with each other and in harmony with the policy of moderation. As Cyprian explained later, they hold to a "sound" middle course between excessive severity and excessive laxity. They safeguard severity by insisting on a "long penance" — *paenitentia plena* — which is to be determined by examination of individual cases, wills and needs — *causae et voluntates et necessitates singulorum* (*Ep.* 55,6; 57,1; 64,1). They allow scope for mildness, first by ratifying the practice which had been in use from the beginning of the persecution, of exempting the dying from the law of *paenitentia plena ;* secondly, by accepting as sufficient the penance already done by the *libellatici* in consideration of their lesser guilt, with the result that there is now no further obstacle to their reconciliation (*Ep.* 55,17): *placuit... examinatis causis singulorum libellaticos interim admitti, sacrificatis in exitu subveniri.* Novatian availed himself of the occasion of both of these "mild" decrees to accuse his rival Cornelius of laxity, after he had been defeated by him in the election to the bishopric of Rome. The charge was indiscriminate reconciliation of those who had offered sacrifice — *passim communicare sacrificatis* (*Ep.* 55,12). That is the reason why Cyprian, who defends Pope Cornelius in *Ep.* 55, selects from the decrees of the Council precisely these two points for special emphasis. It is an unfortunate misunderstanding when, as is commonly the case, the entire legislation of the Council is thought to be contained in the sentence quoted above,

55

and this is taken to mean that all without exception who have offered sacrifice will be reconciled only on their deathbed. On this interpretation the express requirement of a "long penance"[79] does indeed remain intelligible — *legitimum et plenum tempus satisfactionis* — and so does the decision of the Council on the part to be taken by the people in reconciliation (*Ep.* 64,1).[80] However, in actual fact the question of the readmission of *sacrificati* who were in health was left to be decided later, either by the bishop of the region, or by a fresh council.[81] The Easter synod which met in Carthage in 252 under the threat of a new persecution then brought in a general rule. After mentioning the grant of reconciliation by the first synod of 251 to sick penitents who had not completed their penance, it is now decided that for the same motive readmission will be granted to all. For it is not now *infirmis, sed fortibus pax necessaria est, nec morientibus, sed viventibus communicatio a nobis danda est* (*Ep.* 57, 2).[82] The new decision does not represent any change of principle on Cyprian's part. It fits quite easily into the context of the earlier decision. It is not a question whether it is ever justified *de iure* to grant peace in time of health that is now being put, but whether it is permissible *de facto* here and now. The *paenitentia plena* is not yet under consideration. However, if it can be dispensed with in the

---

[79] *Ep.* 57, 1: *agerent diu paenitentiam plenam et, si periculum infirmitatis urgeret, pacem sub ictu mortis acciperent.*

[80] Tillemont (*Mémoires* 14 ed. 2 [Paris 1701] 618, n. 30) was one of the first to reject this interpretation held at that period by Du Pin. In recent times it has also been rejected by J. Stufler, A. Vanbeck, B. Poschmann.

[81] In *Ep.* 56, 2 Cyprian concurs with a bishop who had sought his counsel that for three penitents who had offered sacrifice under torture the three years' penance which they had performed was sufficient to admit them again to communion. Yet he considers the question so important that he wishes to lay it before a synod (56, 3).

[82] The decision of the council of 251 *ut infirmis in exitu subveniretur* (ibid.) was afterwards taken as a kind of precedent for the new more lenient treatment. This provides additional confirmation that this decree does not imply the rigoristic requirement of lifelong penance for all the *sacrificati*, but simply an exemption of the dying from the law of the *paenitentia plena*. Otherwise Cyprian's reasoning in *Ep.* 57, 2 would be quite illogical. See Poschmann I 387 ff.

case of the dying, the same procedure is justified when the living find themselves in a comparable emergency.

This conclusion provides a solution to the problem of the supposed change of mind with which Cyprian was reproached by his opponents even in his lifetime (*Ep.* 55, 3), and which in modern histories of dogma is generally taken as an established fact. There was on his part no fundamental change of mind in the sense that he only gradually came round to the view that ecclesiastical forgiveness for the lapsed was possible, as this possibility was for him an antecedent certainty. However, he is, as he himself admits, "yielding to the needs of the time" (*Ep.* 55, 7), and in the actual assessment of the penance to be performed he advanced more and more in the direction of leniency. Only in this sense is his later confession relevant: *Remitto omnia, multa dissimulo studio et voto colligendae fraternitatis. Etiam quae in Deum commissa sunt, non pleno iudicio religionis examino. Delictis plusquam oportet remittendis paene ipse delinquo (Ep.* 59, 16).[83]

It is not Cyprian who is an innovator in principle, but rather his adversary, Novatian. At the outbreak of the persecution, as we saw, he too was not opposed to the reconciliation of the lapsed, but only to overhasty reconciliation. He even pointed the way to Cyprian in regard to the reconciliation of those who were on the point of death with their penance still unfinished.

---

[83] [M. Bévenot argues that "it may be admitted that, at least before the crisis of the Decian persecution, Cyprian considered the forgiveness of apostasy, being a 'sin against God', to lie beyond the prerogatives of the Church.... We can, perhaps, take it that this was, at the time, his own personal opinion; it does not involve his having derived it from the Church's tradition. Having had no experience of persecution, he will not have put the question to himself as a practical issue.... But what really concerns us is that under the Decian persecution Cyprian never once repeated that threatening heading [in the Testimonia: "There is no forgiveness in the Church for one who sins against God"], nor ever made use of it again.... This seems to show a real progress in Cyprian's thought, the result of his experience during the persecution.... He has passed from his rigorist understanding of the texts which derogated from the Church's powers over sin, to that merciful insistence on discipline, *mitis iustitia,* which, for the repentant, opened the way to reconciliation with the Church and with God." "The Sacrament of Penance and Cyprian's De Lapsis" in *TS* 16 (1955) 188 ff. Tr.'s note.]

The protest which he raised later against the decision of the council sanctioning this practice is, therefore, in flat contradiction to his earlier attitude. Moreover, the dispute about penance has to serve as a justification for his appearance as antipope and for schism.[84] It is significant that he campaigns against the immediate reconciliation of the *libellatici,* and from now on ceases to co-operate in this policy. He contrasts it with the earlier and more dilatory procedure, and is able to represent it with some justification as an innovation.[85] In regard to the reconciliation of the dying he seems at first to have acted with some restraint;[86] in fact, however, he has already repudiated this measure too. He appeals to the purity of the Church as forbidding all contacts with sinners (*Ep.* 55, 27; see Ps.-Cyprian, *Ad Novatianum* 1). However, as Cyprian observed, the principle of purity logically requires the exclusion not only of the lapsed but also of cheats, and adulterers whom Novatian continued to tolerate in his community (*Ep.* 55, 26). The later Novatianists did in fact logically expel all grave sinners from the Church. The wide diffusion of the sect, particularly in the East, is explicable by the fact, already familiar to us, that the tendency towards rigorism had in many places been stimulated by Montanism, and that the practice of refusing reconciliation, which existed even in many Catholic churches, was regarded only as a matter of discipline which did not provide any reason for exclusion from the Church.[87]

b. The Dogmatic Theology of Penance in St. Cyprian

The dogmatic theology of penance in St. Cyprian is quite traditional in character, the only difference being that certain

---

[84] Cf. E. Amann, *DTC* XI 837 with the appeal to A. v. Harnack and L. Duchesne.
[85] Cf. Cyprian, *Ep.* 55, 13—17.
[86] At any rate Cyprian does not feel that he is obliged to defend the conciliar decree on this point too (*Ep.* 55,13).
[87] Thus Cyprian himself, *Ep.* 55, 21; cf. also the question of Antonianus (ibid. 24) asking what was the heresy introduced by Novatian.

aspects are more sharply emphasized. In contrast to baptism, through which pardon of sins is obtained as a sheer act of grace, penance has to earn forgiveness by laborious effort (*Ep.* 55, 22; *De op. et el.* 2 and *passim*). For this reason God alone, and neither bishop nor martyr, has the power to "remit or condone" satisfaction (*De lapsis* 17).[88] Only when adequate penance has been performed should reconciliation be accorded. Otherwise it is an invalid and false peace, dangerous to those who grant it and useless to those who receive it — *irrita et falsa pax, periculosa dantibus et nihil accipientibus profutura* (*De lapsis* 15). Yet the act of reconciliation retains its sacramental significance. Its formal effect is readmission to the Church, and along with this ecclesiastical forgiveness (see *Ep.* 4, 2; 16, 2; 17, 2; 19, 2; 55, 6—29; 57, 1 and *passim*). This effect is by no means restricted to the sphere of the Church on earth. Along with the "peace" of the Church the penitent receives the "Spirit of the Father" (*Ep.* 57, 4), the pledge of life — *pignus vitae* (*Ep.* 55, 13). Although the decision lies with the "Lord when he comes to judgement",[89] yet those who are reconciled have at least an expectation of salvation; whereas those who are outside the Church are without exception excluded from it (*Ep.* 57, 1). Thus ecclesiastical forgiveness is indispensable. Cyprian's theory is, admittedly, imperfect as compared with later doctrine, and it is easy to expose its inconsistencies. However, that makes no difference to the fact that this Father of the Church teaches two incontestable truths: that God alone forgives sins, and that

---

[88] This idea also lies beneath the much misunderstood text of the *Test.* III 28 *"Non posse in ecclesia remitti ei, qui in Deum deliquerit."* The sentence cannot signify: that a "sin against God" is absolutely irremissible (thus, *e.g.* H. Koch, 247 ff.) because from the beginning Cyprian is convinced that even the gravest sin, apostasy, can be forgiven and because the forgiveness of adultery, which he expressly mentions as a "sin against God" (*Ep.* 55, 27), was established practice in his day in Africa (*Ep.* 55, 20—21). For further details see Poschmann I 411—415. [See above n. 83 and M. Bévenot, art. cit. — Tr.'s note.]

[89] [See M. Bévenot, art. cit., who argues strongly against the view of the "supposed delay till the day of judgement for the reward of the just" (ibid. p. 192) — Tr.'s note.]

salvation is linked with forgiveness through the Church. If one of the two series of statements is inadequately considered, or completely ignored, violence is done to the evidence of the texts.[90]

The sacramental character of the act of reconciliation follows also from the fact that its efficacy is dependent on its administration by the official ministers of the Church (*Ep*. 66, 5), and conversely because once it has been officially administered it retains its validity in every case (*Ep*. 55, 13; 64, 1).

As the divine forgiveness presupposes that of the Church, penance must be performed under ecclesiastical direction if it is to be efficacious (*Ep*. 19, 1). The "priests of God" have to determine the appropriate duration of penance — *iustum tempus* — to supervise it, and to examine its sufficiency (*Ep*. 4, 4; 55, 6; 17, 2). The people also have a part to play in the decision concerning readmission. Given this state of affairs, it is obvious that the sinner must also confess or admit his guilt before the Church, that is to say in the first place before the rulers of the Church who are charged with the direction of penance. Fundamentally the entire penitential procedure and its attendant humiliation is a "confession", and in fact is also directly designated

---

[90] Thus some writers, by appealing to the idea that sins are forgiven by God alone, call in question the sacramental efficacy of reconciliation (cf. H. Koch 282). Others see in the passages on the sanctifying power of reconciliation direct evidence of the forgiveness of sins in the sense of the Council of Trent, and thus do not do justice to the texts which attribute the forgiveness to God alone as the fruit of satisfaction. Thus, P. Galtier, *L'Eglise et la rémission des péchés* (1932) 41 ff. [See M. Bévenot, art. cit. p. 212 f.: "The forgiveness that Christ *can* give through His priests is, therefore, a forgiveness given and accomplished here and now upon earth.... If it seems to contradict what he said before, viz., that man cannot remit sins against God; the contradiction evaporates on two separate counts: (a) that 'remit' there meant 'condone, without any personal satisfaction', and chiefly because (b) when the bishop reconciles according to 'Our Lord's commands', it is Christ who is acting through him: 'Only the Lord can grant mercy... who alone has received all power of judgement from the Father.' But 'with the help of the bishop reparation for sin and its remission are pleasing to God', because there is 'one man in the Church who here and now is its bishop, here and now is its judge, deputizing for Christ' (*iudex vice Christi*)." — Tr.'s note.]

by St. Cyprian as a *confessio* or *exomologesis* (*De lapsis* 28, 29; *Ep.* 55, 17, 29 and *passim.*) Along with this general meaning *exomologesis* also has the more restricted sense, known from Tertullian, of the final liturgical act of penance which has to be undertaken publicly before reconciliation in the presence of the bishop, the clergy and the congregation (*Ep.* 15, 1; 16, 2; 17, 2; 18, 1; 19, 2; 20, 3).[91] There is no evidence that a formal confession formed an obligatory part of this public rite. The oral confession which was made before entering on the whole procedure was naturally not a public one. The exomologesis concluded with the imposition of hands by the bishop and clergy. In the Latin Church it is first attested by St. Cyprian, but as an established practice (*Ep.* 16, 2 and the other texts already mentioned). By the commission of the bishop, presbyters who were united with him in the dignity of the priesthood — *sacerdotali honore coniuncti presbyteri* (*Ep.* 61, 3) — and in extreme necessity even deacons (*Ep.* 18, 1) could take his place at the reception of exomologesis and at the imposition of hands for the obtaining of peace.[92]

The penitential procedure which we have described was indispensable for mortal sins, such as apostasy and adultery. It was also made use of for lesser sins — *peccata minora* — which were not "sins committed against God" (*Ep.* 16, 2; 17, 2), in which case a relatively light satisfaction was sufficient for reconciliation.[93] Private ecclesiastical penance is not known to St. Cyprian. Admittedly, however, that kind of private penance which consists in prayer, fasting and especially in almsdeeds plays a very important part in the life of a Christian: *Opus est ... nobis cotidiana*

---

[91] On this see H. Koch 280, excursus on exomologesis.

[92] On the question of reconciliation through a deacon see P. Galtier, *De Paenitentia* (Rome 1956) 464 ff.; Poschmann I 421 f.

[93] *De lapsis* 28 singles out for praise some who do penance — *exomologesim conscientiae faciunt* — merely because they had thought of apostatizing. Ac cording to *Ep.* 4, 4 certain consecrated virgins who had dwelt with men without, however, sexual intercourse, are to be reconciled and readmitted to the Church after they have done penance.

sanctificatio, et qui cotidie deliquimus, debita nostra sanctificatione adsidua repurgemus (*De dom. or.* 12). Good works are parallel with baptism in their power to obtain forgiveness of sins (*De op. et el.* 2—3). But this kind of penance is performed privately without sacramental mediation.

4. The Penitential Doctrine of the Great Alexandrians

LITERATURE: H. Windisch, *Sünde und Buße* (1908). J. Hoh, *Die kirchl. Buße* (1932). G. Anrich, *Clemens u. Origenes als Begründer der Lehre vom Fegfeuer,* Festgabe für H. J. Holtzmann (1902). K. Holl, *Enthusiasmus u. Bußgewalt beim griech. Mönchtum* (1898). P. A. Kirsch, "Die Behandlung der crimina capitalia in der morgenländ. Kirche" in *AKK* 84 (1904). J. Stufler, "Die Sündenvergebung bei Origenes" in *ZkTh* 14 (1907) 193—228; 15 (1908) 542f. B. Poschmann, *Die Sündenvergebung bei Origenes* (1912). J. Hörmann, *Untersuchungen zur griech. Laienbeicht* (1913). A. Vanbeck, "La pénitence dans Origène" in *RHLR* 10 (1912) 544—557; 11 (1913) 115—129. A. d'Alès, *L'Edit de Calliste* (1914) 252-296. P. Galtier, *L'Eglise et la rémission des péchés* (1932) 184—213. Poschmann I 229—260; 425—480. K. Rahner, "La doctrine d'Origène sur la pénitence" in *RechSR* 37 (1950) 47—97; 252—286; 422—456. Th. Rüther, *Die sittliche Forderung der Apatheia in den beiden ersten christlichen Jahrhunderten u. bei Klemens v. Alexandrien* (Freiburg im Br. 1949). W. Völker, "Der wahre Gnostiker nach Clemens Alexandrinus" in *TU* 57 (Berlin 1952). H. Karpp, "Die Bußlehre des Klemens von Alexandrien" in *ZNW* 43 (1950—51) 224—242. A. Méhat, "Pénitence seconde et péché involontaire chez Clément d'Alexandrie" in *Vig Chr* 8 (1954) 225—233. J. Wytzes, "The Twofold Way, Platonic Influences in the Work of Clement of Alexandria" in *Vig Chr* 11 (1957) 226—245; 14 (1960) 129—153. E. F. Latko, *Origen's Concept of Penance* (Quebec 1949). H. v. Campenhausen, *Kirchliches Amt und geistliche Vollmacht in den ersten drei Jahrhunderten* (Tübingen 1953). J. Grotz, *Die Entwicklung des Bußstufenwesens in der vornicänischen Kirche* (Freiburg im Br. 1955). G. Bardy, "Les idées morales d'Origène" in *MSR* 13 (1956) 23—38. G. Teichtweier, *Die Sündenlehre des Origenes* (Regensburg 1958). G. Müller, "Origenes und die Apokatastasis" in *TZ* 14 (1958) 174—190. J. J. O'Meara, tr. and ed., "Origen: Prayer, Exhortation to Martyrdom" in *ACW* 19 (London 1954). J. E. L. Oulton and H. Chadwick, *Alexandrian Christianity* : Selected Translations of Clement and Origen with Introductions and Notes, *Library of Christian Classics* 2 (London 1954). T. J. Manson, "Martyrs and Martyrdom" *BJRL* 39 (1957) 463—484. M. Lods, *Confesseurs et martyrs. Successeurs des prophètes dans l'Eglise des trois premiers siècles* (Neuchâtel; Paris 1958).

Clement and Origen are the first copious witnesses for the institution of penance in the Eastern Church. In essentials their teaching corroborates the western tradition; like it, too, it has been the subject of varying and indeed conflicting interpretations. For some Origen is the impulsive representative of a rigorism like that of Tertullian;[94] according to others he disapproved of the readmission into the Church of those guilty of the capital sins, at any rate during his early period;[95] while yet a third interpretation finds that the forgiveness of all sins is attested by him from the outset.[96] The witness of the great Alexandrian is all the more important because it is a direct report of the tradition of the East, uninfluenced by the controversies generated by Tertullian.[97]

Clement takes over directly from Hermas (*Mand.* IV 3) the doctrine of a second penance which God has instituted in consideration of human frailty, but which is limited to a single concession (*Strom.* II 13, 56f.). Following Heb 10:26 f., he does indeed limit forgiveness to indeliberate sins, but by this all he means to exclude are sins of deliberate malice. These are irremissible, not intrinsically by reason of their objective gravity, but because of the impenitent state of mind which they presuppose in the sinner.[98] In fact, he excludes no sin, however great, from forgiveness (*Quis div.* 38, 4 — 39, 2f.). Penance and forgiveness are open to the bandit chief (ibid. 42, 7), to the adulteress (*Strom.* II 23, 147, 2f.), to heretics (*Strom.* VII 16, 102, 2). Even for one who for the time being is obdurate "instruction" is available from a divine "teacher" (VII 2, 6, 1). A repetition of penance is ruled out because "repeated penances" alternating with fresh sins are merely "sham penance" (II 13, 57, 3—4; 59, 1). Clement is also in complete agreement with Hermas in differentiating the modes of operation of baptism and penance. Baptism simply bestows pardon — ἄφεσις — by free grace,

---

[94] Thus Döllinger and A. v. Harnack.
[95] H. Windisch, K. Holl, P. A. Kirsch, E. Amann.
[96] J. Stufler, B. Poschmann, A. d'Alès, P. Galtier.
[97] On this point see B. Poschmann I 460.
[98] For proof of this see Poschmann I 230—236.

while penance involves a painful process of purification (*Strom.* II 12, 55, 6; 15, 70, 3; IV 24, 1; IV 24, 154, 3; *Quis div.* 40, 1).

Plato's influence on Clement is decisive in the latter's conception of the elimination of sin as a purification or healing. Although it occupies the foreground it does not altogether displace the idea of expiation. Correspondingly the removal of sin does not take place by a single act but by a gradual process (*Quis div.* 40, 3—6). He who in this life has not striven to attain to the grade of a "gnostic" by putting away all inordinate attachment — πάθη (*Strom.* VII 10, 56) — will have to continue the purification by the much more painful punishments of the hereafter (*Strom.* VII 6, 34, 4; *Eclog. proph.* 11; *Quis div.* 42, 18). The purification in the hereafter is only available for repentant Christians, not for unbelievers (*Protr.* 9, 82, 4; 83, 2; 84, 1; *Strom.* IV 24, 154, 3f.; VI 14, 111, 2) or unconverted Christians (*Quis div.* 33, 9; *Paed.* III 11, 83, 4).[99] Consequently, final salvation is in every case dependent on penance done in this life. The chief remedies against sin are once again prayer, fasting and works of charity (*Quis. div.* 42, 14, 15; *Strom.* II 15, 71, 4 and *passim*). The single term ἐξομολογεῖσθαι is used to designate a well-defined procedure which includes the individual acts of penance. The control of ecclesiastical discipline is in the hands of the rulers of the Church in their capacity of pastors of the faithful (*Paed.* I 6, 37, 3; *Strom.* II 15, 69, 2—3). Clement nowhere makes mention of the reconciliation of penitents. However, given the indispensable significance for salvation which he, as clearly as any other writer, attributes to the Church,[100] readmission to communion of those purified by penance must be taken as a fact, quite apart from the evidence from other churches. It appears most clearly in the story of the young man rescued from a life of banditry on whose behalf St. John strove so long by many prayers and fasts until he "brought him back again into

---

[99] Origen's doctrine of the Apocatastasis is not found in Clement. See Poschmann I 244 ff.

[100] For proof of this see Poschmann I 249 ff.

the Church" (*Quis div.* 42, 15). Indispensable though the for-giveness of the Church is, it is not identified with the divine forgiveness. Only God can "make what is done undone ... and wash away previous sins" (*Quis div.* 40, 1). Reconciliation with the Church is an essential element in penance, and a pre-requisite for pardon by God, but it does not coincide with it.

The psychological and therapeutic mode of conceiving it which was introduced by Clement was henceforward to give its special stamp to penance in the Greek Church. It explains the high esteem accorded to "directors of souls" who gave such effective assistance to a penitent in the process of his healing by admonition and prayer. The result was that the "saving of the sinner" and the "forgiveness of sins" were directly attributed to these men. They are the perfect Christians, the "friends of God"; they are to be found principally among the poor members of the community, and they are the embodiment of the ideal of the "gnostic". Every rich or highly placed man in particular should choose such a "man of God" as his own director — κυβερνήτης — and follow his advice without question (*Quis div.* 31, 1; 32, 4; 33, 3; 41, 1—6; *Eclog. proph.* 15, 2; *Strom.* VII 12, 79, 4). To these spiritual guides belong in the first place those in authority in the Church, as the pastoral office is theirs by vocation. How-ever, fitness for this function does not necessarily require the possession of ecclesiastical office, but only personal perfection by which they are "truly" — τῷ ὄντι — priests or deacons according to the will of God (*Strom.* VI 13, 105 f.). This is not meant in the least in an anti-hierarchical sense, as if Clement placed the "gnostic" at the side of, or even above, the bishops in the direction of the Church.[101] He does not think of denying to the presbyters and least of all to the bishop the external direction of the Church, and along with this the right of deciding on exclusion and readmission. But it is otherwise in regard to

---

[101] This is the opinion of R. Seeberg, *Dogmengesch.* ed. 3 I (1920) 497; K. Müller, *ZNW* (1929) 290. On this point see Poschmann I 258, n. 2.

the assistance which they render to penitents by prayer and mortification, with the aim of "obtaining forgiveness from God" for them (*Eclog. proph.* 15, 2). In this function the fruit of endeavour depends on a personal relationship of friendship with God, and consequently the pious layman is on a level with the priest. The only difference is that priests first of all are expected to possess the appropriate qualification.

Origen has the reputation of being an extreme rigorist. The principal reason for this is to be found in the early-Christian concept of pardon (ἄφεσις) which, as we have already seen, was different from that current in present-day speech. As the effect of baptism, it had the meaning of an absolutely gratuitous condonation of guilt, as opposed to expiation of sins by penance. This explains why the harsh utterances in which he excludes all pardon of sins, except that conferred in baptism, do not in the least prevent him from immediately subjoining an exhortation to penance with a view to obtaining forgiveness (*Exhort. ad mart.* 30; *Comm. series in Matth.* 114).[102] The taking away of sins — ἀπολαμβάνειν τὰ ἁμαρτήματα — is in direct contrast with the reception of forgiveness of sins — λαβεῖν ἄφεσιν τῶν ἁμαρτημάτων — in baptism (*In Jer. hom.* 16, 15), and purification through the "baptism of fire" with forgiveness through the "baptism of the Spirit" (ibid. *hom.* 2, 3). Admittedly, the Alexandrian's mention of the "baptism of fire" has its setting in his restoration doctrine, and he is thinking in the first place of the purification even from the gravest sins that is still possible in the hereafter. However, this purification can be anticipated already in this life by penance: "The more he [the sinner] is burnt in the fire of tribulation, the more he finds mercy." A period of chastisement which lasts as long as the punishment imposed by St. Paul on the incestuous man may be considered sufficient (ibid. *hom.* 20, 9). In this effect penance is the counterpart of the blood of Christ

---

[102] His justification of the "irremissibility" is original. He asserts that every sin committed after the reception of the Holy Spirit in baptism is a "sin against the Holy Ghost" (*Comm. in Jo.* 28, 15).

which ransoms us in baptism, but it is the penitent himself who brings the ransom (*In Exod. hom.* 6, 9). Instructive, too, is the comparison of penance with the death penalty imposed in the Old Testament on adulterers. This was an equivalent substitute for punishment in the next life; under the New Testament it is replaced by penance, through which "forgiveness can be merited" (*In Lev. hom.* 11, 2). In particular the public penance of the Church is identical with the punishment of spiritual death which was imposed by St. Paul on the incestuous man. This was not intended for his final ruin, but rather "for the salvation of his spirit in the Day of Judgement". The "handing over to Satan for the destruction of the flesh" is the bodily affliction which is usually suffered by penitents — *quae solet a paenitentibus expendi* (ibid. 14, 4). These passages, which could easily be multiplied, make it quite certain that it is far from Origen's purpose to deny the possibility of obtaining forgiveness of post-baptismal sins through penance.

Not even the gravest offences are excluded from forgiveness. In accordance with 1 Jn 5:16, Origen distinguishes between "sins unto death" and "sins not unto death" (*Comm. in Jo.* 19, 4). To the former belong "idolatry, adultery, and unchastity, deliberate murder and any other similar serious sin" (*De or.* 28, 9—10). These are on a level with the crimes punished by death under the Old Covenant (*In Lev. hom.* 11, 2); in every case they are, therefore, very serious sins, even though they are not restricted to the triad of idolatry, murder and adultery. Even for them, however, there is a possibility of penance, though admittedly limited to a single concession, in contrast to sins of common occurrence — *peccata communia* — which can always be forgiven through penance (ibid. *hom.* 15, 2). It is not possible to draw the boundary between grave sins and those lesser sins which are also mortal in character and which can result in the loss of one's heavenly dwelling (ibid. and *In Ex. hom.* 10, 3). Elsewhere Origen uses the expression "sin unto death" in a sense more in accord with the original meaning of the Johannine text to signify a sin of obduracy which is incurable through lack of repentance. It is incurable through lack of will (διὰ τὸ μὴ βούλεσθαι) and certainly not because of the refusal of penance where the will to undertake it is present (*Comm. in Jo.* 19, 13). He has no hesitation in reckoning repentant sinners among "the righteous", even when they had been guilty of such grave crimes as those of Peter and David (*In Jo.* 36 *hom.* 4, 2; *In Num. hom.* 10, 1). Even Babylon, the embodiment of the deepest iniquity, is according to Scripture, still capable of a cure: *Si est natura, quae pereat, quae alia talis erit ut Babylon? Attamen neque istam despicit Deus (In Jer. hom.* 21, 12).

Equally as evident as the unlimited efficacy of penance is the part played in it by the Church. The rulers of the Church are physicians, helpers of the supreme physician, Christ. For this reason wounds must be shown not only to God but also to the priests (*In Jo.* 37 *hom.* 1, 1). To obtain a cure, recourse must be had to correction (κόλασις, *correptio*) as well as to instruction. In conformity with evangelical precept the correction is to be the severe one of excommunication where this is necessary (*Comm. in Matt.* 13:30; *In Lev. hom.* 3, 2). Failure to impose excommunication because of fear of men or weak leniency is a grave dereliction of duty on the part of priests (*In Jos. hom.* 7, 6). The example of the incestuous man at Corinth is the biblical norm for the penitential procedure, which includes excommunication and reconciliation (*In Ps.* 37 *hom.* 1, 1). This applies also to the duration of the penance (*In Jer. hom.* 20, 9), which should be moderate, lest the sinner in his excessive dejection (2 Cor 2:7) be swallowed up by Satan (*Comm. in Jo.* 28, 7).[103] However, the period of probation for readmission to ecclesiastical communion and to the eucharist is longer than that required for baptism (*C. Celsum* III 51.) Moreover, for the future reconciled penitents are reckoned as Christians of inferior standing, inasmuch as they

---

[103] The identity of the man restored to grace according to 2 Cor 2:5 ff. with the incestuous man of 1 Cor 5 is for Origen beyond doubt. Cf. *Comm. in Ep. ad Rom.* Praef.; *In Ps.* 37 *hom.* 1, 1.

are disqualified from holding any office or position of authority in the Church, This is the earlist evidence we possess for the defamation of penitents.

Essentially, exclusion from the Church is produced by the sinful deed itself, and not just by the sentence of the bishop (*In Lev. hom.* 14, 2). Conversely, a person who is unjustly excommunicated continues to be a member of the Church (ibid. 3). In any case, Origen is insistent that public penance is to be done even for such secret sins (ibid. 4; see also 3, 4; 8, 10). In one place he is at pains to show that Christians have no cause for desperation in spite of the restriction of the baptismal pardon to a single concession. He therefore observes that in the gospels there is mention of no fewer than seven remissions: baptism, martyrdom, almsdeeds, forgiveness of those who have offended us, the conversion of a sinner, the fullness of love, and finally ecclesiastical penance: *Est adhuc et septima, licet dura et laboriosa, per paenitentiam remissio peccatorum ... cum (peccator) non erubescit sacerdoti Domini indicare peccatum et quaerere medicinam* (*In Lev. hom.* 2, 4). Apart from martyrdom, which is an exceptional case, the good works in this list cannot possibly be regarded as sufficient for the expiation of grave sins, if account is taken of the requirements of which we have just heard. It follows that for the mass of those guilty of mortal sin the only way that lies open is the last-mentioned one of official ecclesiastical penance.[104] A much discussed text, *In Ps.* 37, *hom.* 2, 6, also requires voluntary confession of secret grave sins and public penance: Scripture teaches that "sin must not be kept concealed within us" — *quia oportet peccatum non celare intrinsecus.* First a man must make proof of him to whom he would confess his sins. When a true physician of souls has been found his counsel is to be followed in all points: *Si intellexerit et providerit talem esse languorem tuum, qui in conventu totius ecclesiae exponi debeat et curari, ex quo fortassis*

---

[104] Elsewhere only martyrdom and ecclesiastical penance are mentioned beyond baptism (*Sel. in Ps.* 115; *Comm. in Ep. ad Rom.* 2, 1). However, the *remissiones* have found a place in the history of penance.

et ceteri aedificari poterunt et tu ipse facile sanari, multa hoc deliberatione et satis periti medici illius consilio procurandum est.

This passage shows that it is for the spiritual physician to decide whether the sin is so grave as to require public penance.[105] Obviously he has at the same time an opportunity for dealing with lesser sins by making proper use of the *correptio* which forms part of the sinner's penance and helps him to obtain the divine pardon (*In Lev. hom.* 5; *Comm. in Matt.* 4, 16, 8). Some have mistakenly seen in this practice the present-day practice of sacramental confession to a priest. The text makes no mention of a priest; and neither the spiritual counselling nor the assistance in the performance of penance are specifically priestly functions. This holds good even if priests are normally indicated when Origen, like Clement, is speaking of spiritual physicians, as they are in virtue of their vocation charged with the care of souls. But there is no question here of an activity which is in principle reserved to priests, such as is required in the sacramental administration of penance.[106]

In the light of the foregoing exposition a passage of the *De or.* 28, 10, becomes clear. It usually has to serve as the chief proof that the capital sins were excluded from ecclesiastical forgiveness: "I know not how some can presume to do what exceeds priestly power…. They boast that they would forgive even idolatry, adultery and unchastity, as if through their prayer for such sins even the sin unto death could be loosed." The key to the understanding of this passage is the correct conception of the word "forgive" (ἀφιέναι). Origen, as on other occasions, is protesting against an excessively lax administration of the penitential discipline. Certain priests remitted the gravest sins in just

---

[105] See especially *Comm. in Matt.* 13, 30, and on it B. Kurtscheid, *Das Beichtsiegel* (1912) 8.

[106] For a more detailed treatment see J. Hörmann, op. cit. 111 ff. According to Hörmann himself it is "very probable" that the passage refers "practically always to priests". G. Rauschen, *Eucharistie und Bußsakrament* ed. 2 (1910) 221: "primarily only priests"; while A. d'Alès, *L'Edit de Calliste* (1914) 428, and P. Galtier, *De Paenitentia* (1956) 147 f. see in the spiritual physicians priests exclusively.

the same way as lighter faults simply by their prayer; that is through the procedure of the *correptio* along with prayer and a sharing of penance, instead of insisting on the reception of ecclesiastical penance. By way of illustration he cites the Old Testament legislation according to which even priests were only permitted to offer sacrifices "for some unpremeditated offences" but not "for adultery, deliberate murder or any other grave sin" (28, 9).[107] The "sacrifice for sins" is simply the *correptio* which in our text is described as prayer (*In Lev.* 5, 3—4), and which is not sufficient to secure the forgiveness of mortal sins. A fragment on 1 Sam 3:14 (*PG* 17, 40) throws clear light on the matter: "It seems as if God here sets up an obstacle to penance inasmuch as he holds out no hope of forgiveness. But just pay attention to the word. What he says is: I do not pardon them their guilt through sacrifice, I pardon it through works and perfect penance. For it is no ordinary sin, for which animals could be offered in sacrifice, as they were offered for unpremeditated sins or for ordinary offences. God himself is outraged here." Thus the text from the *De oratione* fits quite smoothly into the teaching on the unrestricted power of forgiveness possessed by the Church.[108] In this teaching, too, Origen ever remained consistent. He expounded it throughout all his writings, beginning with the *Commentary on John* of the years 218—238 up to the *Contra Celsum*, 246—248.

The question, however, of the holders of the power of ecclesiastical forgiveness and of its effect remains problematical. First of all, he makes the priestly power of forgiveness dependent on the personal sanctity of its possessor. This will "make him recognizable" as a possessor of the Spirit — πνευματικός (*De or.* 28, 8). On the other hand he ascribes the power of loosing from sins to others also who are not priests, if they, like Peter,

---

[107] Cf. *In Exod. hom.* 4, 8:... *in quibusdam per sacrificia sacerdotum et obsecrationes pontificum nos esse purgandos... in aliis autem, sine dubio, quae difficiliora sunt, ipsius Domini egere virtutem.*
[108] See the detailed proof in Poschmann I 453—460.

possess the appropriate holiness (*Comm. in Matt.* 12, 11—14). Is not the priest thus put on precisely the same level as the layman, in such a way that in principle every Christian has the same power to control penance?[109] To understand Origen, we have to distinguish between two functions which are incumbent on the priest in penance, as we have already established in connexion with Clement. Both of these were described as "loosing from sins". There is the pastoral, intercessory activity, which he shares with pious laymen who are likewise active as "directors of souls", and there is the act of ecclesiastical forgiveness, which he exercises in reconciliation in virtue of his office. Undoubtedly for Origen, even the official power is linked to personal holiness, and indeed unworthy holders of the office of bishop or priest are "hypocritical intruders", just as some persons falsely claim to be martyrs (*Comm. series in Matt.* 24). Yet it does not follow in the least that for him every holy man holds the priestly office. Notwithstanding the sharp criticisms which he levels against its holders, the Alexandrian does not depreciate the authority of the office. On the contrary, he is profoundly conscious of it.[110] It is not depreciation, but on the contrary a high sense of the episcopal office which inspires his severe condemnation of unworthy bishops.[111] The evidence already adduced places it beyond doubt that he considered excommunication and reconciliation as reserved to the bishop.[112]

What is the effect of reconciliation? According to the *De or.* 28, 8 a priest who is filled with the Spirit "forgives whatever God forgives" (ἀφίησιν, ἃ ἐὰν ἀφῇ ὁ θεός). This means that a priest may only grant forgiveness when God grants it, or, what

---

[109] Thus K. Holl, op. cit. 233; K. Müller, *ZNW* (1929) 290.
[110] Cf. *In Luc. hom.* 20; *Comm. in Rom.* 2, 2; *In Jud. hom.* 3, 3.
[111] This is also the later opinion of A. v. Harnack (*Der kirchengeschichtl. Ertrag der exeg. Arbeiten des Origenes* II, Texte u. Unters. 42, 4 [1919] 129 f.) against his earlier view that for Origen as for Clement "the hierarchy was still of no importance for the concept of the Church" (*Dogmengeschichte* I ed. 4 [1909] 413 f., Eng. tr. II 81. On this see R. Cadiou, *La jeunesse d'Origène* (Paris 1935) 386.
[112] See especially above 68.

comes to the same thing, when the sinner has done the necessary penance. The question, which Cyprian found so difficult, when is a penance adequate — *paenitentia plena* — Origen the theorist solves on the principle that the true priest, as a bearer of the Spirit, is enlightened on this point by the Spirit. It might appear from this that priestly forgiveness is merely a consequence of the performance of the penance, and has no influence on divine forgiveness.[113] Against this interpretation there are serious difficulties, if we consider the importance attached by Origen to membership of the Church. Even if he does not emphasize her saving power as strongly as Irenaeus and Cyprian, he does see exclusion from her as the most dreadful of calamities, as indeed the typical formula, *tradere Satanae,* shows. "It is a disgrace *(infamia)* to be cut off from the people of God and the Church" *(In Ez. hom.* 10, 1). Anxiety about readmission to the Church is equivalently anxiety about salvation: "How can I still attain to happiness…. How can I return to the Church?" This makes intelligible the obligation of undertaking public penance with excommunication even for secret grave sins. Origen must, therefore, have attributed to reconciliation a real effectiveness for the forgiveness of sins. In what precisely this consists he does not say. He has received the institution of public penance from tradition; he approves of it, and urges its proper use. In keeping, however, with his whole frame of mind, his interest is centred not so much on the external sacramental operation, as on the interior moral striving after freedom from sin. For him, even when he is thinking of a priest, it is the work of instruction, correction and shared penance of the spiritual physician which occupies the foreground. Laying as he does the greatest emphasis on the spiritual director's function of confessor, he, along with his teacher Clement, can be regarded as the founder of the practice of confession as it later came to be generally practised in monasteries as a means of striving after perfection. This

---

[113] Thus A. Vanbeck, *RHLR* (1913) 127.

practice did not require that the spiritual director should always be a priest, nor that an absolution in the sense of a judicial act of forgiveness should be given. Origen became a figure of far-reaching importance for the development of penance in the Eastern Church.

His doctrine on penance is in substantial agreement with the procedure which we have seen in operation at Rome and Carthage. It is also confirmed by the witness of contemporaries from the East. Mention may first be made of his pupil, the great bishop Dionysius of Alexandria, a leading adversary of Novatianism which was disturbing the whole Church. Dionysius enunciates the principle that readmission to the Church is to be granted to all the lapsed who repent after they have done penance for an appropriate length of time. This will be three to ten years, according to their fervour. To those in danger of death reconciliation will be accorded without regard to the amount of penance they have performed up to that time.[114] In a letter of his to Fabius of Alexandria (in Eusebius, *H. E.* VI 44, 2—6) there is a well known story of the old man, Serapion, who has denied the faith and has sought in vain to obtain admission to penance. Then, when he is at death's door, he sends by night to a priest to come and absolve him from his sin. The priest who himself is sick, sends a boy to him with the eucharist. On this story Dionysius comments that manifestly Serapion was preserved in life just long enough to be "loosed" and "for his sins to be forgiven". This remark indicates that the "loosing" was effected by the concession of the eucharist as the connatural expression of ecclesiastical communion. The restoration of ecclesiastical communion possesses sacramental efficacy.[115] Another pupil of Origen, Gregory the Wonderworker, is, with Dionysius, an early witness for the existence of the penitential degrees of "the Fallers" and "the Kneelers", and so, indirectly, of the

[114] Fragment of a letter to Bishop Conon, in Pitra, *Jur. eccl. Graecorum historia et monumenta* I (1864) 545.
[115] On this see Poschmann I 278 f. against d'Alès, *L'Edit de Calliste* (1914) 346f.

74

concession of reconciliation (Pitra, 562 ff.). Methodius of Phil-
ippi in his work *On Leprosy* (VI 7—9; VII 4—8; X 2—3; *Bonwetsch*) gives information about the individual acts of penance.
Very valuable, too, is the testimony of the *Didascalia,* an anti-
Novatianist work from Syria, dating from the first half of the
third century.[116] It provides a picture of the individual phases of
penance with which we are familiar, and at the same time lays
great stress both on the magnitude of the divine mercy and on
the corresponding duty of the bishop to grant forgiveness to a
penitent who after careful examination is found to be sincerely
repentant (II 10, 12, 13). The imposition of hands is the sign of
reconciliation, and its efficacy is put on the same level as the
effect of baptism: *aut per impositionem manus aut per baptismum
accipiunt participationem Spiritus Sancti* (II 41, 2). It is surprising
to find that for a serious sin involving excommunication all that
is required in the way of penance is fasting for a period of two
to seven weeks (II 16, 2). This bears no relation to the amount of
penance which was normally required at that time. In fact,
however, it does not refer to the whole penance, but only to that
part of it which the sinner had to perform shortly before reconciliation, after he had been admitted to ecclesiastical penance in
the strict sense of the term. Before his admission to penance
proper he would have had to lead a penitential life for a long
period of time.[117]

5. The Martyrs' Privilege in Regard to Penance

In the foregoing exposition attention has already been drawn as
occasion offered to the very influential position which was ac-

---

[116] The opinion advocated by E. Schwartz (*Bußtaufen und Katechumenatsklassen*
[1911, 16 ff.]), that the anti-Novatianist outlook does not represent the original
teaching of the Church-order, but is the product of a revision undertaken after the
Decian persecution, is unsupported by any solid argument. See Poschmann I 478,
n. 1.
[117] Cf. E. Schwartz 20; Poschmann I 477.

corded to the martyrs in the administration of penance. In recent times this question has acquired primary importance for the solution of the problem of the early-Christian concept of the Church. This is because there are many who would see in the martyrs, as the last of the "Spirit-bearers", the proper possessors of the power of forgiving sins. Later, it is claimed, they were supplanted by the holders of the episcopal office.[118] This would seem, therefore, an opportune moment for a brief treatment of this question.

The ancient Church was at one in the special veneration it accorded to the martyrs as the closest imitators and most perfect disciples of Christ.[119] Martyrdom was regarded as the most glorious and the greatest kind of baptism, one which obtained for the sufferer immediate union with God.[120] Even before the consummation of their martyrdom, these holy witnesses, who had borne testimony by their blood, were naturally held in the highest regard; they were the glorious soldiers of the Lord, in whom His power was operative and in whom "the Spirit of the Father speaks" (Cyprian, *Ep.* 10, 3). In particular, the greatest efficacy was attributed to their intercession with God. It is, therefore, intelligible that penitents, who were recommended to seek the assistance of their pious fellow Christians, strove to secure for themselves before all else the intercession of the martyrs when occasion offered. Moreover, the bishops, in their assessment of the amount of satisfaction which was required of a penitent, took account of the promise of intercession which he had received from a martyr before his death, and in consideration of it allowed him reconciliation which was otherwise not yet available.

[118] Thus, among others, A. v. Harnack, *Dogmengeschichte* I ed. 4 ,443 f.; Eng. tr. II 109 ff.; E. Lucius, *Die Anfänge des Heiligenkults* (1904) 67 f.; H. Koch, *Tertullian und Kallist* (1920) 45; K. Müller, *RGG* III ed. 2, 972.

[119] Cf. Ignatius, *Smyrn.* 4, 2; *Polyc.* 7, 1; Tertullian, *Scorp.* 9; Origen, *In Jo.* II 34, 209; Cyprian, *Ep.* 58, 3; 66, 7.

[120] Cyprian, *Ad Fortun.* Praef. 4; *Ep.* 73, 22; cf. *Martyr. Perpetuae et Felic.* 21; Tertullian, *De bapt.* 16, etc.

The earliest direct evidence for this practice is provided by Tertullian (*Ad Mart.* I).[121] He exhorts the martyrs who were confined in prison to preserve peace with one another in order that "when occasion offered, they might be able to bestow it also on others". By way of explanation he adds: *Quam pacem quidam in ecclesia non habentes a martyribus in carcere exorare consueverunt.* He has no more to say on the practice, but the fact of his using it as a motive seems to show that he approves of it. Later, however, as a Montanist he made a bitter attack on it, and poured ridicule on the spectacle of adulterers flocking in crowds to pay their respects to so-called martyrs, as soon as they were put under the easiest confinement, or rushing for succour to the mines in order to return home from them with the status of communicants — *communicatores* — (*De pud.* 22, 1—3). The privilege of the martyrs came into play most prominently in the course of the Decian persecution in Africa, where it degenerated into an abuse. Over a wide area, and indiscriminately, martyrs distributed to the lapsed, without regard to the sincerity of their repentance, so-called certificates of peace — *libelli pacis.* These their possessors relied on to demand immediate readmission to the Church, but this unheard of claim was met by St. Cyprian with a firm refusal (*Ep.* 27). He did, however, give full recognition to the power of the martyrs' intercession within the bounds set by the nature of penance, admitting it as a supplement to the satisfaction made by a sincere penitent (*Ep.* 15, 3; 17, 1 and *passim*). At the beginning of the persecution he found in it a justification for granting reconciliation before the completion of their penance to those among the lapsed who were seriously ill.[122]

In Alexandria, at the same period the intervention of the martyrs had a more peaceful setting than at Carthage. This is evident

[121] The letter of the churches of Vienne and Lyons known to us from Eusebius (*H. E.* V 1—4) has been erroneously interpreted in the same sense. See Poschmann I 270 ff. against A. v. Harnack, E. Lucius, H. Koch, J. Hoh.
[122] See above 55.

from the letter, already mentioned, of Bishop Dionysius to Fabius of Antioch (Eusebius, *H. E.* VI 42, 5—6). He says in it that the "divine martyrs", who were now "possessors of Christ" and who "as partakers of his Spirit pronounce judgement with him", received back fallen brethren, conducted them into the liturgical assemblies and allowed them to take part in their prayers and repasts. In other words, they took it upon themselves to lift an excommunication without waiting for the decision of the bishop. Undoubtedly, that was an encroachment on the rights of the bishop. Later, Dionysius himself had a scruple about the affair and asked his colleagues at Antioch for their opinion. It is clear, however, from the whole tenor of the letter that in principle he concurred in the action of the martyrs. For him it is not a question of possessing authority — but rather one of pastoral care. He is concerned to know whether the lapsed have been legitimately readmitted by the martyrs, that is, by reason of the sufficiency of their penance, and whether they can be considered as validly reconciled. That is the sense of the question: "Shall we concur in this view... or shall we explain that their judgement is unlawful, setting ourselves up as judges over their opinion, wounding their kindness, and annul the settlement which they have made?" Here we have a clear statement of the fact that the decision depends essentially on the bishop, even if in fact he does not exercise his right. Obviously, too, the lenient procedure of the martyrs came at an opportune moment for Dionysius in the defence of the Catholic penitential practice against the rigorism of the Novatians.

Now that we have presented the source material, we return to the question of principle which was posed above. Which authority is the original one: that of the martyrs or that of the bishops? Tertullian's assertions that sinners "seek peace from the martyrs" and that they return home from them with the status of communicants — *communicatores* — do not settle the question whether the martyrs bestowed reconciliation on their own initiative, or whether they merely recommended the sinners to the bishop. Granted that the recommendation was regularly accepted, yet the second alternative makes perfect sense of Tertullian's words. However, in the measure that it became a mechanical procedure, this practice must have led simple folk to imagine that the martyrs themselves forgave sins. This would explain their attitude at Carthage and Alexandria. However, it cannot be denied that St. Cyprian was in the right, both objectively and as a witness of tradition, when he took up a very vigorous stand against this conception. From the very beginning there is evidence from all parts that it is the bishops who are charged with the administration of penance. Moreover, as the responsible rulers of the Church, only they are competent to admit to membership of the Church. The "certificate of peace", therefore, only meant that a penitent could produce a martyr's attestation that he had promised him his intercession, with a view to his reconciliation by the bishop. It was none other than Novatian who drew attention to the inconsistent conduct of the Carthaginian martyrs. "For if the martyrs thought that peace should be granted them, why did they not grant it themselves? Why did they consider, to use their own words, that they had to be referred to the bishop? — *nam si dandam illis pacem martyres putaverunt, cur ipsi non dederunt? cur illos ad episcopum, ut ipsi dicunt, remittendos censuerunt?* (*Ep.* [*int. Cypr.*] 36, 2). Even Dionysius, who in fact gave way to the martyrs, was, as we have seen, aware that the final decision on the validity of the forgiveness which they had granted lay with the bishop. The modern theory which attributes to the martyrs direct power to forgive sins completely fails to see that reconciliation was primarily an ecclesiastical act. Conversely, once the action of the martyrs is seen to have been of purely subsidiary importance, it is in perfect harmony with the conception of ecclesiastical penance. An essential part of this procedure was the assistance rendered by pious fellow Christians. As God's "loved ones" the martyrs have the first place, but on the same level as the other "friends of God": the poor, the widows, the presbyters (Tertullian, *De paen.* 9, 4; *De pud.*

13, 7), along with the "gnostics" and "spiritual guides", of whom Origen says: "holy men can help us and make us worthy to obtain forgiveness of sins" (*De or.* 14, 6).

No objection can be raised against this equivalence by appealing to the charismatic function of these "bearers of the Spirit" in virtue of which the Holy Ghost dwelling within them guarantees the justice of their judgement of sinners. Widespread as this conviction was,[123] it was also assumed that the other friends of God were likewise in possession of the Spirit, and that the power of "loosing" or "binding" was made dependent on it. This is particularly clear from Origen. Moreover, this gift was important, not only for the assistance of a penitent, but also for the charismatic discernment of the state of his soul. Finally, it should be noted that the exercise of the martyrs' privilege was only of sporadic occurrence and was certainly not a typical feature of early Christian penance. In Latin Africa it is only directly attested by Tertullian and Cyprian, and in Alexandria by Dionysius and by him only in a single case which affected only a few penitents. In Rome, at the time of the Decian persecution there is no mention of the practice, as is clear from the correspondence of St. Cyprian, even though it was admitted in principle (see *Ep.* 36, 2). Even in Carthage at the synods held after the persecution there is no mention of the martyrs. With the ending of the persecutions the question ceases to be of practical importance. Veneration of the martyrs and reliance on them is henceforward confined to those in possession of heavenly glory.

---

[123] Cf. M. Viller, "Les martyrs et l'Esprit" in *RSR* (1924) 544—51.

IV. Canonical Penance from the Fourth to the Sixth Centuries: Its Development and Decline

Literature: A. Boudinhon, "Sur l'hist. de la pénitence" in *RHLR* (1897). E. Göller, "Analekten zur Bußgesch. des 4. Jahrh." in *RQ* 36 (1928). Id., "Das spanisch-westgotische Bußwesen" ibid. 37 (1929). Id., "Studium über das gallische Buß-wesen" in *AKK* 109 (1929). Id., *Papsttum u. Bußgewalt in spätröm. u. frühmittelalt. Zeit* (1933). Poschmann II. On this, K. Adam, "Kritische Bemerkungen" in *ThQ* 110 (1929) and Poschmann's reply in *ZkTh* 54 (1930). E. Amann, *DTC* XII 789—845. P. Galtier, *L'église et la rémission des péchés aux premiers siècles* (1932). Id., "Pénitents et convertis" in *RHE* 33 (1937). F. Hünermann, *Die Bußlehre des hl. Augustinus* (1914). K. Adam, *Die kirchl. Sündenvergebung nach dem hl. Augustin* (1917). Id., *Die geheime Kirchenbuße nach dem hl. Augustin* (1921). B. Poschmann, "Hat Augustinus die Privatbuße eingeführt?" (1920) [Vorlesungsverzeichnis der Akademie Braunsberg]. Id., *Kirchenbuße und correptio secreta bei Augustinus* (1923) [ibid.]. Id., "Die kirchl. Vermittlung der Sündenvergebung nach Augusti-nus" in *ZkTh* 45 (1921). Id., "S. Aurelii Augustini Textus selecti de paenitentia" in *Florilegium Patr.*, Fasc. 38 (1934). K. Jüssen, *Die dogmat. Anschauungen des Hesychius von Jerusalem. 2. Teil: Die Lehre von der Sünde u. Sündenvergebung* (1934). J. Gaudemet, "Notes sur les formes anciennes de l'excommunication" in *RSR* 23 (1949) 64—77. P. Galtier, "Les canons pénitentiels de Nicée" in *Gr* 29 (1948) 288—294. C. Vogel, *La discipline pénitentielle en Gaule des origines à la fin du VIIe siècle* (Paris 1952). Id., "La discipline en Gaule des origines au IXe siècle. Le dos-sier hagiographique" in *RSR* 30 (1956) 1—26; 157—186. S. Gonzalez Rivas, *La penitencia en la primitiva iglesia española* (Salamanca 1950). E. Griffe, "Un exemple de pénitence publique au Ve siècle" in *BLE* 59 (1958) 170—175. I. Marzella, "De obligatione S. Eucharistiam indignis denegandi. Expositio historico-doctrinalis" in *Ant* 31 (1956) 25-50. J. Lecuyer, "Les actes du pénitent", in *La Maison-Dieu* 55 (1958) 41—62. P.-M. Guy, "Histoire liturgique du sacrement de pénitence" in *La Maison-Dieu* 55 (1958) 5—21. H. Rondet, "Esquisse d'une histoire du sacrement de pénitence" in *NRT* 80 (1958) 70—82. P. H. Lafontaine, "Remarques sur le prétendu rigorisme du pape Sirice" in *Rev. Univ. Ottawa* 28 (1958) 31*—48*. C. Munier, *Les Statuta Ecclesiae Antiqua. Edition Etudes Critiques* (Paris 1960). H. Dörries, "Die Beichte im alten Mönchtum" in *Judentum Urchristentum Kirche*, Festschrift f. Joachim Jeremias (Berlin 1960) 235—259. K. Aland, "Augustin und der Montanismus" in *Kirchengeschichtliche Entwürfe* (Gütersloh 1960) 149—164. F. Courtney, "The Ad-ministration of Penance" in *CR* 46 (1961) 10—27; 85—98. G. May, "Bemerkungen zu der Frage der Diffamation und der Irregularität der öffentlichen Büßer" in *MThZ* 12 (1961).

There is no sharp dividing line separating the history of penance in the fourth century from the preceding period. The doctrine and practice of penance continue to develop along the same lines. However, the opening years of the century were marked

81

by the epoch-making experience of the Peace of Constantine. This was bound to have the greatest influence on the whole outward life of the Church, and inevitably also on the penitential system. The ancient penitential system had sprung from the heroic age of primitive Christianity at a time when the loss of baptismal grace was still regarded as something exceptional, and when it seemed self-evident that no burden could be too heavy to impose on a delinquent who desired to regain his Christian status. Already in his day, however, Tertullian was forced to complain that "very many" shrank from public penance with its attendant humiliation (*De paen.* 10, 1). If that attitude was to be found among Christians of the Church of the martyrs, who though relatively few did, however, constitute an élite, how much more likely was it to recur among the masses who streamed through the open doors of the Church after the Edict of Milan, and who shockingly lowered the moral level of Christians. The problem was one of adaptation of the ancient institution of penance to these worldly vice-ridden masses. In spite of great pastoral difficulties the ancient severity of the penitential régime was not impaired; on the contrary in certain respects it was even increased.

Severity was guaranteed primarily by the juridical regulation of the whole of the penitential system which was gradually carried through by means of conciliar decisions, papal decretals and collections of private counsels and directives, the so-called "penitential letters" which in time acquired canonical force. In this way the forms and requirements of the penitential procedure were by degrees strictly regulated by canons; hence the term "canonical penance". In the process, individual directives which originally were not at all thought of as hard and fast rules took on the character of rigid legal forms, and as they were unenforceable in practice they finally drove the development of ecclesiastical penance into a blind alley.

The "canonical material" constitutes a primary source for the history of penance during this period. In the Eastern Church account has to be taken of the synods of Ancyra (314), Neo-Caesarea (314—325), Nicaea (325), Antioch (341), Gangra (middle of the fourth century); in the Western Church there are numerous African, Spanish and Frankish synods. By reason of the brisk intercourse between the provinces of the Church, synodal decrees often gained recognition outside the jurisdictional limits of the councils. From the fifth century onwards, for example, Oriental penitential statutes appear in the Western Churches. In Gaul the prestige of the African canons was so great that the *Statuta Ecclesiae antiqua,* an important collection for the organization of penance made in Gaul about the year 500, went under the name of decisions of the African councils.[124] In Rome, too, there appeared about the year 500 the collection of Dionysius Exiguus, which contains legislation deriving from the whole Church. We possess papal decretals concerning penance of Siricius, Innocent I, Leo I, Felix II, Hormisdas and Gregory I. Of special importance is a series of decisions issued by Innocent and Leo. Authors of penitential letters were Gregory the Wonderworker († c. 270), Peter of Alexandria († 311), Basil and Gregory of Nyssa. The three canonical letters of Basil (188, 199, 217) contain no fewer than eighty-four canons in which penances are assigned for the most diverse kinds of capital sins. The very abundant private sources are predominantly of a pastoral and practical type. Dogmatic discussions were conditioned by the struggle against Novatianism which in the fourth and fifth centuries still had its own congregations both in the East and in the West. More extreme than its founder it now excluded on principle from reconciliation not only the *lapsi,* but also all serious sinners. The leaders of the struggle against it are Ambrose and Pacian. In the course of their vindication of the Church's power to forgive sins they give at the same time a graphic picture of the institution of penance as it existed in their day. Richer still are the writings of Augustine, from which it is possible to derive

---

[124] Cf. G. Morin, *RB* 30 (1913) 337f.

quite a comprehensive treatment of the entire penitential system in both its theoretical and practical aspects. In what follows, therefore, his teaching will be considered as typical, except where it is necessary to mention conceptions which conflict with it. For the state of the penitential system in the sixth century Caesarius of Arles († 543) is particularly informative, and for the end of the period Gregory I and Isidore of Seville.

1. The Object of Ecclesiastical Penance

In this later period, as in the earlier one, ecclesiastical penance is only required for mortal or capital sins. Minor offences are treated by the compensatory offering of better deeds — *meliorum operum compensatione curantur* (Pacian, *Paraen.* 4). In keeping with this, Augustine distinguishes three kinds of penance: pre-baptismal penance, penance for sins of daily occurrence, and penance for grave sins. The third is penance in the "proper" sense of the word — *paenitentia maior, insignis* (*Serm.* 351, 4, 7; 352, 3, 8; *De symb.* 8, 16 etc.) which should not occur in a normal Christian life (*De symb.* 7, 15).

It is, however, difficult to draw a hard and fast line between *crimina* and ordinary sins. The division is not covered by the present-day concepts of mortal and venial sins. Thus Augustine exempts all sins of thought (*Serm.* 98, 5, 5), and certain offences against fraternal charity (*Serm.* 82, 3, 5) from the obligation of public penance. There were those who, like Pacian (op. cit.) wished to confine public penance to Tertullian's triad of idolatry, murder and adultery. This view is expressly rejected by Augustine (*Speculum ad Act.* 15, 20 f.) and is in contradiction with tradition.[125] In one place Augustine affirms that all sins against the Decalogue are liable to public penance (*Serm.* 351, 4, 7); in practice he follows the usage of the Church (*De symb.* 7, 15; *Enchir.* 65, 17).

[125] See above 46 f.; on this see Basil, *Ep.* 217 can. 61, 64, 66; Ambrose, *De Elia et ieiunio* 22, 81, 83.

Lesser sins that remain can still be forgiven in the next life by means of the purgatorial fire.[126] When, however, they become very frequent they attain the gravity of a mortal sin and bring eternal death in their train.[127]

As the gravity of a sin depends in the first place on a person's conscience, Augustine holds that only sins of malice — and not sins of weakness and ignorance — *peccata infirmitatis et imperitiae* — are liable to public penance. Consequently sins which in themselves are grave, if committed through frailty and inadvertence, are reckoned venial — *venalia* — and, like lesser sins, can find forgiveness especially by means of the remedies of prayer and almsdeeds practised in private (*De div. quaest.* 83 q. 26). The distinction was, however, difficult to apply and even St. Augustine himself in practice judged sins by an objective norm, such as was provided in Scripture (in the Pauline catalogues of sins) and in ecclesiastical usage. Penance could be undertaken voluntarily, as we have already seen from Cyprian, even for less serious sins (Pacian, *Paraen.* 11). Caesarius recommended all the faithful to undertake it, and in his day it was already customary for all to "receive" penance before death if it were possible (*Serm.* 257, 2; 256, 4; *PL* 39, 2220, 2219 [*CC Serm.* 64, 103, 275 f.; *Serm.* 60, ibid. 265]).

The obligation of doing public ecclesiastical penance for grave sins was binding even though there was question only of secret sins. Private penance for secret *crimina* is still unknown just as it was in the time of Tertullian and Origen (see above, pp. 44, 69).[128] This is evident from the fact that throughout

---

[126] Caesarius, *Serm.* 104 (*PL* 39, 1946 f. [*CC Serm.* 179; 104, 724 ff.]). Augustine holds that this is at least a tenable opinion: *Enchir.* 18, 69; *De civ.* 21, 26.

[127] Augustine, *Serm.* 351, 3, 5; 264, 8 etc.; Caesarius, *Serm.* 104, 1 [*CC Serm.* 179, 1; 104, 724]; Gregory I, *Reg. past.* 3, 3; Isidore, *Sent.* 2, 18.

[128] This question, which is part of the wider problem of the existence of a private ecclesiastical penance alongside of the public procedure, has been the subject of much discussion in modern times. Morinus considered that there was a secret and private penance for less grave mortal sins; Petavius held that even secret capital sins were thus dealt with. The existence of any private ecclesiastical penance

patristic literature, notwithstanding the importance which it attaches to penance as such, not a word is said about the existence of a private form of ecclesiastical penance.[129] Moreover, the Fathers expressly declare that there are only two kinds of penance: daily, personal penance for little sins and public penance for mortal sins. Like Pacian and Augustine, whom we have already heard, Ambrose writes: *Sicut unum baptisma, ita una paenitentia, quae tamen publice agitur ; nam quotidiani nos debet paenitere peccati, sed haec delictorum leviorum, illa graviorum* (*De paen.* 2, 10). There is nowhere mention of an intermediate form, although as a remedy for secret mortal sins it would have stood out prominently. The first certain evidence for private penance is the eleventh canon of the Third Synod of Toledo (589), which we will have occasion to consider in another context. Here it is branded as an abuse — *execrabilis praesumptio* — which has crept into some Spanish churches.

The primary purpose of public penance, even when done for secret sins, was not to humiliate the penitent, but to enlist the support of the faithful on his behalf. Thus, Augustine in *Serm.*

whatsoever has been denied by F. X. Funk, F. X. Kraus, H. Ch. Lea, M. Boudinhon, E. Vacandard, B. Poschmann, E. Göller, E. Amann. P. Batiffol and J. Tixéront claimed that the transition from public to private penance dated from about the year 400. K. Adam sought to show that Augustine was the true founder of private penance in the West. (For the bibliography see above.) A. d'Alès, and especially P. Galtier have been strongly in favour of the early existence of private penance. (For a detailed bibliography see above and Poschmann II 207 ff.)

[129] A passage from Augustine, *De Fide et op.* 26, 48 has been erroneously interpreted in the sense of private penance. Thus K. Adam, *Die geheime Kirchenbuße* 39 f.; P. Galtier, *L'Eglise et la rémission des péchés*, 326 ff. The *quaedam correptionum medicamenta* are simply admonitions intended to stimulate the sinner to do penance and thus indirectly contribute to his cure. They have nothing to do with a secret absolution (B. Poschmann, *Kirchenbuße und correptio secreta* 41—53). The same applies to the notice by Paulinus in the *Vita Ambrosii* 39: *causas autem criminum, quae illi confitebantur, nulli nisi Deo soli, apud quem intercedebat loquebatur.* It only means that the holy bishop discreetly kept to himself the sins made known to him and unlike others did not make them the subject of uncharitable conversations. On other supposed evidence for private penance from Innocent I, Leo I, Hilary of Arles, see Poschmann II 215—229. See also the criticism of Galtier's exposition in *ThR* 32 (1933) 263—267.

392, 3 says: *Agite paenitentiam qualis agitur in ecclesia, ut oret pro vobis ecclesia*.[130] In addition to their intercession, the faithful had a practical part to play in the emendation of the penitent; they kept watch on the progress of his conversion, reported on it to the bishop, and themselves admonished him. In this context, there is an instructive sermon of St. Augustine (*En. in Ps.* 61, 23) in which he brings a soothsayer *(mathematicus)*, who had been admitted to penance, before the congregation and recommends him to their prayers, but also to their supervision.

2. The Organization of Penance

In essentials the penitential procedure preserves the same form as that attested by Tertullian, Cyprian and Origen. Its chief characteristics are the acts of excommunication and reconciliation.[131] Penance proper is preceded by a request for permission to undertake it; this is granted only if the sinner has already shown sufficient proof of the sincerity of his conversion. The expressions *paenitentiam petere, dare, accipere* are everywhere established technical terms. The request to do penance naturally includes acknowledgement or confession of sins. The onerous obligations involved by penance profoundly affected the penitents' mode of life, with the result that in time they are seen as a special body in the Church of inferior legal standing — the *ordo paenitentium*.[132] Enrolment in the order of penitents by the imposition of hands[133] is the characteristic and essential feature of "canonical penance". Confession and acceptance of penance were either spontaneously sought by the sinner or the result of ecclesiastical correction — *correptio ;* in the worst cases this

---

[130] Cf. Tertullian, *De paen.* 10, 6; *De pud.* 2,14; 19, 24.
[131] Augustine, *Ep.* 265, 7; *Enchir.* 65,17; *De symb.* 7,15.
[132] 1 Synod of Orange (441) can. 3: *stent in ordine paenitentium ;* cf. *Stat. eccl. ant.* can. 76; 2 Synod of Arles (443 or 452) can. 11.
[133] Leo I, *Ep.* 167 *ad Rust. inquis.* 2; Synod of Agde (506) can. 15.

had included excommunication.[134] This most extreme measure was only applicable in rare cases, and was adopted from the time when vice notably increased among Christians. Willy-nilly the Church had to tolerate the mass of sinners, as St. Augustine reiterated against the Donatists, and entrust their conversion to the stern mercy of the "divine discipline".[135]

The excommunication which formed part of penance consisted essentially in exclusion from the eucharist; not only from Communion but also from the Offering.[136] In keeping with this, a special place was assigned to the penitents, the *locus paenitentium* ;[137] this was probably at the back of the church, and not in the narthex outside the church proper, as some have thought, relying on Tertullian's *paenitentia in vestibulo*.[138] Their ignominious outward apparel and neglect of their person served further to humiliate the penitents.[139] In time a special penitential dress was developed; it was made from goatskin and was known as the *cilici-*

---

[134] Augustine, *Serm.* 232, 7, 8: *aliqui ipsi sibi paenitentiae locum petierunt; aliqui excommunicati a nobis in paenitentiae locum redacti sunt.* Cf. *Quaest.* XVII *in Matth.* q. 11, 3. The compulsory excommunication, which was a "censure", must be clearly distinguished from the voluntarily undertaken penitential excommunication. The former has achieved its purpose when the latter begins.

[135] *C. ep. Parm.* 3, 14; *Enchir.* 80, 21; *Ep.* 95, 3 ; *Serm.* 17, 3, 3. Similarly Caesarius, *Serm.* 288, 5; 289, 5 (*PL* 39, 2290 f., 2293 [*CC Serm.* 42 f.; 103, 184, 189]); Pomerius, *De vita contempl.* 2, 5.

[136] The 11th canon of Nicaea excludes even the highest degree of penitents from the προσφορά. Augustine, *Serm.* 352, 3, 8: *remoti etiam a sacramento altaris participandi.* See Leo I, *Ep.* 108, 3 *ad Theod.*; can. 2 of Vaison (442); the Lateran Synod under Felix II (487).

[137] Augustine, *Serm.* 232, 7, 8; see Jerome, *Ep.* 77, 2; 1st Synod of Orange can. 3; Epaon (517) can. 29. The ἐκδηλὸς τόπος τῶν ἐν μετανοίᾳ ὄντων is the first thing mentioned by Sozomen in his account of the penitential practice which he had observed at Rome (*H. E.* 7, 16).

[138] Thus P. Batiffol in *BLE* (1902) 5—18. Against this view see H. Koch, "Die Büßerentlassung in der abendländischen Kirche" in *ThQ* 82 (1900) 522 ff.; "Der Büßerplatz im Abendland" ibid. 85 (1903) 254 ff.

[139] Ambrose, *De paen.* 1, 8, 37: *vilia vestimentorum, illuvies sordidatorum.* Jerome, *Ep.* 77, 2 describes the penance of Fabiola in the presence of all the people: *sparsum crinem, ora lurida, squalidas manus, sordida colla submittere.*

um. In Spain its use was already prescribed by the second canon of the First Synod of Toledo (401).[140] In addition to the penitential garment, cropping of the hair came to be a requirement for penance.[141] However, it would appear that the external penitential dress was not everywhere of strict obligation. There is no trace of it in Augustine, nor does Sozomen make any mention of a special penitential garb at Rome. Among the penitential exercises which had to be performed in private, fasting and almsgiving were of course most prominent along with prayer. To these was added renunciation of other pleasures both of the body and of the mind, such as curtailment of sleep, sexual abstinence, and abandonment of the struggle for worldly honours (Ambrose, *De paen.* 2, 10, 96—97). The prohibition of marital intercourse to penitents appears in a decree of Pope Siricius as a law already established (*Ep.* 1, 5 *ad Himerium*), but it is not mentioned by St. Augustine. During the time of penance in the proper sense, that is from its reception until reconciliation, there was a special rite in use for penitents, consisting of a prayer along with an imposition of hands by the bishop in the presence of the whole congregation. Sozomen gives an impressive description of this ceremony which he had observed at Rome.[142] According to his report, the blessing of the penitents took place at the end of the celebration of the liturgy. This shows that in the West the penitents, in contrast to the catechumens,

---

[140] Caesarius explains the symbolism of the *cilicium :* By it the penitent acknowledges that he is not a lamb, but a buck: *Qualis sum foras, talem me intus agnoscite,* *Serm.* 261 (*PL* 39, 2227 f. [*CC Serm.* 67; 103, 284 ff.]).

[141] Cf. can. 15 of Agde: *si autem comas non deposuerint aut vestimenta mutaverint, abiciantur.* Similarly can. 6 of Barcelona (541) and can. 12 of the Third Council of Toledo (589). In contrast to this, Isidore of Seville reports that penitents allow their hair and beard to grow, in order to indicate thereby the enormity of their sins (*De eccl. off.* 2, 17).

[142] Op. cit. Cf. Augustine, *Serm.* 232, 7, 8: *Abundant hic paenitentes ; quando illis manus imponitur, fit ordo longissimus.* The *Vita Hilarii Arelatensis* 13, 16 narrates of the holy bishop: *saepe die dominico paenitentiam dedit.* A decree of Felix II (*Ep. ad episc. Sicil.*) enjoins that the lapsed should for a space of seven years *subiaceant inter paenitentes manibus sacerdotum.* The *Apostolic Constitutions* (VIII 9) also contain

were allowed to remain in the church even during the *missa fidelium*. Unlike the rest of the faithful, however, the penitents had to kneel even on feast-days of joyful character (*Stat. eccl. ant. can.* 80). However, that was the rule for those who were *proprie paenitentes,* that is, those already admitted to penance; it did not affect those who as yet were only seeking admission to it. These, like the catechumens, were only allowed access to the "hearing" of the word of God. The distinction of the two grades of penance is a natural one and is already indicated in Tertullian;[143] but it is first clearly encountered in Dionysius of Alexandria (*Fragment of the letter to Conon,* ed. Pitra, 1, 545) who prescribes that the lapsed shall do penance for three years as "Hearers", and for ten years as "Kneelers". In the *Epistola Canonica* of Gregory the Wonderworker, which dates from the same period, among penitents properly so-called, the "Bystanders" are mentioned in addition to the "Kneelers". They constitute a higher degree and are allowed to take their place with the faithful for the whole of the liturgy, and are only excluded from the Offering and the reception of the eucharist. Thus they differ from the "Kneelers" who, in the eastern rite were dismissed before the *missa fidelium* after receiving the imposition of hands from the bishop. The catechumens had similarly been dismissed before them. Later on, a parallel division, first attested by Basil (*Ep.* 199, 22; 217, 56) was made of the *petentes paenitentiam.* It consisted in the establishment of a grade of the "Mourners" to precede that of the "Hearers". The "Mourners" were excluded altogether from the inside of the church, and only permitted to stand outside in the forecourt where they implored the faithful for their intercession as they made their way into the church.

---

a prayer for penitents. J. A. Jungmann, *Die lat. Bußriten* 15 ff. shows that the *Oratio super populum* provided in the Roman missal for the ferial masses in Lent is none other than the prayer which originally accompanied the blessing of the penitents.

[143] The *paenitentia pro foribus ecclesiae* (*De pud.* 3, 4) and the *paenitentia in ecclesiam inducta* (13, 7 f.). See Poschmann I 316.

The importance of these four penitential stations (στάσεις) has often been exaggerated. The only evidence for them comes from Asia Minor, and they were unknown in the West. From the middle of the fifth century ancient oriental canons, which presupposed the stations, were occasionally drawn upon in the West for the assessment of penance for particularly grave sins.[144] However, these were only exceptional cases, and the canons were suitably adapted to Western penitential law, which only recognized one grade for the whole period of penance from its reception right up to reconciliation.[145]

We have now to define more closely the public character of the penitential procedure. It has already been shown, and indeed is obvious from the fact of enrolment in the order of penitents with its attendant obligations, that in principle it was imposed even for secret sins. However, for these a certain mitigation of publicity was required. This was intended to save an offender from exposure, or, as the case might be, from being handed over to a criminal judge. One such example is that mentioned by Augustine of a murderer whose crime was known only to the bishop (*Serm.* 82, 8, 11). The necessary modification of publicity chiefly affected admission to penance. In this context Augustine lays down the principle: *ipsa corripienda sunt secretius, quae peccantur secretius* (ibid. 7, 10). Accordingly, the normal procedure is that a public rebuke is to be administered to one whose sin is public. Its purpose is either to bring an unrepentant sinner to do penance,[146] or to repair the scandal which he has given.[147] For secret

---

[144] Thus the decree of Felix II already mentioned; can. 10 and 11 of the Second Synod of Arles (442 or 452); canon 29 of Epaon (517).
[145] Cf. F. X. Funk, *Die Bußstationen im Christl. Altertum,* Kirchengesch. Abhandl. I (1897) 182 ff.; also the studies of P. Batiffol and H. Koch mentioned on p. 88, n. 138; E. Schwartz, *Bußstufen und Katechumenatsklassen* (1911); E. Göller, *Papsttum u. Bußgewalt* (1933) 87 ff.; Poschmann I 315 f.; 474 ff.; II 31 ff.; 92 ff.
[146] For reasons of pastoral prudence this procedure was hardly possible in practice in Augustine's day. See above 88.
[147] An example of this is given by Augustine in the case of the soothsayer, mentioned above, of whose activities he gives a vivid account in the sermon (*En. in Ps.* 61, 23).

91

sins, on the other hand, even very grave ones, the rebuke is to be given privately — "between four eyes" — with the purpose of persuading the sinner to submit to penance: *Corripio in secreto... persuadeo paenitentiam*.[148] But the penance itself is none other than the canonical public penance. Because of the preservation of secrecy in regard to the sin for which it is imposed, this kind of penance has been appropriately called "semi-public". Leo I provides evidence from Rome of the same procedure of public penance with secret confession of sins in a directive to the bishops of Campania, Samnium and Picenum (*Ep.* 168, 2). He takes strong exception to an abuse which had crept into those regions. This consisted in the reading out in public of the sins of individual sinners; whereas, says Leo, it is quite sufficient to manifest one's state of conscience by secret confession to priests alone — *solis presbyteris indicare confessione secreta*. Therefore, this intolerable custom — *improbabilis consuetudo* — is to be absolutely abolished. By this decree, Leo neither introduced private penance, as older Protestant scholars considered, nor did he reserve penance for secret sins to a private procedure, as Catholics have held.[149] His action did not modify in the least the existing institution of public penance. By the *praesumtio contra apostolicam regulam* he did not mean the defamation which was attendant on a public penitential procedure — that is unthinkable, given the canonical character of the institution — but the abuse "of publishing in the hearing of the people the state of a penitent's conscience", for this deterred men from doing penance. By itself the public performance of penance did not carry very much defamation with it. It could be undertaken for all kinds of sins,[150]

---

[148] *Serm.* 351, 4, 9: *in notitia multorum ... agere paenitentiam non vereatur.* The phrase *in notitia* implies that the *multi* should know the reason for the performance of penance. For the exegesis of the text see Poschmann, *Kirchenbuße und correptio secreta* 35; *Florileg. Patrist.* XXXVIII, 26 f.; *ThR* 32 (1933) 271.

[149] Thus J. Kirsch, *Zur Geschichte der Kath. Beichte* (1902) 83.

[150] Cf. the caustic observation of Augustine, *Serm.* 232, 7, 8, that many of those in the place of the penitents appeared to be quite content: *nolunt inde surgere, quasi electus sit locus paenitentium.*

even for those which men did not reckon very grave, in particular sins against the sixth commandment, which undoubtedly provided the principal matter for penance; moreover, it was also available for lesser sins. If then there can be no doubt of the sense of this much controverted directive, it is otherwise with the historical question whether the practice of maintaining secrecy in regard to sins is in fact of Apostolic origin as the Pope implies. Some scholars hold that up to about the end of the fourth century public confession of secret sins was commonly required. If this view is correct, it would seem that the practice condemned by Leo was simply a survival of what was earlier general practice.[151] However, the texts from Tertullian, Cyprian, Origen, Ambrose and others adduced in its support are not conclusive; they can be understood either as imposing public penance, or as merely counselling public confession.[152] On the other hand it must be admitted that certain texts *(e.g.* Origen, *In Ps.* 37, *hom.* 2, 6) do seem to tell in favour of public confession as a matter of obligation. It is conceivable that in the earlier period also there was divergency in practice.

It was the responsibility of the bishop to decide on the amount of penance. In principle the necessity of a *paenitentia plena et iusta* was firmly maintained. The greater the guilt, the greater the penance (Ambrose, *De paen.* 1, 3, 10).[153] In making his decision the bishop had to take the disposition of the sinner into account as well as the gravity of the sin: *ac tunc iubere dimitti, cum viderit congruam satisfactionem.*[154] The duration of penance was, therefore, not strictly fixed from the outset; the bishop had to supervise[155] the penance, and in proportion to the fervour of the penitent

---

[151] Thus Morinus lib. 5 c. 12 and 13; J. Kirsch 71 ff.; B. Kurtscheid, *Das Beichtsiegel in seiner geschichtlichen Entwicklung* (1912) 30.

[152] Cf. E. Vacandard, *DTC* III 857; P. Galtier, *De paenitentia* (1956) 220 f., 415.

[153] Leo I severely condemns unjust excommunication for slight faults (*Ep.* 10,8 *ad episc. Vienn.*), Felix II the *immatura curandi facilitas* (*Ep.* 7 *ad episc. Sicil.*).

[154] Innocent I, *Ep.* 1, 7 *ad Decent.*

[155] Augustine, *Serm.* 232: *Discutio paenitentes et invenio male viventes.*

either advance or defer reconciliation.[156] But the bishop was not allowed to render the penitential canons in any way ineffective by an arbitrary use of his power. These canons retained the significance of objective norms; they allowed for a modified application by reason of the circumstances of the subject. On this point Augustine goes to the heart of the matter when he says in the *Enchiridion,* 17, 65: It is not the length of time but the depth of sorrow that has to be measured.[157] Yet, since no one can look into another man's heart and measure the degree of his sorrow, the ecclesiastical superiors were right in determining the *tempora paenitentiae,* in order that satisfaction should also be made to the Church in which the sins are remitted. Two reasons, therefore, are given by the Doctor of the Church for the juridical regulation of penance. In the present context, only the first, the uncertainty of personal judgement, will be developed.[158]

Turning to the penitential legislation in the concrete, we find that in the early part of this period it still breathes a spirit of extreme rigorism. From the time of the Montanist movement this had penetrated even into Catholic circles, and thus had smoothed the way for Novatianism. The Spanish Synod of Elvira (c. 306), which some have accused of being directly Novatianist in character,[159] though without justification, excludes no fewer than eighteen *crimina* from forgiveness for all time, and refuses communion even at the hour of death to those guilty of them. Besides idolatry, these are chiefly various specified sins of unchastity, and murder. In other cases, communion is allowed at the end of life, *acta legitima paenitentia,* and even for penances of limited duration it prescribes five, seven and ten years. It is

---

[156] Leo I, *Ep.* 19, 6 *ad Nicet.;* Felix II, loc. cit.
[157] *Non tam consideranda est mensura temporis quam doloris.*
[158] Augustine indicates, especially in *Ep.* 95, 3, the difficulties and anxiety which lie in wait for a conscientious bishop in preserving a just balance between the claims of objective severity and pastoral indulgence.
[159] Cf. on this J. Morinus lib. 9 c. 11; Bareille, *DTC* IV, 2381 ff.; E. Göller, *RQ* (1928) 236 ff.

impossible to decide to what extent these unparalleled decisions were put into practice. However, isolated examples occur of the denial of communion at the hour of death by a few other synods, even outside Spain, *e.g.* Arles (314) can. 14 and 22; Sardica (343) can. 2; Saragossa (380) can. 2. An absolute denial of communion is unknown to the oriental councils of the fourth century. On the contrary, canon 13 of Nicaea urges, as "an ancient and canonical law" that a dying man "should not be deprived of the last and most necessary viaticum". On other points, however, the regulations are extremely severe. Canon 22 of Ancyra (314) decrees lifelong penance for wilful murder; two to thirty years, divided among the penitential grades, for idolatry and unchastity, in proportion to the gravity of the sins, as determined by the circumstances; for abortion the "earlier law" of lifelong punishment is mitigated to one of ten years (can. 21). Similarly, in the Canonical Epistles the sentences are for the most part in the region of several years' penance. Basil, for example, envisages eleven years for murder, and ten for abortion as the highest penalties (*Ep.* 188, n. 11 u. 2). In the Western Church of the same period lifelong penance was still required for particularly grave sins. This is clear from the decree of Pope Siricius in reference to idolatry, and to concubinage of monks and nuns (*Ep.* 1, n. 3 and 6, Mansi III 657), and those of Felix II concerning the re-baptism of higher clerics (*Ep.* 7, Mansi VII 1057). From rigorist Spain lifelong penance is attested by canon 18 of the First Council of Toledo (400) for re-marriage of the widow of a higher cleric; by canon 2 of Lerida (524) for poisoners; by canon 78 and 79 of the *Capitula* of Martin of Braga (d. 580) for marriage with a deceased husband's brother. Penances of ten years were frequently imposed; canon 81 of the *Capitula* of Martin of Braga, with an appeal to the authority of canon 15 of Ancyra, requires twenty to thirty years for bestiality.

Such exorbitant penalties are, however, only laid down for specific sins of the utmost gravity. For sins of common occurrence, in particular, therefore, for ordinary sins of the flesh, the official period of penance was relatively brief. In Rome at this period it must already have been limited to the forty days of Lent, as it was in the seventh and eighth centuries according to the explicit testimony of the *Gelasian Sacramentary*. As early as the time of Innocent I, Maundy Thursday appears as the established day for reconciliation (*Ep.* 1, 7 *ad Decent.*). According to Leo I, Lent is the proper time for penance; it is a preparation not only for baptism, but also for the forgiveness of sins by reconciliation (*Serm.* 45; 49, 3). For Gaul, too, the same conclusion follows from canon 80 of the *Statuta ecclesiae antiqua,* which prescribes that *omni tempore ieiunii* penitents are to receive the imposition of hands. Naturally, a precondition for reconciliation and the conclusion of penance was the fulfilment of the terms of the penance. If this condition was not verified, then reconciliation was deferred until the following Maundy Thursday. In the decree of Innocent I already mentioned, it is expressly forbidden to proceed with it on another date and only in the case of the sick is an exception provided for.[160]

The rite of reconciliation consisted in the *supplicatio sacerdotalis* with the imposition of hands, that is, in the blessing of the penitents in association with the intercession of the faithful with which we are already familiar. This procedure had been observed in similar fashion during the celebration of the liturgy throughout the whole period of penance (Leo I, *Ep.* 18, 3 *ad Theod.* ; 19, 6 *ad Nicet.*).[161] There is evidence of a gradation of publicity at this ceremony in Africa, just as for the reception of penance. It consisted in the fact that only public sinners received the imposition of hands *ante apsidem,* that is, in the sight of the

---

[160] That is the meaning of the passage: *Ceterum de pondere aestimando delicti sacerdotis est iudicare ... ac tunc iubere dimitti, cum viderit congruam satisfactionem. Sane si quis in aegritudinem inciderit ... ei est ante tempus paschae relaxandum* (see Poschmann II 215 ff.). Cf. also the complaint of Augustine (*Serm.* 232, 7, 8) mentioned above that a great part of the penitents appeared to be in no hurry at all to emerge from the "place of the penitents".

[161] A detailed description is given by St. Jerome, *Dial. contra Lucif.* 5, from which

whole congregation (Synod of Hippo [393] can. 30). For Rome, this distinction appears to be excluded by the decree of Innocent I.

Normally, only the bishop was the competent minister of reconciliation, just as in this period he was the only one to whom the title of *sacerdos* was applied. This is sufficiently clear from the texts which have been discussed up to this point (those from Augustine, Jerome, Innocent I, Leo I). Priests were only allowed to undertake reconciliation as the delegates of the bishop, and in case of necessity. This is prescribed by canon 30 of Hippo. In restricting reconciliation to Maundy Thursday, Innocent I also has in mind the safeguarding of this episcopal right, as is evident from the context of the decree.[162] As, however, in the course of time it was the sick who became more and more the principal applicants for penance, the presbyters did in practice have sufficient scope to occupy themselves with the administration of the sacrament of penance. This state of affairs is illustrated by two notices in the *Liber Pontificalis*. These relate that Pope Marcellus (308—309) *propter baptismum et paenitentiam* divided the Church in Rome into twenty-five titular churches or parishes, and that Pope Simplicius (468—483), for the same reason, introduced into the three basilicas of St. Peter, St. Paul and St. Laurence weekly rounds of ministry for presbyters.[163] These measures were clearly dictated by concern for the dying; they ensured that presbyters would always be at hand to administer baptism and reconciliation to them on request.[164] Apart from the solemn reconciliation which was reserved to the bishop, the presbyters co-operated as a matter of course in the ordinary administration of penance by the advice they gave to the bishop, as well as by their supervision and pastoral care of the penitents. In churches

---

it appears that during the imposition of hands the bishop prays for the return of the Holy Ghost to the penitent.

[162] Poschmann II 216.

[163] I 43 Mommsen.

[164] See ibid. II 50—54; E. Göller, *Papsttum u. Bußgewalt* 23 and 85.

which had grown larger and more difficult to control these duties could no longer be carried out by the bishop alone. No doubt, too, in the majority of cases, sinners made the confession which was a prelude to penance in the first place to a priest of the diocese who was in their confidence, and he would then have arranged for their admission to penance. Moreover, there is no dogmatic reason which would prohibit the delegation to a priest of the function of conferring reconciliation; its reservation to the bishop is only a matter of positive law. In the Eastern Church delegation of this kind was effectively realized in the office of the priest penitentiary. Socrates (*H.E.* 5, 19) and Sozomen (*H.E.* 7, 16) who is dependent on him relate that after the Decian persecution bishops, wishing to spare penitents the hardship of public confession, instituted a special priest for penance who heard the confessions of sinners, imposed appropriate satisfaction on them, and absolved them — [ἀπέ]λυε — after they had completed their penance. This institution is said to have lasted up to the time of Nectarius, Patriarch of Constantinople (381—397). He ill-advisedly abolished the office in consequence of a scandal which had become known through the inquisitorial conduct of the priest penitentiary of the place. The result was that henceforward, in the Eastern Churches, in contrast to the churches of the West, and particularly to the Church of Rome, control over penitents simply ceased to be exercised, much to the detriment of moral discipline, and participation in the holy mysteries was left to the conscience of the individual. As the office of priest penitentiary is mentioned in no other source,[165] it is advisable to treat the judgement of both historians with a certain reserve, both in what concerns the origin and the widespread diffusion of the office, and especially in regard to the assertion that Nectarius' action did away with the office at a

---

[165] P. Batiffol, *Etudes d'hist. et de théol. pos.* I³ (1920) 200; I⁶ (1920) 146 ff. has unsuccessfully attempted to demonstrate and defend (against Vacandard) the existence of the office of priest penitentiary also for Rome, relying on the notices in the *Liber Pontificalis* mentioned above.

single stroke. That can only be accepted for the area immediately subject to the jurisdiction of Constantinople, which at that period was not yet very extensive. Most important of all, however, the abolition of the priest penitentiary is not, as has often been thought, the same thing as the abolition of public penance. In its essence that was unaffected by what was done, and remained in existence.[166] The only difference was that, in the absence of supervision and of official proceedings against sinners, it became progressively less important in practice, yielding to a private therapeutic procedure of which we have still to speak.

3. The Sacramental Efficacy of Reconciliation

Leo I proclaimed as a divine ordinance: *ut indulgentia Dei nisi supplicationibus sacerdotum nequeat obtineri.* Christ, he says, has bestowed on those in authority over the Church power *ut et confitentibus actionem paenitentiae darent et eosdem salubri satisfactione purgatos ad communionem sacramentorum per ianuam reconciliationis admitterent (Ep.* 18, 3 *ad Theod.).* In this classical utterance the indispensability of ecclesiastical forgiveness is enunciated, but at the same time the special difficulty of early-Christian penitential doctrine is also indicated. Is there any place left for the operation of absolution, if the "purification" from sin is produced by personal works of penance? This question still lay outside the purview of the ancients themselves. They were content to teach the necessity of both the one factor and of the other. As they generally laid great emphasis on the performance of penance, the ecclesiastical factor was either treated too briefly or else a certain inconsistency was inherent in their teaching. The therapeutic view of penance, which derived from Clement and Origen, and which was especially cultivated in monastic circles, was transplanted by Cassian († 435) from the Orient into the

---

[166] Cf. also K. Holl, *Enthusiasmus und Bußgewalt* (1898) 277 ff.; H. Koch, *HJ* 21 (1900) 64 f.; P. Galtier, *DAFC* III (1916) 1830; Poschmann II 55 ff.; K. Jüssen, *Die dogm. Anschauungen des Hesychius von Jer.* II (1934) 70 f.

Gallic monasteries. It is, therefore, not a coincidence that precisely in the Church of Gaul which was strongly influenced by the ascetical spirit of monasticism, the Church's power of forgiveness receded considerably into the background in spite of all the recognition which it received in principle.

The Church possesses the juridical title for the forgiveness of sins in the power of the keys which has been delivered to her.[167] The significance of reconciliation is illustrated in practice by the fact that Leo considers penitents who are surprised by death and die without priestly forgiveness as standing outside the Christian community, and withholds from them the suffrages of the Church (*Ep.* 18, 3 and *Ep.* 167 *ad Rust. inquis.* 8). However, the Gallic Church did not share this strict attitude and allowed the *oblatio* for a deceased penitent — *pro eo, quod honoravit paenitentiam* — thus taking his interior disposition as decisive.[168] In Rome, too, a more lenient judgement soon won the day. The *Leonine Sacramentary,* which was completed before the time of Gregory I, already contains proper prayers for unreconciled penitents.[169] The treatment of penitents in danger of death is likewise instructive. We have already heard how it was only with much scruple that Cyprian granted reconciliation even to such sick persons as had already done penance for a considerable time but had not yet completed it. He sharply repelled people who were only converted on their deathbed (*Ep.* 55, 23). The First Synod of Arles (314) adopted the same attitude. In contrast, however, the Council of Nicaea, in the 13th canon mentioned above, affirmed as an "ancient and canonical law, to be observed even now, that the last and most necessary viaticum must not be denied to anyone on the point of death"; in cases of recovery, however, it required that the performance of penance should

---

[167] Thus, with Leo I, Pacian, *Ep.* 1, 6; 3, 11; Peter Chrysologus, *Serm.* 8, 4; Augustine, *Serm.* 392, 3 and others.

[168] Synod of Vaison (442) can. 2; 2nd Synod of Arles can. 12; *Stat. eccl. ant* can. 79.

[169] Chap. 33. *Super defunctos* n. 2. Feltoe 145.

follow. Admittedly, the general recognition of this "law", claimed by the Council, did not exist. It was only gradually that the more lenient practice came to prevail. In Gaul especially, it encountered opposition. Innocent I (*Ep.* 3, 2 *ad Exsup.*) and his successor Celestine I (*Ep.* 2, 2 *ad episcopos Vienn. et Narb.*) still felt themselves obliged to take stern issue with the rigoristic treatment of the dying that existed there. Canon 3 of the Synodal decrees of the First Synod of Orange (441) and canon 2 of those of Vaison (442) show clearly the effect of these papal decrees. They urged the Nicaean law, as also later did canons 76—78 of the *Statuta ecclesiae antiqua*. But even at the end of the century the controversy about the efficacy of *subitanea paenitentia* which was brought to a head chiefly by Faustus of Riez (*Ep.* 5, p. 184 ed. Engelbrecht) and Avitus of Vienne (*Ep.* 4, p. 30 ed. Peiper) disturbed minds profoundly throughout wide circles in Gaul.[170] Admittedly, even Avitus — and he is again typical of the Gallic outlook — in his condemnation of rigorism as "contrary to truth and inhuman", is thinking not so much of the efficacy of reconciliation, as of the atoning power of confession and the limitless mercy of God. In contrast, when Leo I justifies the efficacy of penance which was undertaken only when there was danger of death, it is reconciliation that occupies the foreground: *Multum enim utile et necessarium est, ut peccatorum reatus ante ultimum diem sacerdotali supplicatione solvatur* (*Ep.* 18, 3).[171] Augustine expressly puts it on the very same level as baptism as a necessary means of salvation. This was during the invasion of the Vandals when he

[170] Cf. Poschmann II 111 ff.

[171] Leo I (*Ep.* 167 *inqu.* 7) retained the Nicaean prescription, which is also attested by Felix II (*Ep.* 7 *ad episc. Sicil.*), that a person who made a recovery should afterwards undertake ecclesiastical penance, inclusive of reconciliation. This was not felt as a difficulty against the operation of the power of the keys. The concept, first worked out by the scholastics, of the forgiveness of sins as an act completed in an instant, was not yet available, and anthropomorphic thought envisaged the possibility of a gradual elimination of guilt before God. Obscurity and inconsistency in theory must inevitably affect the practical organization of penance. Cf. Poschmann II 44 ff.

obliged priests to remain at their posts with their flocks and prevent the terrible disaster that, after the flight of the priests, the dying *vel non regenerati exeunt* (*i.e.* without baptism) *vel ligati* (*i.e.* without reconciliation).[172]

We are also indebted to the great doctor of Hippo for the first theory on the efficacy of reconciliation. He is fond of comparing the process of justification to the raising of Lazarus from the dead, in order to show what part belongs to God and what to the Church in the elimination of sins. God's exclusive prerogative is the reawakening of the sinner through the *magna gratia,* which stimulates him to contrition and penance. The reawakened man is, however, *adhuc ligatus, confitens et adhuc reus,* the loosing from the *vincula ipsius reatus* is the business of the Church,[173] and in this connexion the *reatus peccati* is nothing else than the sin itself, inasmuch as after the act has taken place it abides in the man and renders him liable to punishment.[174] The formal cause, however, of the pardon of the *reatus* is the Holy Ghost, and the man becomes worthy to receive Him by his incorporation into the Church. It is not only for baptism but universally valid that: *Ecclesiae caritas, quae per Spiritum Sanctum diffunditur, participum suorum peccata dimittit, eorum autem, qui non sunt eius participes, tenet* (*In Jo. tr.* 119, 4).[175] Living fellowship with the Church is the factor ensuring the forgiveness of sins and the communication of grace.

Here we have the sacramental efficacy of reconciliation expounded even more clearly than in Cyprian. In so far as the priest, and he alone, confers it validly (*Serm.* 71, 23, 37), it can be said of him that he forgives sins. But he is always no more

---

[172] *Ep.* 222, 8; cf. *De civ.* 20, 9, 2; Victor of Vita, *De persecutione Vandalica* 2, 11; Gregory I, *Registr.* 1, 15.

[173] *In Jo. tr.* 49, 24; ibid. 22, 7; *Serm.* 67, 1, 2; 98, 6; 295, 3, 2; 352, 3, 8; *Serm. Mai.* 125 (*Misc. Agostiniana* I 355).

[174] *De nupt. et concup.* I 29; cf. *Retract.* 1, 15, 2. In addition B. Poschmann, *ZkTh* 45 (1921) 214—228; 405—420.

[175] *De bapt. c. Donat.* 3, 18, 23: *Pax ecclesiae dimittit peccata et ab ecclesiae pace alienatio tenet peccata. C. Cresc.* 2, 16: *Quos civitas Dei recipiendo efficit innocentes.*

than the official executor of the power of the keys: its proper holder is the universal Church, that is the collectivity of its members who are animated by the Holy Ghost. Not Peter alone, *sed universa ecclesia ligat solvitque peccata (In Jo. tr.* 124, 7; *Serm.* 99, 9 and often). Here we have the starting-point for an understanding of the prayer which along with the imposition of hands symbolized the act of reconciliation. It is not without qualification to be equated with the "deprecative absolution" in the sense of the later doctrine of penance.[176] Its significance is much more that of an aid to the penitent in his efforts to obtain the divine mercy, and in this it resembles the blessings previously bestowed on the penitents. That is the reason why there was great emphasis on the necessity of persevering prayer, united with personal works of penance.[177] Sacramental efficacy belongs to it only in so far as the priest has the intention of conferring reconciliation along with it. In other words, the sacramental cause is reconciliation as such; the prayer is simply its accessory rite.

[176] It is thus understood by E. Göller, *Papsttum und Bußgewalt* 63; P. Galtier, *L'Eglise et la rémission* 78 ff.
[177] Cf. Pomerius, *De vita contempl.* 2, 1; Gregory I, *Moral.* 20, 36, 71; *In Ez.* II *hom.* 9, 22; I *hom.* 11, 28 and above. See also B. Poschmann, *ThR* (1934) 356 f.; Id. *Der Ablaß im Licht der Bußgeschichte* (1948) 10—13.

4. *The Law of One Penance : Life-long Obligations of Penance*

The doctrine of a single penance, introduced into theology by Hermas, and justified on psychological and moral grounds, was already regarded as an established principle by Tertullian, Clement and Origen; and it continues to be inflexibly applied. As the *secunda post naufragium miseris tabula* (Jerome, *Ep.* 80, 9), penance in this respect stands on the same footing as baptism: *sicut unum baptisma ita una paenitentia* (Ambrose, *De paen.* 2, 10, 95). When a man has broken for the second time his vow of fidelity to God, he can count no more on a further offering of the remedy. *Suffugium non habent paenitendi* are the words in a decision of Pope Siricius on a question of Bishop Himerius of Tarragona which arose out of this rule (*Ep.* 1, 5), and even two centuries later the Third Synod of Toledo (589) condemned the custom of granting repeated reconciliations which had arisen in some Spanish churches as an *execrabilis praesumptio*. In justification of the severe practice, Augustine brings forward the disciplinary reason: *ne medicina vilis minus utilis esset aegrotis, quae tanto magis salubrius erit, quanto minus contemptibilis fuerit* (*Ep.* 153, 7). In the Eastern Church, too, the principle of the *paenitentia una* is still in operation at the beginning of the fifth century, as is shown by the accusations brought against Chrysostom by his enemies, that he had granted sinners penance and forgiveness over and over again.[178]

Not all hope of salvation is as yet cut off from the recidivists by the denial of penance. Augustine *(loc. cit.)* indignantly repudiates such an idea. Nor does the Church withdraw herself from them altogether. According to the decree of Siricius, they may take part in the prayer of the faithful and in the celebration

---

[178] Socrates, *H. E.* 6, 21. Similarly the 6th charge of the "Synod of the Oak", which had been convened against the Doctor of the Church (Mansi III 1145). Cf. K. Jüssen, *Die dogm. Anschauungen des Hesychius von Jerusalem* II (1934) 83 f. Jüssen shows that Hesychius taught that there could be a repeated admission to penance of a recidivist sinner, but not a repetition of reconciliation (81 f.).

of the holy mysteries; but they are excluded from the eucharist. But at the hour of death they will receive the consolation of the viaticum. By this provision canon 13 of Nicaea is applied to the recidivists, and they are put on the same footing as those who were converted only at the approach of death. These too, in default of all performance of penance receive viaticum only and not regular reconciliation.[179] The idea of viaticum not preceded by absolution, which is so strange to us today, becomes intelligible if we consider that the efficient sacramental cause of the forgiveness of sins is the act of readmission to the Church as such, and that in the concession of the eucharist this act is performed in an eminent, *i.e.* implicit way.

As the counterpart of the "one baptism", so, too the "one penance" impresses on a man a kind of "character" which lasts beyond his period of penance in the proper sense, and adheres to him for the rest of his life. A person who has once undertaken penance remains forever a Christian of inferior juridical status. He is not to be admitted to the clerical state,[180] and he must submit to restrictions which profoundly affect the conduct of his life. To these belong the prohibition of holding public offices, in particular of engagement in military service, and, most important of all, abstention from marital intercourse. In other words, the "status of a penitent" requires a renunciation of the "life of the world", not different in kind from that of the "religious state". *Qui mortui et sepulti in Christo sunt, non debent iterum velut viventes de hoc mundo decernere* (Ambrose, *De paen.* 2, 10, 95). Moreover, the obligations are so strictly interpreted that

---

[179] In contrast to the *communio* of viaticum which *morientis sufficit consolationi,* Gallic synods describe reconciliation given after the completion of penance as *reconciliatio absolutissima* (Vaison can. 2) and as *legitima communio cum reconciliatoria manus impositione* (1 Orange can. 3). Cf. Poschmann II 107 ff.

[180] Siricius op. cit. c. 14; Augustine, *En. in Ps.* 61, 23; *C. Crescon.* 2, 16, 19; Innocent I, *Ep.* 6 *ad episc. Apul.*; Synod of Rome (402) can. 5; Hormisdas, *Ep.* 25, 1 *ad episc. Hisp.* (517); *Statut. eccl. ant.* can. 68; Synod of Agde, can. 43; Epaon (517) can. 3; 4th Synod of Arles (524) can. 3; the earliest evidence comes from Origen, *C. Cels.* III, 51 (above 69).

their infringement is equivalent to a relapse into sin. It is in fact the infringement of these penitential laws, and not fresh mortal sins, that Siricius has in mind in his decree on recidivism.[181] The existence of the lifelong obligations is established with certainty for the period from the fourth century onwards.[182] There is no hint of them in the source material of the first three centuries, and yet in some respects this is quite rich. Augustine nowhere mentions them; indeed what he says about the practical organization of penance, and especially about the great number of penitents[183] seems to rule them out. Yet, according to the witness of Fulgentius they are also in operation in the African Church. In contrast, it seems that in the Orient they simply did not arise. The origin of these obligations, which added such a heavy burden to penance, is to be explained by the legalistic tendency of the Roman mind. What was earlier a mere matter of counsel gradually took on the character of a rigid law, much in the same way as the rule of one penance which originally was based only on moral and psychological grounds. These excessive demands, more than anything else, were the shoals on which the system of canonical penance would inevitably be wrecked. How could average wordly Christians be persuaded to renounce forever, not only sin, but life in the world, in itself permissible, in exchange for a kind of monastic life?

---

[181] ...*Qui acta paenitentia tanquam canes et sues ad vomitus pristinos et ad volutabra redeuntes* (2 Pet 2:22) *et militiae cingulum et ludicras voluptates et nova coniugia et inhibitos denuo appetivere concubitus. Quorum professam incontinentiam generati post absolutionem filii prodiderunt* (*Ep.* 1, 5). Göller's claim (28 n. 11) that what is meant is a relapse into previous serious sins is in contradiction with the text of the decree.

[182] Leo I, *Ep.* 167 *inqu.* 9 and 13; Synod of Tours (461) can. 8; Angers (453) can. 5; 1st Orleans (511) can. 11; Epaon can. 23; 2nd Synod of Arles (443 or 452) can. 21; Barcelona (541) can. 6 and 8; Toledo (638) can. 8; Caesarius, *Serm.* 249, 6; 258, 2 (*PL* 39, 2208, 2222 [*CC Serm.* 65, 2; 103, 280]); Fulgentius, *Ep.* 1, 2 (*PL* 65, 303). In the face of this evidence it passes comprehension how A. Ehrhard (*Die katholische Kirche im Wandel der Zeiten und Völker* II [1937] 276 f.) can deny the existence of these lifelong obligations.

[183] Cf. *Serm.* 232, 7—8: *Abundant hic paenitentes; quando illis imponitur manus fit ordo longissimus.*

The immediate consequence of this was the postponement of penance for as long as possible. The Church had to be content with this; even herself recommend this practice within certain limits; and indeed absolutely prohibit the admission of young people to penance. Ambrose says that penance is to be undertaken *eo tempore quo culpae defervescat luxuria* (*De paen.* 2, 11, 107). Canon 15 of the Synod of Agde is even clearer: *Iuvenibus paenitentia non facile committenda est propter aetatis fragilitatem*. Canon 24 of the Second Synod of Arles and canon 24 of the Third Synod of Orleans decree that married persons must only be allowed to do penance with the consent of their partners. This means in principle that ecclesiastical penance is equated with a vow of perpetual chastity, as indeed Avitus of Vienne expressly described it (*Ep.* 4, p. 30; ed. Peiper). Difficulties arose, especially when young men received penance in danger of death and then after recovery were bound forever by the regulations imposed on penitents. Leo I felt himself obliged on that account to adopt a more lenient attitude and declared that it is excusable if a young man in such a case contracts marriage.[184] The Pope, however, does not wish to "establish any rule, but rather to ponder what is bearable". Similarly, even two centuries later, the Sixth Synod of Toledo (630) in canon 8, cited Leo in allowing penitents of this kind to resume married life after recovery: *quousque possint adipisci temporis maturitate continentiae statum,* but it also observed that this was not *legitime praeceptum sed constat a nobis pro humana fragilitate indultum*.

As a result of such impracticable requirements, ecclesiastical penance gradually ceases to have any part in the ordinary course of life, and becomes merely a means of preparing for death. Caesarius propounds this objection to his recommendation of penance: *Ego in militia positus sum, uxorem habeo et ideo paenitentiam*

---

[184] *Ep.* 167 *inqu.* 9. Other penitential obligations, too, are interpreted leniently by Leo. Lawsuits and trading are discouraged rather than forbidden. Only the prohibition of military service is strictly enforced, because *contrarium est omnino ecclesiasticis regulis* (*inqu.* 10—12).

agere quomodo possum? (*Serm.* 258, 2, *PL* 39, 2222; [*CC Serm.* 65; 103, 278]). In remarkable fashion, the preacher admits that this retort, with its appeal to the claims of military service and matrimony is justified. The only reservation he makes in his reply is that neither the one state nor the other should put any obstacle in the way of leading a truly penitential life. He makes a sharp distinction between *paenitentiam agere* and *paenitentiam accipere,* that is between the practice of penance as it is done throughout life by good Christians — *per omnem vitam a bonis Christianis agitur* — and formal ecclesiastical penance, such as all men desire to receive at the end of their life — *omnes homines volunt in finem vitae suae recipere* (*Serm.* 256, 4). Now that ecclesiastical penance is postponed to the end of life he is content with what is obviously required, urging only immediate conversion, in order that the late "reception of penance" might be fruitful.[185] There were also of course at that period cases where penance was voluntarily undertaken even in time of health. These, however, were exceptions.[186] In the whole of the writings of Gregory I, in which penance fills so large a place, the only certain evidence for ecclesiastical penance is in the form of penance of the sick, even if it be admitted that one or two passages could also be taken to refer to public ecclesiastical penance.[187]

In proportion as penance was postponed until the end of life it was progressively transformed; whereas it had been an extraordinary spiritual remedy, primarily relied on only for mortal sins, it became a normal one, sought by all, for on the threshold

---

[185] Similarly Avitus, *Ep.* 18 p. 50 ed. Peiper: *Quod ad paenitentiam spectat, moneatur interim agere, accipere non cogatur.... Patiatur paenitentiam cum perdit peccandi occasionem.* Even for admission to Communion it seems that in this later period the *paenitentiam agere* was considered sufficient. Cf. Caesarius, *Serm.* 229, 2, 3 (*PL* 39, 2166 f. [*CC Serm.* 227; 104, 897]). A different practice is still found in Ambrose, Augustine, Leo and even in Gennadius. For further details see Poschmann II 240—247 and *ZkTh* 44 (1930) 248 ff.

[186] Cf. *e. g.* Caesarius, *Serm.* 261 (*PL* 39, 2227 [*CC Serm.* 67; 103, 284]).

[187] Cf. E. Amann, *DTC* XII 835; Poschmann II 260—267 and his reply to Göller's denial (*Papsttum und Bußgewalt* 153 ff.) *ThR* 33 (1934) 355 ff.

of eternity all were desirous of obtaining for themselves the blessing that went with it. Augustine, like Tertullian (*De paen.* 7, 2), warned the faithful against the second penance — *hoc genus paenitentiae nemo sibi proponat, ad hoc genus nemo praeparet* (*Serm.* 352, 3, 8) — but in the sixth century its reception before death was not only in general use, but actually a law.[188] A natural consequence of the change was that ecclesiastical penance more and more lost its defamatory character. The penitents were no longer held up as warnings but rather as models. True, the ancient laws, which also covered the penance of the sick, still remained in force in principle, but in keeping with the new attitude to penance, they must have permitted a certain relaxation. Thus Spanish penitential law decreed that sick persons who were not guilty of a grave sin and who had undertaken penance out of devotion, need not submit to the public rite of penance after recovery, and could be admitted to the clergy.[189] But the *vita paenitentium,* in what concerned their mode of life, dress and sexual abstinence, continued to be demanded with ancient severity even of them for the rest of their life.[190] The reception of penance is indeed associated with entry into the religious state. "Apostasy" from penance to the way of life of the "laity" is cursed by an "anathema".[191] In respect of its ascetical obligations the order of penitents is on the same level as the priestly and religious states.

---

[188] Cf. can. 9 of Barcelona (541); Isidore of Seville, *De eccl. off.* 2, 17, 6.

[189] Synod of Gerunda (517) can. 9; 4th Synod of Toledo (633) can. 54; see also E. Göller, *RQ* 37 (1929) 291 ff. Moreover the numerous decrees of councils and popes which urge the ancient law of irregularity show that bishops in selecting candidates for the clergy will often have fallen back even on penitents in the strict sense of the word.

[190] Cf. can. 6—8 of Barcelona.

[191] 4th Synod of Toledo can. 55; 6th Toledo can. 7.

5. The Penance of Clerics and Religious

The emphasis in canonical penance is on the sincerity of the spirit of penance, despite a rigid adherence to legal requirements. This is, indeed, quite clear from the development which has been traced at the close of antiquity. However much the necessity of canonical penance is stressed, yet salvation is not unconditionally attached to it. This is open, for example, even to recidivists, even though penance is denied them. It is therefore intelligible if in other cases too, where there are special reasons, some other way of penance is substituted for the canonical procedure.

The first case of this is the penance of clerics: *Paenitentiam agere cuiquam non conceditur clericorum.* These words are found in the same decretal of Pope Siricius (*Ep.* 1, 14 *ad Himer.*), in which he forbids the admission of penitents to the clergy. Leo I (*Ep.* 167, *inqu.* 2) is even more definite: *Alienum est a consuetudine ecclesiastica, ut qui in presbyterali honore aut in diaconii gradu fuerint consecrati, ii pro crimine aliquo, per manus impositionem remedium accipiant paenitendi.... Unde huiusmodi lapsis ad promerendam misericordiam Dei privata est expetenda secessio, ubi illis satisfactio, si fuerit digna, sit etiam fructuosa.*[192] Leo believes that he can trace the law back to Apostolic tradition. Against this there is quite clear evidence showing that n the first centuries clerics had to undertake it in just the same way as laymen.[193] We meet the earliest prohibition of penance for priests in a decision of a Roman Council of the year 313, which according to the account given by Optatus of Milevis (*C. Parmen. Donatist.* 1, 24 p. 21 ed. Ziwsa) condemned Donatus of Casa Nigra on the ground that he im-

---

[192] Cf. also can. 12 of the Synod of Carthage (401).
[193] Thus especially Cyprian, *Ep.* 64, 1; 65, 1; 67, 6; also can. 76 of Elvira (306); can. 1 of Neo-Caesarea (314—325). Morinus long ago demonstrated this (op. cit. 1, 4. c. 12).

posed hands on fallen bishops, *quod ab ecclesia alienum est*.[194] At that time, therefore, the custom was well established in the Roman Church. In Africa it found in Optatus a strenuous defender against the Donatists, who compelled sinning bishops and priests to do penance (ibid. 2, 21, 24, 25). No certain reason can be given for the special treatment of the higher clergy in regard to penance. According to Optatus and Augustine, it is a dogmatic one. The dignity of the priesthood and of the sacrament on which it is based forbid the imposition of penance.[195] The imposition of hands, given to a priest at ordination, may not be repeated any more than baptism. For this reason, maintains Augustine, clergy who are converted from heresy, unlike lay converts, do not receive imposition of hands, *ne non homini, sed ipsi sacramento fiat iniuria* (*C. Ep. Parm.* 2, 13, 28; *De bapt. c. Donatist.* 1, 1, 2). However, the imposition of hands which was given in public penance is a far greater "dishonouring of the sacrament" than the one which took place at the conversion rite, for the latter involved no penance. On the other hand, the exceptive law appears less of a privilege than a disadvantage for clerics: penance is "not granted" them; they have no claim on the *remedium paenitendi*. The text of 1 Sam 2:25 applies to them: *sacerdos si peccaverit, quis orabit pro eo?* (Leo). They are not let off a thing in the way of punishment and humiliation. Instead of public penance the far more painful punishment of degradation is incurred. This is regarded as equivalent to public penance. The offender must not be visited with a double punishment, both that of degradation and that of excommunication. The principle is enunciated in the 25th *Canon of the Apostles,* and is attested as an ancient canon — ἀρχαῖος κανών — by Basil in his Canonical Letters (*Ep.* 188, can. 3; 217, can. 51). It is also frequently met

---

[194] For proof that the passage refers to penance and not reordination (thus Morinus and Hefele) see Poschmann II 176 ff.

[195] *A vobis occisi sunt de honoribus Dei sacerdotes :* Optatus, ibid. 2, 25.

with in western penitential ordinances.[196] However, the prin- ciple *ne bis in idem* does not assure clerics of immunity from excommunication in every case. This is imposed in addition to degradation for specified sins and for recidivism.[197] In the Gallic Church it is quite often combined with degradation even for ordinary mortal sins.[198] In this connexion, however, excom- munication, which is constantly mentioned by itself, must not simply be equated with public penance,[199] for the ancient Church was also familiar with an excommunication which did not in- volve public penance.[200] According to the decretal of Leo the substitute for public penance in the case of clerics is the *privata secessio,* which, like penance, has to be requested from the Church.[201] It consists in the offender's withdrawal to a quiet place where, without being excluded from communion he does penance in private. In practice, this is usually a monastery, so that from the beginning of the sixth century relegation to a monastery is also directly linked with degradation.[202] By the very fact that the Church must give permission for penance of this kind, the penitential exercises acquire an ecclesiastical character. Apart from this, there is no mention of any ecclesiastical inter-

---

[196] Siricius, *Ep.* 1, 7, 9 *ad Him.*; Innocent I, *Ep.* 3, 1 *ad Exsup.*; can. 12 of Carthage (401).

[197] Felix II, *Ep.* 7 *ad univ. episc.* (Mansi VII 1057).   [198] Examples in Poschmann II 186 ff.

[199] Thus Morinus, op. cit.; P. Hinschius, *System des kath. Kirchenrechts* IV (1888) 740; H. J. Schmitz, *Die Bußbücher* I (1883) 134 ff.

[200] Canon 4 of the 1st Synod of Orange, which is repeated in Canon 21 of the 2nd Synod of Arles, appears at first to conflict with Roman law: *Paenitentiam desider- antibus clericis non esse negandum.* This canon, however, is not treating of penance for mortal sins, but of penance undertaken out of devotion in danger of death which, as we have heard, did not carry the defamatory effect of canonical penance. The fact that doubts had been raised even against such penance of the sick for clerics shows that they were excluded from ordinary penance in Gaul as well as in Italy and Africa. See Poschmann I 189 ff.

[201] The phrase is a term of canon law. Cf. John II, letter to the bishops of Gaul, Mansi VIII 807:... *ut habeat paenitendi licentiam, petitorium dare vobis censemus.* Agapetus I (535—536) to Caesarius of Arles, ibid. 856: *privatam magis potuit secun- dum canones expetere paenitentiam.*

[202] Cf. can. 22 of Epaon (517), can. 7 of 3rd Synod of Orleans (538).

vention. The details of the satisfaction are left to the penitents themselves: *Ubi illis satisfactio, si fuerit digna, etiam sit fructuosa.*[203]

From the fifth century religious are put on the same footing as clerics in regard to penance. This applies primarily to monks, but also includes ascetics living in the world who bind themselves by vow to the religious life. An indirect proof of this is the fact that there is no trace of ecclesiastical penance in ascetical instructions destined for monks, such as the sermons addressed to them by St. Jerome, or the teaching of the monastic father, Cassian. It is expressly said, first by an anonymous writer of the fifth century,[204] that it is only necessary for people in the world; whereas *abrenuntianti publica paenitentia non est necessaria.* The monk's vow is a kind of second baptism, through which he who makes his profession is inserted afresh into the Body of Christ, so that he may partake of the eucharist without any further requirement.[205] Gennadius of Marseilles († c. 492—505) makes a very similar claim for religious in general as that made by the anonymous writer for monks. After having demanded public penance for the pardon of *capitalia et mortalia peccata,* he continues: *sed et secreta satisfactione solvi mortalia crimina non negamus, sed mutato prius saeculari habitu et confesso religionis studio per vitae correctionem et iugi imo perpetuo luctu miserante Deo veniam consequatur...* (*De eccl. dogm.* 53). In this passage it is directly taught that the religious life is a form of private penance and as such is a fully equivalent substitute for ecclesiastical penance. Its starting-point is the *conversio* by which a person binds himself by a vow made before the Church to a life of perpetual penance in prayer, mortification, sexual abstinence etc., and manifests externally in

---

[203] Cf. also the description of the penance which Jerome, *Ep.* 147, 8, requires of the deacon Sabinianus who had committed adultery. On the attempt of H. Brewer (*ZkTh* 45 [1921] 7 f.) to read into the word *fructuosa* a reference to ecclesiastical absolution, see Poschmann II 199 n. 1.

[204] In a fragment falsely attributed by Migne to Faustus of Riez as *Sermon* 3 (*PL* 58, 875). See Poschmann II 128 n. 4.

[205] On the sacramental estimate of profession as a "second baptism" cf. O. Casel, "Die Mönchsweihe" in *JLW* 5 (1926) 1 ff.

his dress the exchange of the secular for the religious life. Like a monk, a *conversus* ceases to belong to the laity and henceforth has to regard himself as a "penitent".[206]

The ecclesiastical act which initiates the *conversio* is accordingly styled *benedictio paenitentiae,* just like the prayer which was pronounced over public penitents with imposition of hands.[207] It is, therefore, often difficult to decide whether penance proper or *conversio* is indicated, all the more so as at that time ordinary penitents, too, were classified as religious. Moreover, the reception of penance was regarded as religious profession, and infringement of the penitential regulations as *relabi ad saecularia.*[208] In spite, however, of their similar character and obligations, ecclesiastical penance and *conversio* were juridically regarded as quite distinct. The former, too, still continued to be defamatory, at least in theory, the latter was regarded as a state of perfection. Whereas penance carried irregularity with it, *conversio* became a preliminary condition for admission to the clergy.[209]

Undoubtedly the original motive force behind *conversio* was zeal for perfection. That is why it was pre-eminently Christians of exemplary piety who resolved to undertake it. From the fifth century we hear of a succession of persons of high standing who led lives of penance and self-denial while remaining in their families.[210] It was very popular as a way of preparing for death, either under the impulse of sickness or old age. Despite the arduousness of the commitment that it involved, *conversio* was an easier state than that of public penance which imposed similar

---

[206] Can. 6 of the 3rd Synod of Orleans speaks of *conversio ex laicis;* cf. Ruricius, *Ep.* lib. 2, 32, p. 415 f. ed. Engelbrecht; Salvian, *De gub. Dei* 5, 10; ed. Pauly 118.
[207] Can. 44 of Agde; can. 21 of Epaon, can. 24 and 25 of the 3rd Synod of Orleans.
[208] Can. 11 of the 1st Synod of Orleans; can. 23 of Epaon; can. 55 of the 4th Synod of Toledo.
[209] On penance, cf. can. 3 of Epaon; on conversion, can. 6 of 3rd Synod of Orleans; can. 2 of 4th Synod of Arles (524) and can. 9 of 5th Synod of Orleans (549).
[210] Thus Eucherius, later bishop of Lyons, and his wife Galla; the ecclesiastical writer Salvian and his wife Palladia; Agricola, a member of the Gallic court aristocracy; the praetorian prefect, Felix, to whom Faustus of Riez addressed a letter, and others. See Poschmann II 131 ff.

ascetical demands, and for this reason it tended more and more to replace it. The result was that voluntary reception of public penance became an exceptional and edifying event.[211] In any case the far-ranging criticism levelled against the *conversi* by Salvian and Pomerius — including charges of outward show and hypocrisy[212] — proves that their number must have been quite considerable. The penance of the sick was not normally regarded as *conversio,* as is clear from the numerous synodal decrees subjecting those who make a recovery to the law of canonical penance. Even here, however, a change was introduced inasmuch as in Spanish penitential law of the sixth century, as already mentioned,[213] sick persons who receive penance out of devotion and not on account of grave sins, are not obliged to do public penance but simply to the observance of the *vita religiosa.* As a result, between them and the *conversi* there was in fact no distinction. From the point of view of dogma the difficulty arises as to how the existence of the sacrament is safeguarded in the penance of clerics and *conversi;* here there is neither excommunication nor corresponding reconciliation. In fact the sacrament is not dependent on the outward form of readmission but on the forgiveness actually granted by the Church, on the *pax ecclesiae,* and this is verified in both cases. According to Leo I and John II, an indispensable preliminary for the *privata secessio* of clerics is that it be "obtained by prayer" from the Church; and similarly the ecclesiastical *benedictio paenitentiae* is necessary for the profession of the *conversi.* In both cases the Church gives her blessing to the promise of a life of penance, and thereby proclaims that she on her side pardons the sinner. Fundamentally, this is simply an anticipation of the practice, later to become general, and which today is taken for granted,

---

[211] When Caesarius, *Serm.* 261 (above 108) in praising the heroism of penitents emphasizes that: *Et ille quidem, qui paenitentiam publice accepit, poterat eam secretius agere,* he is almost certainly alluding to *conversio.* See Poschmann II 139 ff.; *ZkTh* 54 (1930) 239. [212] Cf. Salvian, *De gub. Dei* 4, 10; Pomerius, *De vita contempl.* 2, 4. [213] Above 109.

of granting absolution before the performance of penance. The reason for the exceptive treatment of the clergy was, no doubt, the impossibility of repeating the imposition of hands received at ordination, for this carried with it an even greater obligation to a life of penance than the imposition of hands which was bestowed on penitents. Accordingly, clerics guilty of serious sins were put on the same footing as relapsed penitents in regard to ecclesiastical penance. These, too, were simply ordered to do penance in private. Religious, on the other hand, including monks and *conversi,* owed this special treatment to the high esteem of their religious profession which bound them to the closest union with God. Consequently, grave sins after profession put them also among the "relapsed", and disqualified them for ecclesiastical penance. However, the Nicaean law which urged the concession of viaticum to all the dying ensured that thenceforth all the relapsed, whether *penitentes, conversi* or *clerici,* also received the forgiveness of the Church even if they were not granted *reconciliatio absolutissima.*[214]

6. Reconciliation without Ecclesiastical Penance.
Therapeutic Direction of Souls

Although excommunication was an essential element in ecclesiastical penance, it does not follow that every excommunication was linked with this procedure. On the contrary, excommunication was also used as a disciplinary measure in the case of serious offences of lesser gravity, which were not subjected to public penance. There is ample evidence for cases of this kind from the fourth century onwards. Thus canon 14 of Elvira decrees that, if fallen virgins marry the men with whom they have sinned, *eo quod solas nuptias violaverint, post annum sine paenitentia reconciliari debebunt;* failing this, they are to be reconciled only after five years, *acta legitima paenitentia.* Similarly, in connexion with other, shorter excommunications imposed by

214 Above 105, n. 179.

the Synod there is no mention of ecclesiastical penance.[215] Apart from such cases foreseen by law, bishops made use of excommunication at their discretion, so much so that Leo I felt obliged to urge that no one should be deprived of fellowship for slight offences (*Ep.* 10 *ad episc. Vienne.*). Excommunication was of its nature simply a disciplinary measure and a means of emendation, and as such was not restricted to the ecclesiastical penitential procedure. In its application in practice, however, a further and substantial development is to be noted towards the end of our period, one which is parallel to the development of public penance. For the removal of an excommunication, even when imposed for grave offences, it was no longer necessary as a general rule, as it had been formerly, to undertake ecclesiastical penance — *accipere paenitentiam* — of which there was question only at the end of life. All that was required was conversion and personal penance in the conduct of a Christian life — *agere paenitentiam*. Thus Gregory I normally abstained from the imposition of public penance, and was satisfied with sentence of excommunication or other punishments, such as suspension, incarceration or corporal chastisement.[216]

The correlative of excommunication is reconciliation, assuming that a real exclusion from the Church is involved, and not just a short-term prohibition of participating in the eucharistic liturgy and particularly in Communion. This latter is undoubtedly the sense of a number of the synodal decrees which have already been adduced.[217] All the same, canon 14 of Elvira

---

[215] Cf. can. 21 for absence on three occasions from the Sunday liturgy, can. 79 for playing dice for money (Hinschius IV 713 n. 2 also associates with this canons 40, 54, 55, 57); further, canon 11 of Arles, (314); from a later period can. 13 and 14 of Vannes (465); can. 55 of Agde (506); *Stat. eccl. ant.* can. 24 and 88. From the Eastern Church, Basil, *Ep.* 199 can. 24; *Ep.* 217 can. 55; can. 1 of Laodicea (c. 380).

[216] See Poschmann II 259 ff.; cf. above 108.

[217] Thus no doubt can. 14 of Vannes which by way of punishment for a cleric who is absent from matins without being excused by sickness decrees: *Septem diebus habeatur extraneus.* A special act of reconciliation can hardly have taken place in this case.

shows that there were cases in which reconciliation was conferred even though there had been no sentence of ecclesiastical penance. This is commonly found where bishops had imposed excommunications for serious offences at their own discretion. An effect for the next life also was undoubtedly attributed to a reconciliation of this sort, as also to the excommunication which was lifted by it. Consequently, this disciplinary procedure against a sinner can, with a certain amount of justification, be regarded as a kind of ecclesiastical penance alongside canonical penance. However, it does not by any means stand alongside of it as an independent institution with parity of right. In the first place, it is only an extraordinary form of penance, not the ordinary one; resort is had to it only occasionally, in cases involving grave scandal, and not for secret sins which do not incur ecclesiastical censure. It does not, therefore, render ecclesiastical penance superfluous. Excommunication and its removal, which was the procedure for public sinners, could certainly not have meant that in principle these enjoyed any advantage over others who did penance on their own account, either spontaneously or in response to the admonitions of priests. For an understanding of the situation it is also necessary to take account of the imprecise notion that existed of the effect of reconciliation.[218]

It was general and traditional practice to grant reconciliation without ecclesiastical penance to converted heretics, provided they were not originally Catholics who had lapsed from the Church.[219] The reason for this discrimination between those born in heresy and lapsed Catholics was twofold: first there was absence of guilt;[220] in addition the effect of baptism outside the Church was still not clearly recognized. It was a

---

[218] Cf. above 100. On Gregory I's view see Poschmann II 254 ff.

[219] The earliest evidence is the edict of Pope Stephen against Cyprian in the controversy on heretical baptism: *Ep. Cypr.* 74, 1. Similarly can. 8 of Arles (314). Augustine produced a thoroughgoing defence of the practice against the Donatists.

[220] Augustine, *Ep.* 43, 1; *De un. eccl.* 73.

firm principle, even for Cyprian's adversaries,[221] that baptism administered in heresy did not confer the Holy Ghost, *i.e.,* forgiveness of sins and grace, and this conception persisted throughout antiquity. It was taught that those who had been thus baptized only received the Holy Ghost through the imposition of hands in the *Catholica.* Consequently, this imposition of hands took the place of the laying on of hands which had been invalidly received in heresy at confirmation.[222] It was, therefore, described both as *manus impositio in paenitentiam* and also as *manus impositio ad accipiendum Spiritum.*[223] As a completion or revalidation of baptism it should be interpreted as an initiation rite rather than a penitential procedure, in spite of its outward resemblance to the latter.[224] That this reconciliation was sacramental in character, even though all performance of penance except conversion was dispensed with, requires no proof.

There were, therefore, in Christian antiquity certain other forms of ecclesiastical penance in addition to the institution of canonical penance. However, they were designed only for extraordinary cases. In a normal Christian life in the West, even in the fifth and sixth centuries, only penance in the strict sense, *paenitentia proprie dicta,* came into question. It is inappropriate and only makes for confusion of the facts, to gather these forms together under the concept of "private penance", on the ground that the characteristic feature of canonical penance, enrolment in the order of penitents, is not found in them.[225] The reason is, that by private penance we understand, in accordance with

---

[221] Cf. *Ep. Cypr.* 73, 6, 9; 74, 5; 70, 2, 3, and above.
[222] Augustine, *De bapt. c. Don.* 3, 16, 21; 5, 23, 33; *Serm.* 71, 19, 32 and above; Leo I, *Ep.* 167, 18 *ad Rust.*; 166, 2 *ad Neron.*; 158, 7 *ad episc. Aegypt.*; 1st Orange (441) can. 1; Epaon (517) can. 16.
[223] Cf. F. J. Dölger, *Das Sakrament der Firmung* (1905) 144 ff.
[224] Innocent I undoubtedly describes the nature of the rite most felicitously when he says that the converted Arians were received *sub imagine paenitentiae ac sancti Spiritus sanctificatione per manus impositionem* (*Ep.* 18, 3 *ad Alexandr. Antioch.*).
[225] Thus P. Galtier, *L'Eglise et la rémission des péchés* (1932).

linguistic usage, a secret procedure *in foro interno* which is outside the sphere of external ecclesiastical law. As against this, the reconciliation both of excommunicates and of converts was public in character, and has not the slightest connexion with present-day confessional practice.[226] Private penance in this sense is unknown right up to the end of our period. What has been produced as proof for its existence does not stand up to critical examination.

It was not sacramental confession, but confession as a therapeutic measure in the direction of souls, and already known to us from Clement and Origen, which continued in use to a certain extent. Under the influence of St. Basil monastic confession became a regular institution in the Eastern Church.[227] The born "physician of souls" or "confessor" was the προεστώς. He was ordinarily a priest, but not always. Through the influence of Cassian, who laid great emphasis on spiritual therapy and on confession to superiors,[228] the practice was transplanted to the West. In similar fashion the Rule of St. Benedict obliged monks to "reveal their evil thoughts to the spiritual father" — *spiritualis senior* — who likewise did not have to be a priest.[229] From the monasteries confession spread to pious lay circles as an ascetical practice. Augustine, for example (*De div. quaest.* 83, n. 26), Pomerius (*De vita contempl.* 2, 7, 1), but especially Gregory I, whose *Pastoral Care* is a specimen of comprehensive spiritual direction of the individual, provide proof that zealous Christians submitted even slight faults to the bishop or priest,

---

[226] The penance of the sick, which is also counted as private penance by Galtier (ibid. 381 ff.), was indeed not performed in public, but, as already shown above (100 f. and 109), it involved all the juridical obligations of canonical penance and was expressly spoken of as *paenitentia maior et insignior* (Augustine, *Ep.* 15, 1, 9).
[227] Cf. J. Hörmann, *Untersuchungen zur griechischen Laienbeicht* (1913) 171 ff.; K. Holl, *Enthusiasmus und Bußgewalt* (1898) 262 ff.
[228] Cf. e. g. *Institut.* 4, 9, I 53 ed. Petschenig.
[229] *Regula* c. 4, 7. On the question of the priestly character of the abbot, cf. J. Tixéront, *L'Université catholique* 69 (1912) 138; P. Bihlmeyer, *Regel des hl. Benedikt*, *BKV* 20 (1914) 35 n. 3.

and applied to him for counsel in regard to the appropriate remedy. In this function priests did not limit themselves to receiving the confession and giving the appropriate instruction; they also assisted the efforts of the sinner to obtain forgiveness from God by their constant prayer and personal works of penance.[230] The emphasis on persevering prayer and participation in penance is already evidence that the intercession of the priest is to be evaluated from the point of view of vicarious satisfaction, and not from that of sacramental absolution.[231] Further, the fact that the efficacy of the intercession is made dependent on the personal relationship of the priest to God[232] also tells against an *opus operatum*. Priestly intervention was only sacramental when a reconciliation of the sinner took place. Apart from the lifting of a simple excommunication unconnected with ecclesiastical penance, the only case where this occurred was in public penance and in the penance of clerics and religious which was its equivalent.[233] The priest's mediation in other respects was within the sphere of functions proper to the "physician of souls"; these were incumbent on a priest in virtue of his vocation, but they could also be exercised by laymen. Even though a higher efficacy was attributed to the prayer of a priest because of his special relationship to God no one thought that in this respect it should be put on the same level as reconciliation, which was an act indispensable for salvation.[234]

---

[230] Cf. Pomerius, ibid. 2, 1.

[231] Gregory I, *Mor.* 20, 36, 71: *suos ei oratione continua fletus iungit.* It is an *opus onerosum* (*In Ez.* I *hom.* 11, 28) and *laboriosum* (*In Ez.* II *hom.* 9, 22). Hence some priests repel sinners from among simple folk *eisque compati culpam suam fatentibus nolunt* (*In Ez.* II *hom.* 22). When the people beseech the priest *ut ipse orando deleat culpas* (*In Ez.* II *hom.* 9, 20), this no more signifies a sacramental remission than when he says, *Mor.* 13, 6: *corripiendo a culpa liberat.*

[232] *Reg. past.* 1, 10: ... *aut quomodo aliis veniam postulat, qui, utrum sibi sit placatus, ignorat?*

[233] For Gregory I see especially B. Poschmann, *ThR* (1934) 355 ff. (against E. Göller).

[234] On the whole question see Poschmann II 204—247: *Die angebliche kirchliche Privatbuße* ["The alleged ecclesiastical private penance"].

Chapter Two

PENANCE IN THE EARLY MIDDLE AGES

LITERATURE: A. Boudinhon (see above 81). E. Göller, "Das spanisch-westgotische Bußwesen" in *RQ* 37 (1929) 298—313. A. Amann, *DTC* XII 845—948. Poschmann III. A. Teetaert, *La confession aux laïques dans L'Eglise latine depuis le VIIIᵉ jusqu'au XIVᵉ siècle* (Bruges-Paris 1926). L. Gougaud, ed 2. *Christianity in Celtic Lands* (London 1932), rev. and enlarged edn. of Id., ed. 1. *Les chrétientés celtiques* (Paris 1911). H. Wasserschleben, *Die Bußordnungen der abendl. Kirche* (1851). H. J. Schmitz, *Die Bußbücher und die Bußdisziplin der Kirche,* 2 vols. (1883/98). P. Fournier, "Etudes sur les pénitentiels" in *RHLR* VI—IX (1901—1904). W. v. Hörmann, "Bußbücherstudien" in *Ztschr. d. Savigny-Stift. für Rechtsgesch. Kan. Abt.* 1/4 (1911/14). Th. P. Oakley, *English Penitential Discipline and Anglo-Saxon Law in their Joint Influence* (New York 1932). P. W. Finsterwalder, *Die Canones Theodori Cantuariensis und ihre Überlieferungsformen* (1929). J. A. Jungmann, *Die lateinischen Bußriten in ihrer geschichtlicher Entwicklung* (Innsbruck 1932). J. T. McNeill and H. M. Gamer, *Medieval Handbooks of Penance* (New York 1938). P. Galtier, "Les origines de la pénitence irlandaise" in *RechSR* 42 (1954) 58—85; 204—225. J. Ryan, *Irish Monasticism* (London 1921). O. D. Watkins, *A History of Penance* vol. II (London 1920). G. Mitchell, "The Origins of Irish Penance" in *ITQ* 22 (1955) 1—14. Id., "Columbanus on Penance" ibid., 18 (1951) 43—54. G. S. M. Walker, *Sancti Columbani Opera,* Scriptores Latini Hiberniae II (Dublin 1957). J. Laporte, "Le Pénitentiel de Saint Columban" in *Mon. Christiana Selecta* IV (Tournai 1958). *Mélanges Columbaniens,* Actes du Congrès International de Luxeuil 1950 (Paris n. d.). G. Le Bras, "Pénitentiels" in *DTC* XII (1933) 1160—1179. H. Weisweiler, "Die Auffassung von der Buße in Spanien und Gallien bis zur späten Merovingerzeit" in *Sch* 30 (1955) 229—233. Abundant material also listed in W. Bonser, *An Anglo-Saxon and Celtic Bibliography* (450—1087) (Oxford 1957).

At the close of Christian antiquity canonical penance had come to a dead end in its development. The increasing rigidity of its forms had gradually conducted it to the utopian objective of obliging all the faithful sooner or later to a kind of monastic renunciation of the world. The result of such an excessive demand was that ecclesiastical penance ceased to play any practical part in life, and was almost exclusively regarded simply as a means of preparation for death. Precisely in the years when sins importuned men most strongly there was no sacramental remedy at their disposal. No amount of pastoral care by way of preaching, personal admonition or penal measures could make up for the privation of the sacrament. In the absence of a penitential institution which was obligatory on all and repeatedly available to all, the great mass of men in that age of brutalized morals put off not only the *accipere paenitentiam,* but also the *agere paenitentiam.* The situation is illustrated by a brief remark of the monk Jonas in the *Life of Columban* (c. 11) stating that on the arrival of the great missionary in Gaul, about 590, *paenitentiae medicamenta et mortificationis amor vix vel paucis in illis reperiebatur locis (PL* 87, 1018f.).

An effective reform of ecclesiastical penance was only possible if there was a retreat from the rigid principle which forbade its repetition. This was the chief cause of the whole peculiar development. We have already heard that Chrysostom was accused by his enemies of having acted contrary to the principle.[1] It remains an open question to what extent the reproach was justified. Undoubtedly it is a possibility not to be ruled out that the great bishop set aside the law which was not founded on the doctrine of faith, and which was such a grave handicap in pastoral care, and that he granted repeated forgiveness in a

---

[1] Above 104 n. 178. According to Socrates he said: "even if you have already done penance a thousand times nevertheless come back."

private mode of procedure. However, this is the sole evidence that exists. In the continental Western Church two full centuries elapsed before this new procedure was mentioned for the first time, and, significantly, once again in the form of a sharp condemnation. The well known canon II of the Third Synod of Toledo (589) rejects as an *execrabilis praesumptio* the practice that *per quasdam Hispaniarum ecclesias non secundum canonem, sed foedissime pro suis peccatis homines agere paenitentiam, ut quotiescumque peccare libuerit, totiens a presbytero reconciliari expostulent.* The observance of the canonical form, including excommunication, the penitential dress, the status of a penitent, the penitential blessing and reconciliation, is most emphatically enjoined. It is, however, noteworthy that the "abuse" had already gained ground in all the churches of Spain. Now, at the very time that the sixty-four bishops and the seven episcopal delegates delivered their verdict on it, private penance began its triumphant migration to the European mainland. Its home were the Celtic churches in Britain and Ireland. Our first task, then, is to describe Celtic penance, and to give an account of its transplanting on to the Continent.

1. Penance in the Celtic and Anglo-Saxon Churches

Because of its isolation the Celtic Church occupied a special place apart in questions of worship and discipline, and for centuries remained fixed in its usages which differed from those of the rest of the Church.[2] Also peculiar to it was the fact that it had no knowledge of the institution of a public ecclesiastical penance which could not be repeated, and which involved canonical obligations. It had not shared in the faulty development which has been described, nor blocked the way for itself for an effective prac-

---

[2] Cf. L. Gougaud ed. 1, 175—211. Also given here are references to literature on the supposed "independence from Rome". [Fuller treatment in Gougaud ed. 2, 185—216. Tr.]

tice of penance. Penance is here private in character. Its "reception" consists in confession, in the acceptance of the satisfaction fixed by the priest, and finally in reconciliation. It has no defamatory or juridical consequences, and is available to all at any time. The sources for Celtic penitential practice date from the sixth century. In essentials they consist of the penitential books, native to the islands, which provide precisely determined penances for all offences, whether grave or slight in character (Tariff penance). Casuistical in form, they were for the use of confessors. In contrast to the canonical decisions of councils and popes their authority is purely private, and they carry weight only in virtue of the prestige of their authors, rather like the so-called "canonical letters" of the ancient Eastern Church.[3] The oldest comprehensive collection is the Irish *Penitential of Finnian* dating from the sixth century, of which the prescriptions passed in large part into the later penitential books. Among these are the *Penitential of Cummean,* and the *Penitential of Columban,* named after the famous missionary. Best known, however, is the Anglo-Saxon *Penitential of Theodore* named after the Greek Theodore († 690) who as archbishop of Canterbury exercised a strong influence on the penitential discipline, with the result that his pronouncements, mingled with decisions deriving from other sources, were propagated in a number of collections. The author of the penitential, who in the preface describes himself as the *discipulus Umbrensium,* intends to give a critical and ordered compilation of the prescriptions of Theodore. The origin of the work is not to be put before the middle of the eighth century. Essentially more imperfect are two other Anglo-Saxon penitential books which also erroneously bear the names of famous men. These are the *Penitential of Bede* († 735) and the *Penitential of Egbert,* Archbishop of York († 767); both are jumbled compilations from older collections dating from

---

[3] See above 83.

about the year 800.[4] It is significant that the Anglo-Saxon Church took over the arrangement of penance from the Celtic Church, even though the latter had for long sharply separated itself from the Germanic conquerors. The *Penitential of Theodore* is the very first to express the difference between the arrangement of penance which is observed in Rome and that "in this province". *Reconciliatio in hac provincia publice statuta non est, quia et publica paenitentia non est* (I, c. 12).

Among the penitential prescriptions fasting joined with fervent prayer occupies the most prominent place, so that in the penitential books *paenitere* simply means "to fast". It admits of different degrees, both in regard to abstinence from certain foods and drinks and also in the restriction of eating and drinking to a small amount. Thus there is fasting "on bread and water", and abstinence from flesh meat, from solid food and from wine; there are stricter fasts on certain days of the week *(feriae legitimae)* or times of the year (the three *quadragesimae*) [the forty days before Easter, and those before Christmas and after Pentecost. Cf. *Pen.* II, xiv, 1. Tr.]. For the shedding of blood and sins of unchastity abstention from marital intercourse and renunciation of weapons were normally required, and for certain specially heinous sins exile *(peregrinatio perennis)* was also imposed in addition to other penitential works. Naturally almsgiving is not forgotten. The duration of these penances is graded according to the gravity of the sins, and varies in the different books. In Theodore penances are generally greater than in the Celtic collections and in Bede and Egbert; these two are clearly seeking to mitigate the harshness of the Theodorean discipline. Starting from sentences of lifelong penance for certain specific crimes, we find others of fifteen, twelve, ten or seven years downwards to one year; and for lighter sins of forty, twenty, seven days or

---

[4] The critical work of the researchers mentioned in the bibliography — Wasserschleben, Schmitz, Fournier, v. Hörmann, Oakley, Finsterwalder — has performed a heavy and successful task in the clarification and arrangement of the chaotic material. Cf. Poschmann III 3 ff.

one day (*e.g.* for drunkenness, seven days; for immoderate eating, one day); and in the case of repeated offences each individual act is taken into account.[5]

The value of the individual penitential acts is determined by the degree of self-denial which they entail. Consequently a longer penance can be replaced by a shorter one of a more intensive character. In this case the fasting is carried to the point of complete abstinence from food, and is combined with vigils, continuous recitation of psalms in a standing posture with arms outstretched, genuflexions and other similar complications. In this way, for example, a *triduanum, i.e.* a forced fast of this kind lasting for three days, is reckoned as the *arreum anni,* that is as the equivalent of a normal penance of one year.[6] A substitution of this sort often proved necessary for the reason that, owing to the high scale of the tariff penance, the whole length of a man's life would not have sufficed for the fulfilment of a normal penitential burden. Redemptions represented a special kind of commutation. Their original purpose was to adapt penance to personal circumstances and needs. That was necessary in the first place for the sick, for whom there could no longer be any question of fasting. The most convenient substitute was almsgiving (cf. *Pen. Cummeani* VIII, 21). The redemption was taken over from Celtic tribal law, and was the equivalent of the "wergeld" [O. Ir. éric. Tr.] by payment of which every offence could be expiated. Quite early, however, it came to be employed in other cases,[7] and this obviously involved the danger of externalism and moral worthlessness.

The Synod of Cloveshoe (747) spoke out against the practice, characterising it as a "new invention" and as a "dangerous

---

[5] For examples see Poschmann III 12—18; 43 ff.
[6] Cf. the instruction printed by Wasserschleben p. 139 which gives a whole list of similar commutations.
[7] The oldest example is the decision of an Irish synod, supposedly presided over by St. Patrick, according to which a penance of seven years can be redeemed by the price of seven *ancillae.*

127

custom" (Mansi XII 403). Nevertheless it continued to develop. In the penitentials of Bede and Egbert the penances proper are already practically replaced by the redemptions which are immediately subjoined. Sufficient justification is now seen in the fact that the proper penance *ardua et difficilis est* (*Pen. Bedae* c. XI). The most dubious case was when a person paid money for others to take his place in the performance of penance. The principle of penance by proxy could have a certain justification when a person was hindered from performing it (cf. *Pen. Bedae* c. X, 8). In practice, however, its outcome is shown by the direction in the [spurious-Tr.] penitential canons of King Edgar dating from the second half of the tenth century, which indicates how a magnate could finish his seven-year penance in three days by means of an equivalent number of fasts by hired men (Mansi XVIII 525).

In evaluating the penitential books and their strange, even revolting, prescriptions, account has to be taken of the historical situation in which they had their origins. It was a matter of waging war on the savagery and vice of still half pagan children of nature, on bloodshed, drunkenness and all kinds of natural and unnatural forms of unchastity. The robust discipline, and what may be called its homely directness, with its drastic remedies and strenuous exercises was admirably adapted to the violence of instinct. The size and strict standardization of the punishments become intelligible to us when we remember that the penitential laws also represented secular penal law. The penitential books sought to meet the danger of penance becoming a mechanical business by laying the greatest emphasis on the truth that the performance of penance is only efficacious where there is sincere contrition and conversion. Constant prayer, in conjunction with tears and sighs, is for them indispensable, in the same way as in ancient Christian penitential practice. An unprejudiced judge must at any rate recognize the deep moral earnestness and the stern and unrelenting notion of atonement on which the system was based. In this respect the disappearance of publicity in the procedure

128

had brought no change in its spirit of severity. The practice of redemptions was a concession to human weakness, and we may find its numbering and balancing of good works little to our taste; but underlying it there was a firm belief in the reality of the concepts of guilt and atonement. Precisely because for the men of that age these realities were indistinguishable from the concrete things of life they "reckoned" also with these, and this they did in the rough and ready way appropriate to their stage of cultural development. Contemporary critics should hesitate to bring forward the charge of laxity, all the more so when it is considered that what was demanded for a redemption goes far beyond what could be expected of modern man in the way of expiation.

Although in ancient Celtic penance great emphasis was laid on penitential works, yet the ecclesiastical and sacramental aspect of penance stands forth clearly. It is only efficacious through the ministry of the priest; as judge he has to adapt the punishment to the gravity of the guilt and to individual circumstances in the light of the penitential book. The phrase *iudice sacerdote* constantly recurs in the canons (*Finnian* 9, 23; *Cummean* III 3, 12; IV 4; V 2; VIII 2, 3, 20). In contrast to ancient ecclesiastical practice, priests appear from the outset as the ordinary ministers of the sacrament of penance alongside of the bishop (*Theodore* II 2, 15), and only in exceptional cases is a particularly grave sin reserved to the bishop (*Cummean* X 18; *Columban* B 25). The judical function of the priest presupposes confession, which makes known to him the state of soul of the sinner. In this system with its personal mode of procedure and its provision of a special punishment for every individual offence, confession is naturally more strongly emphasized as compared with the old canonical penance; although, precisely because it is so obvious a matter it is seldom mentioned in the penitential books. A novelty appears in that now even slighter sins in the greatest variety are submitted to confession. Here we have a link between this sacramental ecclesiastical penance which allows of repetition

129

and the frequent confession which was practised in monasteries and pious lay circles with a view to spiritual therapy. As the care of souls among the Celts was largely in the hands of monks,[8] the extension of monastic practice to the laity occurred quite naturally. Here and there the ancient penitentials reveal the connexion with monastic discipline quite clearly.[9]

But it is wrong to exaggerate this connexion and to regard monastic confession as the primary source of the entire later institution of penance.[10] Confession of grave sins was also of strict obligation in the ancient Church, and in regard to the other essential parts of the sacrament — contrition, satisfaction and reconciliation — Celtic penitential practice is also in complete harmony with that of the ancient Church. Further, exclusion from the eucharist until reconciliation is likewise required, as also are special penitential obligations, such as abstention from marital intercourse and renunciation of military service. In view of all this, the differences which we have described, however important in themselves, are only of an accidental character, and do not abolish the historic connexion of the new system with the old one. According to the *Penitential of Theodore* it is the same penance *in hac provincia,* except that it is differently organized than *apud Romanos.*[11] The clear attestation of the act of reconciliation is of special significance; this had its place only in canonical penance, and not in "monastic confession". In canons of all kinds, after the determination of the penance, the note is found, *et reconcilietur altario* or *recipiatur ad communionem* (*Finnian* 6, 14, 35, 36; *Columban* B 3, 13, 15, 18, 25). Canon 14 of the first synod under St. Patrick has the formula *et postea resolvetur a sacerdote,* an undeniable reference to the power of the keys. Strictly speaking, after the disappearance of the excommunication which

---

[8] See Gougaud ed. 1. 82 ff.
[9] See Poschmann III 27 f.
[10] Thus especially since E. Loening, *Geschichte des deutschen Kirchenrechts* (1878) 468 ff.
[11] Cf. E. Amann 857 ff.

was linked with public penance, the concept of "reconciliation" is no longer quite appropriate. However, as the exclusion of a penitent from the eucharist was still kept up, the phrase *reconcilietur altario* could still be used in reference to the renewed concession of Communion. The very fact of the application of a concept which is no longer quite appropriate to a differently organized penitential institution is a clear proof of its connexion with canonical penance.

2. The Transplanting of the Celtic Penitential System on the Continent

Among the primitive people of the British Isles Christianity attained to an unexpectedly early flowering. Notwithstanding their wild and passionate character they were fundamentally unspoiled, and unlike the Germanic tribes on the Continent they were not exposed to the corrupting influence of a decadent ancient society. They were, therefore, in a position to employ some of their surplus energy in the service of other churches. It is impossible to overestimate the historic importance of the Irish and the Anglo-Saxons as new fertilizing agents on the widest scale of the religious and intellectual life of the West; thereby they made a decisive contribution to the establishment of medieval civilization.[12] Great numbers of monks followed in the wake of Columban († 615), that ardent, eccentric and strongwilled pioneer of the missionary activity,[13] and they became the apostles and teachers of the Continent which was then showing signs of the most serious religious decay. Naturally the immediate aim of their work of reformation was the awakening of the spirit of penance and, as was only to be

---

[12] Cf. A. Hauck, *Kirchengeschichte Deutschlands* I 3./5. Aufl. (1904) 243 ff. 400 ff G. Schnürer, *Kirche u. Kultur im Mittelalter* I (1924); but especially L. Gougaud *Gaelic Pioneers of Christianity. The Work and Influence of Irish Monks and Saints in Continental Europe* (Dublin 1923).
[13] Cf. Th. Concannon, *The Life of St. Columban* (Dublin 1915). J. J. Laux, *Der hl. Kolumban* (1919).

expected, in this activity they retained the organization of penance which was native to them. Proof of this is seen in the *Penitential of Columban* which was entirely composed on Frankish soil, and which at least in regard to its nucleus is correctly named.[14] Its whole content places it in the Celtic system of penance and we have, therefore, put it without hesitation in that category. Boudinhon says with justice: "The route taken by the tariff penance in Gaul and Germany is easy to follow: it is none other than that of the missionary monks."[15]

Generally speaking, the introduction of the new penitential procedure passed off without friction and without opposition, in sharp contrast to the severe condemnation which the same innovation had encountered in the Third Synod of Toledo. There is nowhere mention of an alteration introduced by the Celtic missionaries. There is no reference at all to the *Penitential of Columban* even though many Gallic synods dealt with questions concerning penance. The interest of contemporaries was centred on the energy and emphasis with which the northern monks insisted on penance as the most elementary requirement of the Gospel, and not on the ecclesiastical form of penance.[16] The first ecclesiastical document to adopt an attitude to the new procedure is canon 8 of the Synod of Chalon about the year 650: *De paenitentia vero, quae est medela animae, utilem hominibus esse censemus; et ut paenitentibus a sacerdotibus data confessione indicatur paenitentia, universitas sacerdotum noscitur consentire.* The declaration, as Loening[17] and Hinschius[18] have perceived, can only refer to a new institution. The obvious truth of the usefulness of penance does not need a synodal decree, but the new form of penance

---

[14] Thus against J. Schmitz, who questions Columban's authorship, Hauck, Seebass, Fournier. See Poschmann III 5 65.

[15] Op. cit. 502.

[16] It is therefore inadmissible because of this silence to reject with J. Schmitz (II 146f.) as "in the highest degree improbable" Celtic influence on Western penance.

[17] II 776 n. 2.

[18] *System des kath. Kirchenrechts* IV (1888) 826 n. 2.

with its special characteristics does. The sense is that the faithful confess repeatedly to the priest, are instructed by him, and receive from him appropriate penances for individual sins; whereas formerly, apart from the penance received once only at the end of life, they were left to themselves to do personal works of penance.[19] Yet the fact that the question was a subject of deliberation shows that even at Chalon certain scruples had been felt against the new practice. However, the synod adopted the opposite attitude to that of the fathers of Toledo half a century earlier and unanimously approved the new procedure. It is worth noting that amongst those who took part in the synod were men who were products of Columban's famous monastery at Luxeuil, such as St. Giles of Noyon, Donatus of Besançon and Chagnoald of Laon. In them the method of penance sanctioned by their master had its most effective advocates.

The best proof for the adoption of the tariff penance is provided by the Frankish penitential books which were already numerous in the second half of the eighth century. Thanks to the thorough research work which has been done, we now have a fairly clear view of their origin and interdependence. They derive from three sources: 1. Canonical material, chiefly taken from the collection of Dionysius which was received in Gaul, and from the ordinances of Gallo-Merovingian synods — *iudicia canonica*; 2. Celtic statutes — *iudicia Cummeani*; 3. Anglo-Saxon statutes — *iudicia Theodori*.[20] As was to be expected, there has

---

[19] Galtier overlooks this *indicare paenitentiam* when in the course of a long exposition he tries hard to prove the continuity of the practice of the northern missionaries with the penitential form of the *conversio* which was in use in Gaul (*RHE* 33 [1937] 291—301). As evidence for the necessity of confession at the admittance to penance he attaches extraordinary importance to a text from the *Vita Eligii* (I 7 p. 673 Krusch): *omnia adulescentiae suae coram sacerdote confessus est acta ; sicque sibi imponens paenitentiam coepit fortiter conluctationes carnis spiritus fervore resistere.* But he overlooks the word *sibi,* which is of decisive importance for the question: ecclesiastical or personal penance? (ibid. 296).

[20] The thesis, defended with great emphasis by J. Schmitz, that the canonical

been a fusion of the penitential statutes used in Gaul with those brought with them by the missionaries. In connexion with this Fournier has established a very significant fact. This is the inclusion of a considerable number of texts from the *Penitential of Columban* among the *iudicia canonica*. This means that the decisions of the celebrated abbot of Luxeuil were from the first put on a level with the canonical norms.[21] This is further confirmation that his practice was by no means regarded as something new in principle, but simply as the continuation and further development of the ancient procedure. The borrowings from Celtic and Anglo-Saxon penitentials are primarily to be attributed to the practice of the missionaries, who continued to make use of their native form of penance. These penitentials must have been welcome to the Frankish priests as a supplement to their scanty canonical decisions. Above all, however, they commended themselves by their greater mildness as compared with the canonical decrees. This appears not only in regard to the amount of penance, but still more in reference to the redemptions, particularly as set forth in the penitentials of Bede and Egbert which from the turn of the eighth century had a wide circulation in the Frankish kingdom.[22]

Naturally the penitentials were very convenient in practice, but their indiscriminate use necessarily led to confusion in the administration of penance and to a serious relaxation of ecclesiastical discipline. A reaction against this made itself felt in the so-called Carolingian reform. The reforming synods of Tours, Chalon and Rheims which were held in the year 813 expressly decreed that the penitential books should be repudiated, and

series must be referred back to a *Paenitentiale Romanum* as its source, with the result that the procedure underlying the penitential books is not of Celtic origin but common to the Roman Church, at once encountered strong opposition, and must, especially after Fournier's studies, be regarded as finally disposed of.

[21] Fournier, op. cit. VIII 534 ff.

[22] For examples and literature see Poschmann III 76—83.

that a return should be made to the ancient canonical procedure.[23] With a view to implementing the decrees a series of new penitential ordinances was drawn up which substantially were restricted to a systematic compilation of the *sententiae patrum*, and of canons and decretals.[24] Circumstances were, however, stronger than the will to reform. The penitential books proved indispensable to the average clergy. Consequently the Synod of Tours (Canon 22) in its verdict allowed from the outset the retention of a single authorized book chosen from them all, and Halitgar appended a proper penitential as the sixth book to his collection of canons, giving as a reason: *simplicioribus qui maiora non valent capere, poterit prodesse*.[25] However, the ancient penitential books also continued in existence and were augmented by new ones. As late as the opening of the eleventh century the *Decretum Burchardi* provides in the *Corrector* a new and very extensive penitential containing extracts from earlier books.[26] It was not until the great reform of Gregory VII that the penitential books were effectively withdrawn from circulation.

Public penance, of which the voluntary reception was already in the sixth century a rare event,[27] had practically disappeared by about the year 800, to judge from the complaints of the reforming synods.[28] These insist on its reintroduction, with the

---

[23] Can. 38 of Chalon: ... *repudiatis ac penitus eliminatis libellis, quos paenitentiales vocant, quorum sunt certi errores, incerti auctores.* The synod of Paris, 829, ordered in can. 32 the burning of the books.

[24] To these belong the *Collectio Dacheriana,* the *Collectio Vaticana,* the *Collection of Halitgar of Cambrai,* the *Liber paenitentium* of Rabanus Maurus and his *Epistola ad Heribaldum,* the *Capitulare secundum Theodulfi Aureliensis,* the *Capitula Rodulfi Bituricensis.* See Wasserschleben 79 f.

[25] Schmitz II 266. Halitgar's statement that this sixth book was taken *de scrinio Romanae ecclesiae,* on which Schmitz built his theory of an original *Paenitentiale Romanum* belongs to the age of the falsifications of the pseudo-Isidore. See Fournier VIII 533 ff.

[26] Schmitz I 762 ff.

[27] Above p. 107f.

[28] Can. 25 of Chalon: *Paenitentiam agere iuxta antiquam canonum institutionem in plerisque locis ab usu recessit.* According to Jonas of Orleans († 843) they are *perrari*

sanctions of the civil power when occasion demands (e.g. in regard to *incestuosi et parricidae*).[29] Here public penance is from the first restricted to public sinners. The reformers are no longer aware that in the past it was required for all mortal sins, and do not even suspect that private penance even for secret sins was first introduced through the despised penitential books in contravention of the ancient canonical ordinance. In reality the axiom which they proclaimed: public penance for public sins, private penance for secret sins, is an important innovation in the development of the administration of penance.[30] Henceforth public and private penance go forward together with equality of right. In principle they are equivalent, both in their effect and in their demands. For this reason the leaders of the reform require that in private penance the same punishments shall apply as in public penance.[31] Admittedly care had to be taken here to preserve secrecy, although on this point there was no scrupulosity. In any case the redemptions provided a convenient means of sparing a secret sinner embarrassing penitential exercises.[32]

In public penance the form of administration was the old canonical rite, but now further developed. The imposition of hands at the commencement of penance was linked with the distribution of ashes, and followed by the expulsion of the penitents from the church.[33] Specially noteworthy is the prescription which already occurs in the *Gelasian Sacramentary* (at the beginning of the eighth century) and in a great variety of

hodie in ecclesia who submit to canonical penance (*De institutione laicali* 1, 10 [*PL* 106, 138]).

[29] Can. 25 of Chalon, can. 3 of Tours.

[30] On the difficulty of fitting secret penance into the framework of ancient Christian penitential law, which was of a different kind, and the impossible attempts to defend it by patristic evidence, see Poschmann III 98 ff.

[31] Theodulf of Orleans, *Capitul.* II (*PL* 105, 212); can. 10 of Mainz (851).

[32] On the preservation of secrecy in regard to sins confessed and the development of the seal of confession, see B. Kurtscheid, *Das Beichtsiegel in seiner geschichtlichen Entwicklung* (1912) 38 ff.

[33] Cf. Regino of Prüm († 915), *De synod. causis* I 295; Wasserschleben 136 f.

later *ordines* that the penitent is to be kept in confinement from the beginning of his penance on Ash Wednesday until Maundy Thursday, the ancient date for reconciliation.[34] The detailed observance of the regulation will have varied according to local circumstances. The essential point was the detection and punishment of the criminals, and the control of their penance in custody, whether in the bishop's residence or in their own dwelling-place. Only criminal cases such as murder, incest, adultery and perjury were involved.[35] The Carolingian reform took stringent measures to enforce the law in this respect. On Maundy Thursday the penitents were again brought before the bishop by their "deans", and he then decided whether they should be admitted to reconciliation or continue to do penance during Lent of the next year. The reason for this was that often, in fact in the majority of cases, in view of the gravity of the crimes penance during one Lent was insufficient.[36] In the *Gelasian Sacramentary* a more elaborate arrangement of the rite of reconciliation is already visible. The penitent lies prostrate on the ground in the presence of the congregation, the deacon presents him to the bishop and begs for his readmission, whereupon the bishop pronounces over him the prayers of reconciliation. From the ninth century a further development appears, corresponding to the rite of expulsion on Ash Wednesday; this is the solemn readmission of the penitents into the church, a ceremony which gives vivid and moving expression

---

[34] The prescription of incarceration was an amalgamation of religion and penal law, illustrating the state of affairs at one stroke; and it is the most effective confirmation of our conclusion that at the close of antiquity public penance was normally only in use as a compulsory penance, and that recourse was had to it only rarely. In principle the measure was not new. Outside public penance not only clergy (see above) but also laymen were frequently consigned to a monastery to do penance. Examples in Poschmann III 118ff.

[35] *Capitulare* of Aachen 801/13 c. 1; Hincmar of Rheims, *Capitula synodica* III (856) c. 1.

[36] Cf. Regino, *De eccl. discipl.* 1, 142: On Ash Wednesday all have to be present *qui publicam suscipiunt aut "susceperint" paenitentiam.*

both to the original meaning of reconciliation and to its immediate effect.[37]

The earliest information on the arrangement of private penance is found in the penitential books of the eighth century which were composed in Frankish lands. Appended to these was an instruction for the reception of confessions. About the turn of the ninth century there were already formal *ordines* for confession with directions for the conduct of the penitent and the confessor, along with rubrics and formulae, after the manner of other church functions which were regulated by their corresponding *ordines*.[38] We will examine these more closely in the next section.

VI. CONFESSION

IT HAS already been remarked that in the private administration of penance confession came into greater prominence. When public humiliation ceased to be practised it is seen as the concrete expression of the sinner's penance in the sight of the Church. Here we have the explanation of a change in linguistic usage which is discernible from the eighth century. From that time onward *confessio* was used to designate not only acknowledgement of sin to a priest, but also with increasing frequency ecclesiastical penance as a whole.[39] A repeated reception of penance was a basic innovation, and gives rise to our first question which is concerned with the obligation of confession.

In principle the ancient Christian requirement that ecclesiastical penance should be undertaken for the forgiveness of mortal sins

[37] It is first attested in the *Pontifical of Poitiers* (end of the 9th century) and elaborated in the *Ordo Romanus Antiquus* (10th cent.). Further details in Jungmann 44—109.

[38] Cf. Jungmann 144f.; 170ff.; Poschmann III 102ff.

[39] Instances in Boniface, Pirmin, Chrodegang, Theodulf, Alcuin. See Poschmann III 168f.

remained in force, the only difference being that now it was to be done not only once in a lifetime, but as often as anyone had committed a serious offence.[40] The best proof for the practice of frequent confession is the fact that in the eighth century there is already mention of persons of rank having their own confessors.[41] In practice confession of grave sins before the reception of Communion was required as a matter of course. Admittedly, insistent admonitions and complaints seem to show that many received Communion without going to confession, even though they were in serious sin.[42] In any case it was still left to the conscience of the individual to judge beforehand whether his moral condition at the time was such as to require confession as a preparation for Communion. Soon, however, pastoral considerations led to confession being made obligatory on all at fixed times, quite apart from the gravity of their sins. The earliest example is provided about the year 760 by Chrodegang of Metz. He required his canons and also the *matricularii, i.e.,* the poor who were supported by the Church, to confess twice a year, at the beginning of Lent and in the autumn (*Regula can.* 14 and 34). About 800 Theodulf of Orleans testifies that in Gaul confession at the beginning of Lent is general practice.[43] Often more was demanded, with three confessions a year as a minimum requirement; thus the interpolated recension of the *Rule of Chrodegang,* dating from about 900, which even says that the monks should confess every Saturday.[44] In the formulary for episcopal visitations Regino provides for the case where certain Christians either do not confess at all or only once a year.[45]

---

[40] Cf. Boniface, *Serm.* 3, 4; *Serm.* 8; Bede, *In Ep. Jac.* 5 et al.

[41] Examples in E. Vacandard, *DTC* III 864.

[42] Cf. Pirmin, *Scarapsus, PL* 89, 1043; Boniface, *Serm.* 11. Further instances in P. Browe, *ZkTh* (1932) 382 ff.

[43] *Capitul.* I c. 36; similarly the *Penitential of Egbert* (Wasserschleben 34) and the instruction *Praemonere debet,* which occurs in various penitential *ordines* from the end of the ninth century.

[44] C. 32 Mansi XIV 337.

[45] Qu. 56 & 65 *PL* 132, 285.

Undoubtedly the law of three confessions a year was difficult to enforce. Alan of Lille († c. 1202) complains: *sed hodie invaluit, ut vix laicus vel clericus semel confiteatur in anno.*[46] Shortly after his death the Fourth Lateran Council made confession *saltem in anno* a general law of the Church.

The obligation of periodical confession was something new. Formerly there was no law requiring confession of every Christian. However, the necessity of getting rid of grave sins by ecclesiastical penance before Communion, and on the other hand, the general consciousness of sin, naturally led to periodical confession once the law of only one penance was given up. This explains why so difficult an ordinance, which intimately affected every individual, encountered no opposition worthy of mention. However the literature of the period contains a few indications which show that the introduction of the practice did not pass off altogether without friction. Thus Alcuin writing of a habit which had established itself in West Gothic Gaul says: *neminem ex laicis suam velle confessionem sacerdotibus dare (Ep.* 112); Jonas of Orleans testily rejects the "inquisitive question", where is the authority in the New Testament for confession to a priest; the reforming synod of Chalon, 813, (can. 33) observes: *Quidam Deo solummodo confiteri debere dicunt peccata, quidam vero sacerdotibus confitenda esse percensent, quod utrumque non sine magno fructu intra sanctam fit ecclesiam.*[47] The theoretical question indeed continued to be discussed in the twelfth century, although by that time the law of confession was to all intents and purposes universally enforced.[48]

In spite of all the emphasis which was laid on it, confession

---

[46] *De arte praedicatoria, PL* 200, 171.

[47] The formulation recalls can. 8 of Chalon of about 650 (above 132). Further details in Poschmann III 181 ff.

[48] Gratian in particular gives a list of reasons for and against — among the latter is can. 33 of Chalon, 813 — and leaves the decision to the judgement of the reader. *Decr.* c. 87—89 C 33 *de paen.* d. 1. Similarly Hugh of St. Victor deals with the objection, on what authority and what text of Scripture the requirement of confession is based. *De sacr.* 1, 2, p. 14, 1.

was by no means considered as the most important factor in the performance of penance. As in the past, satisfaction was still the real efficient cause of the forgiveness of sins. Confession was primarily a means, the purpose of which was to enable the priest to determine the penance appropriate to the quantity of the sins. The *Regula coenobialis* of Columban (c. 10) exactly delineates the scope of confession with the words: *interrogare debitum paenitentiae,* and similar expressions continue to recur occasionally in the later period, and for that very reason are more significant.[49] However, in face of the gradual decline in the severity of penance, confession itself began to be considered in its aspect of a penitential work and its expiatory value to be stressed. This is found in the humiliation and self-conquest that it involves. It is a thought already familiar to ancient Christianity,[50] and one which naturally had greater actuality after the introduction of compulsory confession. A Bavarian synod of the middle of the eighth century lays down the proposition, later incorporated in the popular catechism: *melius est hic in praesenti erubescere in conspectu unius hominis quam in futuro iudicio coram cunctis gentibus.*[51] The pseudo-Augustinian tract *De vera et falsa paenitentia* goes further. Dating from about the middle of the eleventh century, this work was assured of unquestioned credit during the scholastic period by reason of the authority of the great doctor of the Church to whom it was universally attributed up to the fifteenth century.[52] It affirms that the forgiveness of sins is a direct fruit of confession: *erubescentia enim ipsa partem habet remissionis... fit enim per confessionem veniale, quod criminale erat in operatione.... Qui erubescit pro Christo, fit dignus misericordia.* For this reason a man obtains

[49] Can. 8 of Chalon, 650; Bede, *Expos. sup. Ep. Jac.* 5; Concil. Germanicum 742 can. 2; Pirmin, op. cit.; Theodulf, *Capitul.* I c. 30.
[50] Tertullian, *De paen.* 9 & 10; Augustine, *In Jo. tr.* 1, 6; 12, 13; *Serm.* 67, 1, 2; Cassian, *Coll.* 2, 11.
[51] C. 2 Mansi XIII 1026. Similarly Alcuin, *Ep.* 225; *De conf. pecc. ad pueros* (*PL* 101, 651, 655f.); Rabanus Maurus, *hom.* 55 (*PL* 110, 102f.).
[52] On the tract see K. Müller, *Der Umschwung in der Lehre von der Buße während des 12. Jahrh.,* in Festschr. F. Weizsäcker (1892) 292ff.

141

the grace of forgiveness more easily if he confesses the shame of his sin to several persons. In such a case the priest's action is more effective and he can be more merciful. Indeed, so great is the power of confession, *ut, si deest sacerdos, confiteatur proximo.* Even though the layman does not possess the power of absolving like the priest, yet one who confesses to him becomes worthy of forgiveness *ex desiderio sacerdotis.* The mercy of God always knows how to spare the just, *etsi non tam cito, sicut si solveretur a sacerdote.*[53] Thus confession is no longer just one of the means in penance alongside of others, but, as this evaluation of confession to laymen shows, the most important of these means, and one which in case of necessity is an adequate substitute for priestly absolution.[54]

Confession to laymen, which, as we are aware, was a traditional practice in spiritual therapy, now came to have greater general importance. After the introduction of the obligation of periodical confession to a priest, an obligation which applied to mortal sins, confession to laymen was assigned as the ordinary means for the remission of venial sins. Here Bede was particularly influential, as he justified the practice from Jas 5:16. In his *Exposito sup. Ep. Jac.* he says: *In hac sententia illa debet esse discretio, ut quotidiana leviaque peccata alterutrum coaequalibus confiteamur eorumque quotidiana credamus oratione salvari. Porro gravioris leprae immunditiam iuxta legem sacerdoti pandamus atque ad e us arbitrium, qualiter et quanto tempore iusserit, purificare curemus.* This sentence was constantly cited by theologians in later centuries.[55] In practice, however, it seems clear that the custom of mutual confession gained only slight acceptance.[56] On the other hand, the ancient principle that ecclesiastical penance is indispensable for grave sins was universally recognized.

[53] C 10, *PL* 40, 1122f.
[54] Further details in A. Teetaert 44ff.
[55] Instances in Teetaert 33ff.
[56] Jonas of Orleans, *De instit. laic.* 1, 16; *perrari sunt qui invicem confessionem faciunt, exceptis monachis qui id cotidie faciunt.*

The rite employed for confession to a priest corresponded liturgically to the one for the reception of penance in the canonical procedure, except that the acts which symbolized excommunication were dropped. The imposition of the penance took place at the confession, and was followed by the penitential blessing along with prayers, the same as, or similar to, those used in public penance. At this point the confessional procedure was terminated.[57]

Reconciliation was an independent act, and for the time being still separated from confession as it had been in the past. The Celtic order of penance required in principle that the sinner should only be admitted to the altar after the fulfilment of the penance laid on him.[58] In practice, it is true, the treatment was milder; there was a deliberate departure from the strictness of the rule, and reconciliation was granted after a part of the period of penance had elapsed.[59] In the Frankish Church likewise this procedure was adopted.[60] Reconciliation was to be granted immediately after confession only in extreme danger of death; otherwise, even in the penance of the sick, a longer or shorter interval was observed depending on the condition of the sick person.[61] The oldest *ordines* for confession (dating from the end of the eighth, and from the ninth century) as a rule give no direction whatsoever for reconciliation. It appears that it was only taken in hand for *causae criminales,* and these called for a procedure of excommunication which was decided on by the confessor and terminated by reconciliation.[62] If no *crimina* were

---

[57] There is a detailed exposition of the development of the rite in Jungmann 143—201.

[58] Thus the last canon in the *Penitential of Finnian.* Wasserschleben 119.

[59] *Praefatio Gildae* (6th cent.) and *Paenitentiale Theodori* I 12, 4. Wasserschleben 105 and 196.

[60] While Benedict the Levite (1. c. 116) requires that the penance be completed, Theodulf (*Capitul.* II, *PL* 105, 215) allows Communion after one year of a seven-year penance.

[61] Cf. *Decret. Burchardi* 18 (*PL* 140, 935 f.).

[62] *Paenitent. Floriacense* (end of the eighth century), *Pontifical of Poitiers* (9th cent.), of *Jumièges* (first half of tenth cent.). Jungmann 267.

confessed the proceedings came to an end with the imposition of a penance. This was not "proper penance" in the ancient Christian sense; it was rather in line with the ancient monastic confession or the confession to laymen mentioned above.[63] As, however, the majority of penitents had in any case to accuse themselves of serious sins, the practice of confession not followed by reconciliation could not last long. The instruction *Praemonere debet,* which is included in many penitential *ordines* from the end of the ninth century, lays on all who confess at the beginning of Lent the strict obligation of appearing for reconciliation on Maundy Thursday.[64] This means that they were included in the Maundy Thursday reconciliation of the public penitents.[65] Yet the instruction itself provides for a private reconciliation in immediate conjunction with the confession as an exceptional case, when the penitent is prevented from appearing at the Maundy Thursday reconciliation, or when through his mental obtuseness the obligation cannot be made clear to him.[66]

The difficulty here indicated of summoning people a second time, and the danger thus involved that many would forego reconciliation, naturally led to confession and reconciliation being brought together as one whole. Canon 31 of the so-called *Statuta Bonifatii* shows this, when, alluding to the impossibility of putting the canonical rule into practice, it orders: *Curet unusquisque sacerdos statim post acceptam confessionem paenitentium singulos data occasione reconciliari.*[67]

---

[63] It cannot be accepted however that even after a confession of secret grave sins a reconciliation did not take place (Jungmann 269). Against this there is the Celtic practice (above 130) and the fact that in Benedict the Levite 1, 116 and in the *Capitula* of Herrard of Tours (858) c. 59 (Hardouin V 454) provision is made for a private reconciliation.

[64] For the text see Jungmann 178.

[65] See Jungmann 271.

[66] Similarly the *Excarpsus Egberti : Si vero simplicem vel brutum eum intellexeris, statim reconcilia eum* (Jungmann 272).

[67] Mansi XII 386. Jungmann (273 n. 137) precisely because of this development

If the new practice is here still regarded as a makeshift, a hundred years later the *Decretum Burchardi* takes it completely for granted, and the contemporary confessional *ordo* of Arezzo provides a direction in the ritual that the priest, after hearing the confession and imposing the penance, *per stolam, qua indutus est, in dextera manu paenitenti faciat remissionem.*[68] From this time onwards — round about the year 1000 — the contraction of the penitential procedure into one act can be said to be general practice. This marks one of the most important stages in the history of penance. At first account was still taken of the ancient conception, inasmuch as the binding effected through the imposition of the new penance was only formally lifted through the absolution at the next confession. However, to meet the eventuality of the penitent dying beforehand, a provisional absolution was also imparted to him from the penitential obligation that had not yet been fulfilled.[69]

VII. The Ecclesiastical Power of the Keys

In the procedure of private penance, where excommunication did not come into question, reconciliation no longer took effect in its original sense; yet men continued to see in it as in the past the decisive sacramental factor in penance. Works of penance and confession were held in high regard, but it was a firm principle that grave sins could only be forgiven through the keys of the Church — *claves ecclesiae* — which had been

---

in the history of penance would like to put the definitive redaction of the *Statuta* at the earliest towards the end of the 9th century. The canon is also found in the collection of Benedict the Levite (2, 206).

[68] Jungmann 193 & n. 104.

[69] Thus the penitential *ordines* of Arezzo, of *Cod. Paris.* 3880, of the *Paenitent. Vallicellanum* II (Jungmann 194 220 199). Cf. B. Poschmann, *Der Ablaß im Licht der Bußgeschichte* (1948) 24.

handed down from Peter and the Apostles to the bishops and priests.[70] As in the ancient Church the official minister of penance was the bishop, and an ordinary priest officiated only with his permission. This applies not only to public, but also to private penance. The *Capitula Herardi* c. 59 (Hardouin V 454) expressly require: *ut presbyteri de occultis iussione episcopi paenitentes reconcilient*. In practice, however, the administration of private penance was entrusted to priests. Herard's prescription does, however, show that the distinction between the power of order and that of jurisdiction was already applied in principle even though it was not yet formally taught. The synods of Piacenza and Clermont under Urban II in the year 1095 (Mansi XX 803) expressly decreed that: *nullus presbyter sine licentia episcopi aliquos ad paenitentiam recipiat*. The first example of a sin reserved to the bishop (sodomy) occurs in Canon 20 of the Synod of London, 1102; of one reserved to the pope (assault of a cleric or a monk) in canon 10 of the Synod of Clermont, 1130, reiterated in canon 15 of the Second Lateran Council, 1139.[71]

The keys of the Church — *claves ecclesiae* — signify in substance judicial power, which includes the two functions of binding and loosing. According to the conception of the ancient Church binding consisted primarily in excommunication, but also included the positive obligation of doing penance. Later, with the disappearance of excommunication in private penance, binding through the imposition of penance came into the foreground.

---

[70] Thus Bede, *hom.* 2, 16 and, citing him, Rabanus Maurus, Christian Druthmar, Walfrid Strabo, besides Halitgar, Haymo of Halberstadt, Benedict the Levite, Rather of Verona and others. Instances are given in Poschmann III 1944ff. H. Ch. Lea arbitrarily asserts that the doctrine of the effectiveness of the power of the keys for the hereafter derives in essentials from pseudo-Isidore: *A History of Auricular Confession* I 127.

[71] According to some medieval documents deacons were also called on to take part in the administration of penance in cases of necessity. The dogmatic difficulty that is involved in this is resolved, as Jungmann shows, 157f., by the fact that the right of reconciliation was not ascribed to deacons, but only that of receiving confessions and of admitting to Communion if no *causae criminales* are involved. In accordance with this my judgement in III 104 n. 1 and 201f. is to be corrected.

Indeed, the emphasis laid on it was incomparably greater than today, when the power of the keys is thought of as hardly anything except loosing. The predominantly judicial character of the act finds expression in the phrase *iudice sacerdote* which constantly recurs in the ancient Celtic penitential books, and in the designation of the prescribed penances as *iudicia paenitentiae*. In reference to the unrepentant, binding — *ligare* — acquires the sense of condemning — *damnare*. Loosing, on the other hand, means both liberation from an excommunication (in public penance) and from the obligation of doing penance. This is effective for the after-life when, and to the extent that, the sinner has discharged the obligation laid on him. The priest absolves — *absolvit* — the sincere penitent from the fear of perpetual death — *a timore perpetuae mortis*.[72] Thus the power of the keys is still equated with the power of forgiving sins in an altogether Augustinian sense: *In ecclesia, quae habet clavem regni caelorum, fit remissio peccatorum*.[73] Ecclesiastical forgiveness is the "absolution" from sin — an expression which gained ever-growing currency after the introduction of private penance and the consequent obscuring of the concept of reconciliation which this entailed.[74]

A basic difficulty bequeathed by antiquity was how scope still remained for a real act of absolution if the forgiveness of sins is primarily the effect of personal works of penance. Understandably, the theologians of the early middle ages whose activity was purely receptive did not solve it. Confronted with the ever-threatening danger of an outward show of penance they often laid such one-sided emphasis on the efficacy of personal penance that in the last analysis absolution appears devoid of content. A source of particular confusion in this respect was a

---

[72] Bede, *hom.* 2, 16.
[73] *Paenitent. Halitgar.*, Schmitz II 266. Cf. Benedict the Levite 1, 16; Isaac of Langres 1, 11; Alcuin, *Ep.* 112 and others.
[74] On the linguistic use of the composite word *absolvere* cf. Jungmann 203; B. Poschmann, *Der Ablaß* 15.

text, constantly cited, from Jerome's commentary on Matthew (16:19) dealing with the healing of the lepers: *non quo sacerdotes leprosos faciant et immundos, sed quo habeant notitiam leprosi et non leprosi et possint discernere, qui mundus quive immundus sit.* This appeared to attach to priestly absolution not a causal but a merely declarative significance. It would, however, be erroneous to attribute this opinion to all the authors who appeal to the text; they include Bede, Druthmar, Smaragdus, Rabanus, Walfrid Strabo, Paschasius and Haymo of Halberstadt. Such an interpretation is excluded by the uncritical, compilatory character of their handling of traditional material. Indeed, not infrequently, the selfsame authors contradict themselves on the same matter by using different responses taken from tradition. Thus, even in the question under consideration, a succession of the same theologians who rely on the text from Jerome stress no less emphatically, as has already been observed, the effectiveness of the power of the keys for the hereafter and its indispensability.[75]

Moreover, at that time there was not the slightest tendency to regard absolution and penitential works as mutually opposed; rather they were seen as equally necessary means on the same level for the forgiveness of sins.[76] The term *absolvere* was by no means already reserved exclusively to sacramental absolution. It had rather the general sense of an intercessory prayer emanating from one who possessed the power of loosing, and for this reason of special efficacy. As conveyed in the form of a blessing this was of ancient usage. The word gained relatively late entry into the liturgy of penance,[77] and even here retained the meaning of a priestly intercession of which the efficacy depended on

---

[75] Another allegory taken from the Fathers and much made use of was that of the raising of Lazarus from the dead. It also was expounded in a sense derogatory to the power of the keys.

[76] Isaac of Langres, *loc. cit.* : *Criminalia peccata multis ieiuniis et crebris manus sacerdotum impositionibus eorumque supplicationibus... placuit purgari.*

[77] Cf. B. Poschmann, *Der Ablaß* 18f. 27ff.

perseverance in prayer and in doing penance along with the sinner. This was the same conception as that prevalent in antiquity.[78] As in the past one still seeks in vain for a fixed formula of absolution. The sacramental power of reconciliation consisted, as has been shown, in the act of readmission into or reconciliation with the Church as such. The prayer which accompanied the act was still in principle an aid for the sinner in making satisfaction, just like the prayers at the introduction to the penitential procedure. Admittedly, in the measure that understanding of the real meaning of reconciliation was lost, the conception of the judicial and sacramental meaning of the act of reconciliation was necessarily obscured. The outcome of this was a jumble of theories when the early scholastics applied themselves to the speculative examination of the sacrament of penance. In practice the difficulty first found expression in connexion with the general absolutions as conveyed from the tenth century onwards, not only on Maundy Thursday, but also on Ash Wednesday and on other occasions. Besides those who had made their confession, others among the faithful were included in their scope after a mere general acknowledgement of sins, with the idea of applying also to them the fruit of the bishop's prayer. In consequence the distinction between sacramental and non-sacramental absolution was visibly endangered.[79]

VIII. Medieval Forms of Penance. Paenitentia Solemnis

The Carolingian reform insisted on the greatest strictness in penance, with the result that the requirements at this period

---

[78] Cf. the *Instructio "Quotiescumque christianis"* (c. 800), Schmitz II 193—203; Chrodegang, *Regula can.* c. 32.

[79] An anonymous writer from Speyer about the middle of the eleventh century sent in consequence a letter of protest to the archbishop of Cologne against these new absolutions (*PL* 151, 693 ff.). About 1120 Honorius of Autun provided an instruction for preachers concerning the form of such absolutions and the general confession of sins which preceded them. See Poschmann, ibid. 40 ff.

were harder than ever, the early Church not excepted.[80] However, their severity was such that they proved to be impracticable. Consequently the reform itself had likewise to tolerate redemptions which in themselves were uncongenial to it, as it was no longer able to abolish the penitential books which it despised in principle. In the instruction *Quotiescumque christianis* the *Penitential of Halitgar* gives a direction for the commutation of fasting through almsgiving; the Synod of Tribur (895) directly commends a limited use of redemptions (can. 54—58); the collections of Regino and Burchard provide a whole series of detailed regulations for redemptions. In these, among other elements, feats of endurance taken from Celtic penitential ordinances appear once again.[81] Absolutely speaking, however, redemptions were money redemptions, as is clear from the constantly recurring phrase: *si habet unde redimat*. It was the business of the confessor to adapt the penance to the individual circumstances of the sinner. The penitential tariffs became more and more general directives for the assessment of penance at the discretion of the confessor. In the course of this development it was often emphasized that a misplaced mildness should not hold sway. The best evidence of the actual survival of genuine penitential zeal in spite of the practice of redemptions appears in some forms of practising penance which at this period came into more general use.

Mention must be made first of the pilgrimage — *peregrinatio* — with which we are already familiar from Celtic penance. It meant that a man cut himself off for ever or for a lengthy period from his home, his occupation and his family in order to devote himself exclusively to God. Frankish penitentials prescribed it for murder and occasionally too for specific sins of unchastity, particularly on the part of clerics. Many, however, decided on it voluntarily out of pure zeal for perfection, while others again

---

[80] There is a comparison in Morinus I 7, c. 9, 10; some examples are given in Poschmann III 133.
[81] See above 126 f.

undertook it as a substitute for public penance to which they would otherwise be liable. Its penitential value consisted in the perpetual hardships of such a life of pilgrimage; and a further motive was the hope of obtaining the help of the saints whose tombs were the goal of the pilgrims. In addition to Jerusalem, they resorted especially to Rome, Santiago de Compostela, Mont-St.-Michel and Tours. The number of pilgrims to Rome grew considerably, especially after the establishment of the close political connexion between the kingdom of the Franks and Italy in the eighth century.[82] As a result confidence in the Apostolic power of the keys now also became centred on the absolving power of the representative of Peter. Some of the penitents did not have their penance imposed on them until they reached the pope, although ecclesiastical laws forbade going beyond the jurisdiction of one's own bishop — *episcopus proprius* — as an abuse.[83] Occasionally bishops themselves sent penitents to Rome with the purpose of leaving the decisions in especially difficult questions to the pope. In consideration of the high level of penitential effort involved in making the pilgrimage and trustful prayer to the Apostles, the popes either granted a certain mitigation of the penance or sent the penitent back to his bishop with a recommendation that he on his side should reduce the penance on these grounds.[84] Pilgrims to other places sought and obtained from the local bishops a corresponding reduction of penance in the same way as the Roman pilgrims from the pope. As for the religious value of making a pilgrimage, it is certain that many were very earnest about it, and manifested a truly heroic spirit of penance. However, like everything human, the practice also had its dark side. Love of adventure was often

---

[82] J. Zettinger, "Die Berichte über Rompilger aus dem Frankenreich bis zum Jahre 800" in *RQ*, Supplementheft 11 (1900) 105ff.

[83] Cf. can. 45 of Chalon, 813; *Haitonis Capitula* c. 18 (814); can. 16 and 18 of Seligenstadt, 1022.

[84] Cf. N. Paulus, *Geschichte des Ablasses im Mittelalter* I (1922) 22ff.; Poschmann III 140ff.

concealed under the appearance of penance, and uncontrolled roving was a moral danger for many; instead of doing penance they gave way to dissipation and vice. As a result the Church became mistrustful of pilgrimages, and here and there even issued decrees against them,[85] without however succeeding thereby in preventing the penitential pilgrimage from being adopted with ever greater frequency as a substitute for canonical penance.

Another substitute for it was entry into a monastery. Already in antiquity this value was attached to the step as is clear from the appreciative designation of it as *conversio*. The *Penitential of Theodore* (I 7, 1; 4, 5) recommends it especially in cases of grave crimes. Paulinus of Aquilea († 802) allows a wife-murderer the option of choosing the monastic life in place of lifelong public penance which would be much more oppressive and more onerous.[86] Peter Damian, the strenuous protagonist of the Gregorian reform, admittedly attacks this conception and the practice based on it as a disastrous abuse founded on an exaggerated notion of ordinary monastic life (*De perfect. monachorum* 6).

Finally, a typical medieval kind of penitential exercise is flagellation. From the fifth century onwards numerous synodal decrees and other documents provide evidence of corporal chastisement as an ecclesiastical penalty. It was often applied to clerics, but also to laymen, chiefly to slaves and persons of low estate, occasionally to freemen also. More than anywhere else it played a part in monastic discipline.[87] In these cases chastisement

---

[85] Worthy of note is a *Capitulare* of Charlemagne of the year 783 n. 78 (*MGH* Leges in fol. I 66 Pertz.): *non sinantur vagare et deceptiones hominum agere, nec isti nudi cum ferro* — often the pilgrims wore iron rings round their necks and on their hands and legs — *qui dicunt se data sibi paenitentia ire vagantes : melius videtur ut, si aliquid inconsuetum et capitale crimen commiserint, ut in uno loco permaneant ... paenitentiam agentes, secundum quod sibi canonice impositum est*. Similarly Rabanus Maurus and the Synod of Mainz presided over by him, 847, in can. 20, which later found a place in Regino 2, 28 and Burchard 6, 35; cf. also can. 45 of Chalon, 813, already mentioned.
[86] *Ep. ad Heistulfum, PL* 99, 181 ff. The counsel was embodied in the canon law; Burchard 6, 40; Ivo 8, 126; Gratian c. 8 C. 33 q. 2.
[87] The Rule of St. Benedict only makes provision for it in exceptional cases of obstinate incorrigibility (c. 23 and 28); in contrast the *Regula coenobialis* of Colum-

appears as a disciplinary measure, but in the Anglo-Saxon penitentials and later books influenced by them it occurs as a method of obtaining a redemption, and is thus recommended as a voluntary work of penance. The penitentials of Bede and Egbert provide copious instances. Gradually self-flagellation came to be practised not only by penitents in the technical sense of the term, but also by other zealous Christians as a method of mortification and penitence, particularly in monasteries. Its most ardent advocate was Peter Damian; with his approval a direct redemption system was drawn up for assessing in juridical fashion the penitential value of flagellation combined with the recitation of the Psalter.[88] Understandably the new kind of penance with its severity and its peculiar system of calculation did not meet with universal approval. In a sharp letter Damian was thus induced to defend it against the clerics of Florence who made fun of "the new penance unheard of up till now throughout so many centuries".[89] At all events his energy contributed to making "the discipline" a permanent institution in monasteries. Moreover, the practice also found approval among layfolk,[90] the best proof of this being the extent of the later flagellant movement.

Over against the new forms of penance the ancient canonical penance declined progressively in importance in spite of the strenuous effort of the reform movement to revive it. The ancient ecclesiastical laws, prohibiting a repetition of penance and imposing its lifelong effects, continued to be included in medieval canonical collections, but in practice after the introduc-

ban prescribes it even for the smallest faults, and by the gradation of the number of strokes enjoined for particular offences establishes a veritable system of corporal punishment. See Poschmann III 147; other instances are also given here.

[88] *Opusc.* 14; *PL* 145, 332. Three thousand strokes of the discipline are a substitute for one year's penance, and as a thousand strokes are possible during the recitation of ten psalms, by correct calculation a discipline of a single psalter yields a penance of five years, and if it is repeated twenty times of a hundred years. *Vita S. Dominici Loricati* 8; *PL* 144, 1015 f.

[89] *Ep.* 1, V. 8; *PL* 144, 350 ff., 415 ff.

[90] *Vita S. Dom. Lor.* 10.

tion of private penance they had completely lost their significance. What is the meaning of the non-repetition of public penance when alongside of this there is the much more pleasant method of private penance? Moreover, public penance gradually became so rare that it now played hardly any part in the general life of the Church.[91] It is significant that from the twelfth century the name *paenitentia solemnis* came into use for it in contrast to private penance, and this places it as something extraordinary.[92] Then very soon *paenitentia solemnis* is contrasted not only with private penance but also with "public penance". This last form was merely a pilgrimage — *peregrinatio*[93] — while *paenitentia solemnis* now only came into consideration for monstrous sins such as parricide: *pro peccatis enormibus, ut pro parricidio*.[94] Its characteristic form is the Ash Wednesday and Maundy Thursday rite provided for in the rituals and reserved to the bishop, while the simple *paenitentia publica* is imposed by a priest *in facie ecclesiae* without any solemnity by the bestowal of the pilgrim's garb and staff.[95] *Paenitentia solemnis* is the last genuine offshoot of the "canonical" penance, the form in which an illusion of existence was still for a while made possible for it. How slight its importance was in the thirteenth century is illustrated by the fact that Thomas Aquinas has only devoted a single question to it in the appendix to his doctrine on penance after the doctrine on indulgences.

---

[91] For further detail on the after-effects of penance in the ancient system see Poschmann II 153—160.

[92] See among others Peter Lombard, *Sent.* IV d. 14 c. 3 and the *Decr. Gratiani,* c. 61 D 50.

[93] Thus earliest in the *Penitential* of Robert of Flamborough (between 1207 and 1215), and the *Summula fratris Conradi* (of the time of Honorius III; on both of these unprinted documents see Dietterle, *ZKG* 24 [1903] 363 ff. and 520 ff.).

[94] *Penitential* of the Augustinian canon Peter of Poitiers (between 1180 and 1230); cf. A. Teetaert in: Festschr. M. Grabmann I [1935] 310—331.

[95] Raymond of Peñafort, *Summula de paenit. et matrim.* 1. 3 tit. 34, 3. Similarly the great scholastics: cf. St. Thomas, *Suppl.* q. 28 a. 3.

154

Chapter Three

THE THEOLOGY OF PENANCE FROM THE EARLY

SCHOLASTIC PERIOD TO THE COUNCIL OF TRENT

Literature: P. Schmoll, *Die Bußlehre der Frühscholastik* (1909). M. Buchberger, *Die Wirkungen des Bußsakr. nach der Lehre des hl. Thomas von Aquin* (1901). J. Göttler, *Der hl. Thomas von Aquin u. die vortridentinischen Thomisten über die Wirkungen des Bußsakr.* (1904). M. A. Koeniger, *Die Beicht nach Cäsarius v. Heisterbach* (1906). N. Krautwig, *Die Grundlagen der Bußlehre des J. Duns Skotus* (1938). C. Feckes, *Die Rechtfertigungslehre des Gabriel Biel* (1925). E. Amann, "Pénitence", *DTC* XII 894—948. A. Michel, ibid. 948—1050. R. Schultes, "Die Lehre des hl. Thomas über das Verhältnis von Reue u. Bußsakr." in *JPhTh* 21 (1907) 72—110; 143—178; 273—290. J. Périnelle, *L'attrition d'après le concile de Trente et d'après saint Thomas* (Bibliothèque thomiste X, Le Saulchoir 1927). P. de Vooght, "La justification dans le sacrement de pénitence" in *EThL* 5 (1928) 225—256; ibid. 7 (1930) 663—675. E. Neveut, "Valeur du repentire du pécheur" in *DThP* (1927) 264—297. H. Dondaine, *L'attrition suffisante* (1943). V. Heynck, "Zur Lehre von der unvollkommenen Reue in der Skotistenschule des ausgehenden 15. Jahrh." in *Franzisk. Studien* (1937) 18—58. Id., "Der hl. John Fisher und die skotist. Reue-lehre" ibid. (1938) 105—133. Id., "Die Reuelehre des Skotusschülers Johannes de Bassolis" ibid. (1941) 1—36. Id., "Die Begründung der Beichtpflicht nach Duns Skotus" ibid. (1941) 65—90. Id., "Attritio sufficiens" ibid. (1949) 76—134. J. Klein, "Zur Bußlehre des seligen Duns Skotus" in *Franzisk. Studien* 27 (1940) 104—113; 191—195. B. Poschmann, *Der Ablaß im Licht der Bußgeschichte* (1948). P. Anciaux, *La théologie du sacrement de pénitence au XIIe siècle* (Louvain 1949). Z. Alzeghy, "La penitenza nella scolastica antica" in *Gr* 31 (1950) 521—532. F. Courtney, *Cardinal Robert Pullen: an English Theologian of the Twelfth Century* (Analecta Gregoriana 64, Rome 1954). U. Horst, "Das Wesen der potestas clavium nach Thomas von Aquin" in *MThZ* 11 (1960) 191—201. A. M. Landgraf, "Grund-lagen für ein Verständnis der Bußlehre der Früh- und Hochscholastik" in *ZkTh* 51 (1927) 161—194. Id., *Dogmengeschichte der Frühscholastik* (Regensburg 1952—1956) Teil III/2 244—276. R. Ohlmann, "St. Bonaventure and the Power of the keys" in *Franciscan Studies* VI (1946) 293—315. B. Poschmann, "Zur Bußlehre Bonaventuras" in *MThZ* 4 (1953) 65—78. V. Heynck, "Zur Bußlehre des hl.

Bonaventura" in *Franzisk. Studien* 36 (1954) 1—82. A. Vanneste, "La théologie de la pénitence chez quelques maîtres parisiens de la première moitié du XIIIᵉ siècle" in *EThL* 28 (1952) 17—58. Ch. R. Meyer, *The Thomistic Concept of Justifying Contrition* (Mundelein [Ill.] 1949). M. Flick, *L'attimo della giustificazione secondo S. Tommaso* (Analecta Gregoriana 40, Rome 1947). E. H. Fischer, "Bußgewalt, Pfarrzwang und Beichtvaterwahl nach dem Dekret Gratians" in *ThQ* 134 (1954) 39—82. R. Blomme, *La doctrine du péché dans les écoles théologiques de la première moitié du XIIᵉ siècle* (Louvain 1958). L. Hödl, *Die Geschichte der scholastischen Literatur und der Theologie der Schlüsselgewalt* Teil 1 (Beitr. z. Gesch. d. Phil. u. Theol. d. MA 38/4, Münster 1960).

IX. The Doctrine of Penance from the Beginning of Scholasticism to St. Thomas Aquinas

WITH the bringing together of confession and reconciliation, which had been completed by the eleventh century, the external procedure of penance had in essentials attained the form in which it is practised to this day. It consists of confession, the imposition of penance and absolution, and its characteristics are that it can be repeated at will and is binding on all. But the speculative doctrine of penance presents a very different picture. Of this it can be said with a certain justification that at the very time when the external development has come to an end it is really just beginning. It is true that individual points of doctrine, in accordance with the needs of pastors, or of protection against false conceptions, were expounded even earlier both by the Fathers and by early-medieval authors. In addition to the penitential laws, the canonical collections often also indicated their sources in Scripture and tradition. However, a uniform synthesis and a scientific penetration of the vast range of the material were lacking. They were all the more urgently required as the decretals and "sentences" were not infrequently self-contradictory. These had been handed down from a great variety of periods, and in part could only be interpreted by taking account of assumptions which in the meantime had become obsolete. Yet they were set out side by side as if possessing equal authority. In penance, therefore, early scholasticism had ready to hand a very productive field for study. Two questions were urgent: the intrinsic relationship of the different factors in penance to each other, and then the subsumption of the entire process under the concept of a sacrament, which at that period had recently been worked out. The combination of theology with dialectic, and especially the adoption of the Aristotelian conceptual system, contributed considerably to clarification. On the other hand it also gave rise to a number of new problems which were worked out in a maze of theories.[1] In addition to the interest in scientific theology which at that time was vigorously awakening, there was another powerful incentive which assisted the clarification of the doctrine of penance. This was the practical need of defending ecclesiastical teaching against the heresies of the Waldensians, and particularly of the Catharists, which were undermining its foundations.[2]

An unsolved problem which had been bequeathed by the Fathers and the Carolingian theologians to the scholastics was that concerning the relation of the subjective or personal factor in penance to the objective or ecclesiastical one. This was now approached from a new angle, inasmuch as among the personal factors the emphasis was no longer laid on works of penance *(paenitentia, satisfactio)* but on sorrow *(contritio)*. This was due to the further evolution which the administration of penance had undergone in the meantime. For after the bringing together of confession and reconciliation it was no longer possible to represent the penitential works (which still remained to be done) as the cause of the forgiveness of sins expressed by reconciliation. The only cause of forgiveness which came into consideration was antecedent and concomitant repentance or sorrow. Before this time such sorrow had been taken for granted as present in all sincere penance, and had hardly received any special treatment independently of satisfaction *(paenitentia)*. From the start,

---

[1] Cf. Morinus, lib. 8 c. 2. In his opinion the application of the doctrine of "habits" to penance is a source of many grave difficulties *(ebulliunt difficultates)*.
[2] See P. Schmoll 11 ff.

therefore, the problem as now presented was the question of the relation between sorrow and absolution; or between sorrow and confession, since in ordinary speech absolution and confession stood for the same thing. From this time onwards sorrow is at the centre of the doctrine of penance. Another new perception, which is explicable on the same grounds, concerned the concept of forgiveness. If satisfaction still remained to be made, then the effect produced through sorrow and absolution could no longer be "forgiveness" in the sense of the remission of all punishment. That was the immediate and primary meaning of the word in the mind of the ancient Church. Now the concept had to be made more precise by distinguishing between eternal and temporal punishment. The forgiveness of temporal punishment continued to be attributed to satisfaction as its direct effect. On the other hand, all that precedes it, namely, contrition, confession and absolution, is the cause of forgiveness in the sense that the eternal punishment which has been merited is remitted, or rather, converted into temporal punishment, and the sin is made "pardonable". This is the teaching of the pre-scholastic treatise *De vera et falsa paenitentia,* which is typical of the eleventh-century outlook on penance.[3]

Among the speculative thinkers who endeavoured to set forth the causality of forgiveness in this narrower sense, Abelard, the pioneer of the scholastic method, exercised the greatest influence. He attributes the forgiveness of sins in one-sided fashion to the subjective factor of contrition, confession and satisfaction (*Ethica* 17), holding, however, that contrition is properly speaking the cause of forgiveness. When it is sincere, that is, motivated by the love of God, it straightway annuls sin, which consists in

---

[3] 10, 25; *PL* 40, 1122: *fit enim per confessionem veniale, quod criminale erat in operatione.* 18, 3, ibid. 1128: *quaedam enim peccata sunt, quae sunt mortalia et in paenitentia fiunt venialia, non tamen statim sanata.* The distinction adds nothing really new to traditional teaching. According to this, sinners who are sincerely converted and reconciled do not incur eternal punishment, even if their penance has still to be completed in the next life. This has been abundantly demonstrated in the course of this exposition.

the contempt of God — *contemptus Dei* — and also eliminates the cause of eternal damnation (ibid. 20). Temporal punishment, on the other hand, must be expiated by satisfaction or in purgatory (*Serm.* 14). Confession and the imposition of penance by a priest are indispensable, as they are remedies ordained by God (*Eth.* 24). The will to undertake them is an absolutely essential constituent of sincere contrition, and consequently a prerequisite for the forgiveness of eternal punishment (*Serm.* 8). However, although the intervention of the Church is necessary for salvation, yet essentially its scope is limited to indicating to the sinner the due measure of satisfaction, in order that all may be expiated here on earth and nothing left over for purgatory — *nihil ibi purgandum restet* (*Eth.* 25). Abelard rejects an authoritative ecclesiastical forgiveness based on the power of the keys. Absolution has the significance of a supplication for sinners in accordance with Jas 5:16; and in agreement with Origen he teaches that in its effect it is dependent on the moral character of the priest (*Eth.* 26). Only inasmuch as it lifts an excommunication does it possess the significance of a judicial act. In this sense it grants readmission to ecclesiastical fellowship to one who has already been reconciled with God through contrition and confession (*Serm.* 8). The denial of the episcopal power of the keys is found among the heretical propositions — *capitula haeresum* — on account of which Abelard was condemned at the Synod of Sens in 1140 at the instigation of St. Bernard. Belief in the power of the keys undoubtedly belonged to the ancient heritage of ecclesiastical tradition. Yet at the same time the notion of what this power involved was both obscure and capable of various interpretations. Account must be taken of this if one is to do justice to Abelard. The original idea that the formal effect of loosing was peace with the Church — *pax ecclesiae* — had gradually disappeared from the consciousness of the Church. It is, therefore, intelligible that a critical theologian like Abelard no longer found a place for an authoritative priestly power of forgiving sins, and that he demanded personal holiness for the

159

effectiveness of the supplications. In regard to the excommunicated, that is, where there was notoriously question of a public reconciliation with the Church, he recognized the power of the keys more markedly.[4]

With the exception of his attitude to the power of the keys, Abelard's doctrine on penance exercised a predominant influence for more than a century. It penetrated the work both of the canonists and the authors of books of sentences. The *Decretum* of Gratian and the *Sentences* of Peter Lombard both contributed to its diffusion. The liberation from eternal wrath, the latter teaches, is not effected through the priest at the moment of confession: it is on the contrary already present beforehand from the moment when a man has begun to love God and to bewail his sins (IV d. 18 c. 4). In treating of the power of the keys he distinguishes between the key of knowledge — *clavis scientiae* — and the key of power — *clavis potestatis;*[5] the first qualifies the priest to form a correct judgement of the state of conscience of the penitent, the second empowers him to impose a penance and to grant admission to the sacraments. Quite manifestly the power of the keys thus conceived remains extrinsic and does not extend to the forgiveness of sins. In accordance with the pattern of the healing of the lepers, and the allegorical interpretation of the raising of Lazarus, the priest has not himself to forgive sins; his function is rather to certify that they are forgiven (ibid. 5). The same doctrine had already been taught by Anselm of Canterbury, *hom.* 13: *qui iam coram Deo sunt mundati, sacerdotum iudicio etiam hominibus ostenduntur mundi.*[6]

---

[4] Cf. A. Teetaert, *La confession aux laïques,* 90 and 118f. He is in favour of a milder verdict on Abelard.

[5] The distinction arose in the ninth century. It was disseminated chiefly because of its incorporation into the *Glossa interl.* of Anselm of Laon († 1117). P. Schmoll 19.

[6] On other authors who have essentially the same theories, see P. Schmoll 35ff.; E. Amann, *DTC* XII 941ff.; H. Weisweiler, "Die Bußlehre Simons von Tournai" in *ZkTh* 56 (1932) 190—230; [F. Courtney, *Cardinal Robert Pullen: an English Theologian of the Twelfth Century,* 228—232; P. Anciaux, *La théologie du sacrement de pénitence au XIIe siècle,* 275—353, 492—586. Tr.]

However, wide as its popularity was, the theory of a merely declarative meaning of absolution did not go unchallenged even from the beginning. Hugh of St. Victor was the first to reject such an emptying out of the content of the power of the keys, and to look for a real inherent efficacy in absolution. He distinguished a double bond in sin: one is interior, consisting of impiety or obduracy of heart — *impietas (vel) obduratio cordis;* the other exterior, consisting of liability to future damnation — *debitum futurae damnationis.* Only the first bond is removed by contrition; the second one is loosed by absolution (*De sacr.* II 14, 8). With this conception Hugh has in effect, even if not formally, introduced into theology the distinction between guilt — *culpa* — and punishment — *poena* — which henceforward is fundamental for the doctrine of penance.[7] His theory of the effect of absolution was, however, untenable because, as the Lombard proved, the forgiveness of eternal punishment cannot be separated from the forgiveness of guilt. For this reason it did not gain acceptance outside the bounds of his school. Richard of St. Victor tried to save the position of his master by making a further distinction in the bondage of punishment between the bond of damnation — *vinculum damnationis* — which in fact can only be loosed by God, and the bond of expiation — *vinculum expiationis* — where a combined activity of God and the priest takes place. In it the priest in absolution by the power of co-operating grace — *gratia cooperandi* — converts eternal punishment into temporal — *poenam non purgatoriam in purgatoriam* (*De pot. lig. et solv.* c. 3).[8] The bond of damnation — *vinculum damnationis* — is already loosed by God by reason of the preceding contrition, but only provisionally — *conditionaliter* — on condi-

---

[7] The substance of the distinction is already found in Augustine (*In Jo. tr.* 124, 5; *De pecc. mer. et rem.* 1, 32, 61; 2, 34, 56), but is not used by him for his doctrine on penance. Hugh's pupil, Richard of St. Victor, often speaks directly of *culpa* and *poena* instead of *obduratio* and *damnatio* (*De potest. lig. et solv.* c. 4 and *passim*), similarly Peter Lombard (IV d. 18 c. 4).

[8] This is the teaching of the tractate *De vera et falsa paenitentia,* above 158.

tion of the subsequent absolution; while the priest in absolution looses it entirely — *integraliter* (c. 19—20). The theory obviously was only feasible before the elaboration of the concept of sanctifying grace. For the development of doctrine it had however the merit of holding fast to a real efficacy in the sacramental action. The idea of a conditional forgiveness of sins based on contrition comes to the same thing as the doctrine of the *sacramentum in voto,* and was also adopted outside the Victorine school.[9] It shows at least the need that was felt to establish an intrinsic connexion between the forgiveness of sins and the power of the keys, at the point where in the more generally accepted theory of the Lombard the two were sundered.

Not even the concept of a sacrament opened the way at once to a solution of this problem. The septenary number of the sacraments had an established position in theology since the time of Peter Lombard, with penance in the fourth place. However, even though this meant that the different parts of penance were considered as a whole, it did not yet settle the question of the contribution of the individual parts.[10] At first a sacrament was conceived after the manner of Augustine as a sign of grace, but this point of view appeared to be a direct confirmation of the merely declarative meaning of reconciliation.[11] As against this, substantial progress was made when the Lombard opened the way for another conception alongside of it. He taught that not only exterior penance, or the outward manifestation of penance, was included in the concept of the sacrament, but also interior penance or contrition, and in so doing established the

---

[9] Especially by Praepositinus († c. 1210), Caesarius of Heisterbach († c. 1240). Texts in Schmoll 58 f.; Koeniger 82. See on this A. Landgraf, *Das sacramentum in voto in der Frühscholastik* in Mélanges Mandonnet II (Paris 1930) 97—143.

[10] Some canonists *e.g.* Rufinus († c. 1190), Robert of Flamborough wished, moreover, to attribute sacramental quality only to *paenitentia solemnis* which could not be repeated, and not to private penance. Further details in P. Schmoll 56 f.; E. Amann 944 f.

[11] Cf. Robert Pullen († 1146): *absolutio remissionem peccatorum, quam antea peperit cordis contritio, designat, Sent.* VI c. 61; *PL* 186, 910.

causal efficiency of the latter. On this view the outward acts in penance are signs of interior contrition; they are the *sacramentum tantum*. Contrition, in its turn, is a sign, but in addition a cause of the forgiveness of sins; it is the *sacramentum et res*. Finally, the forgiveness of sins is the ultimate effect of the whole process; it is the *res tantum* (IV d. 22 c. 2). Admittedly here too justice is not done to absolution, since the exterior penance is simply regarded as a sign of interior penance. Yet the formulation offered a starting-point for the more advanced speculation of the thirteenth century. The concepts of matter and form were taken up into the doctrine of the sacraments from the beginning of the thirteenth century. They presented considerable difficulty when applied to penance owing to its special character and its difference from the other sacraments. They did not advance the solution of the principal problem, as is at once apparent from the contradictory conceptions of what was to be regarded as the matter and form of penance. But an important step was taken when from this time forward grace came to be regarded as an "information" of the soul. This made it easier to conceive how the efficacious divine factor in absolution could co-operate with the one present in contrition. On the other hand, the development of the doctrine of contrition was naturally also of importance.

Since the time of Anselm sorrow was called *contritio* (cf. Ps 50:19) instead of the earlier customary *compunctio*. Substantially it corresponded to the later Tridentine definition (Denz. 897). In agreement with Augustine it was already established doctrine that contrition was only possible through grace, or, seeing that up to the end of the twelfth century grace was equated with the theological virtues, that it was the effect of faith and charity. Here faith and charity signify essentially the same thing as the concept of sanctifying grace which was first introduced at the beginning of the thirteenth century.[12] The

[12] For proof of this see A. Landgraf, *ZkTh* 51 (1927) 168ff.

interest of the early scholastics was concentrated on the act of justification; the preceding preparatory acts and along with them the motives of sorrow remained in the background. Although all held that true contrition was inconceivable without the love of God, yet no one thought of excluding fear from the starting-point of sorrow. On the contrary, because of *Eccles* 1:27 it was regarded as necessary for justification.[13] But mere fear of punishment is servile fear — *timor servilis* — and is insufficient for justification; for this it must become filial or initial fear — *timor filialis* or *initialis* — through the advent of love of righteousness.[14] At the beginning of the thirteenth century the term attrition emerged as a designation of the sorrow which is insufficient for salvation.[15] However, the criterion distinguishing *contritio* and *attritio* was by no means, as in the later view, the motive of sorrow. Originally it was rather a distinction based on the degree of affliction of soul, according as this included a resolution strong enough to confess and make satisfaction.[16] Later, as the doctrine of informing grace — *gratia informans* — became established, it was based on the relation of the sorrow to justifying grace. *Contritio* for the high scholastic period and for pre-Tridentine theology is penance "formed" by grace; *attritio* is "unformed" penance *(paenitentia per gratiam formata, paenitentia informis)*.

Forgiveness of sins was universally taken to be inseparably connected with contrition. Consequently, the question concerning the influence of absolution on the forgiveness of sins amounts to asking whether, and to what extent, absolution has the power of producing contrition, or, in other words, of changing one who is *attritus* into *contritus*. From the time of Peter of Poitiers a fixed scheme had been available for the treatment of

---

[13] Anselm, *hom.* 1; *Summa Sententiarum* (c. 1156) 6, 10; *PL* 176, 146.
[14] P. Lombard III d. 34 c. 34 c. 4—6. Similarly other authors.
[15] It is first attested in the *Quaestiones* attributed to Praepositinus, and is later found in Simon of Tournai and Alan of Lille. See Landgraf, art. cit. 164. *LThk* VIII[1] 850.
[16] Cf. Alan of Lille, *Regulae theol.* 85; *PL* 210, 665.

the process of justification, and it was still employed by St. Thomas Aquinas. This consisted in an analysis of justification into four moments, simultaneous in time but distinguishable in regard to their content. These were: the infusion of grace, the movement arising from free will, contrition, the remission of sins *(infusio gratiae, motus surgens ex libero arbitrio, contritio, peccatorum remissio)*.[17] As has already been observed, by grace the theological virtues are to be understood up to the time of the elaboration of the concept of sanctifying grace. By the movement of free will was meant the active co-operation of man towards faith by conversion to God. St. Thomas Aquinas combines this movement with contrition to form a double movement of free will: a movement towards God and against sin *(motus liberi arbitrii in Deum et in peccatum, Summa theol.* I II q. 113 a. 6). Accordingly, in adults there can in principle be no justification without both of these movements of the will. But how can absolution now produce not only the habit — *habitus* — but also the corresponding acts of faith and contrition *(fides et contritio),* if these are already the indispensable presuppositions for the bestowal of absolution? This question was the culminating point of the difficulty with which the scholastics saw themselves confronted in the doctrine of the sacrament of penance.

The first to attribute to absolution the effect of making an attrite man contrite was William of Auvergne *(ex attrito fit contritus).* On this point, however, he is thinking not of the *opus operatum,* but of the *opus operantis,* inasmuch as he holds that priests impetrate the grace of contrition for the attrite in absolution *(De sacr. paenitentiae* c. 19).[18] Both the great Franciscan theologians Alexander of Hales and St. Bonaventure, who held substantially the same views on the doctrine of penance, adopted the same standpoint. They too denied to absolution any

---

[17] Peter of Poitiers, III *Sent.* c. 2; *PL* 211, 1044. Other authors in Landgraf, *ZkTh* (1927) 183.

[18] Cf. A. Teetaert, *La confession aux laïques,* 261 against P. Schmoll 128 and W. Rütten, *Studien zur mittelalterl. Bußlehre* (1902) 18—20.

sacramental power for the forgiveness of guilt and eternal punishment. The priestly power of the keys operates in regard to this only after the manner of one entreating absolution and not after the manner of one conveying it *(per modum deprecantis absolutionem [non] per modum impertientis)*. Noteworthy in both is the interpretation they give to the deprecative and indicative formulae of absolution, which at that time were used side by side. First the priest ascends to God as intercessor for the sinner in order to beg for grace; he is qualified for this *(ad hoc est idoneus)*. Only after this does he come down from God in the rôle of superior and judge. The supplication entreats grace and the absolution supposes it *(deprecatio gratiam impetrat et absolutio gratiam supponit)*.[19] His authoritative, judicial power first comes into operation *ex opere operato* in the remission of a part of the punishment for sin,[20] but principally in reconciliation with the Church, because the sinner has not only offended God, but also the Church.[21] This is an echo of the ancient conception of reconciliation, but one of which the relevance for the problem of the sacramental forgiveness of sins was no longer understood.[22]

St. Albert the Great equally with the leading Franciscans underestimated the function of absolution, notwithstanding the emphasis with which he insisted on the sacramental mediation

---

[19] Alexander, *Summa theol.* IV q. 21 memb. 1. Bonaventure adds: *Numquam enim sacerdos absolveret quemquam, de quo non praesumeret, quod esset absolutus a Deo, Sent.* IV d. 18 p. 1 a. 2 q. 1.
[20] Alexander, q. 21 m. 2 a. 1; Bonaventure (ibid.) q. 1 and 2.
[21] Bonaventure, d. 15 p. 2 a. 1 q. 2; 17 p. 1 a. 2 q. 4.
[22] The ancient Christian idea that sin of itself cuts off the offender from the Church was, as A. Landgraf has shown, *Schol* (1930) 210—247, alive right up to the high scholastic period. As it was impossible to regard sinners as absolutely outside the Church, a distinction was made between exterior and interior membership *(numero et merito)*. But if sin as such causes separation, it follows that this will cease when the sin is forgiven through contrition. Hence absolution has no more part to play for interior reunion with the Church than for the forgiveness of guilt. It only retained that signification for the external forum, as a readmission of one who had been publicly excommunicated. Cf. Poschmann, *Der Ablaß* 29 f.

of forgiveness. It is true that he combined contrition, confession and satisfaction in one effective principle, yet in such a way that the power of justification inheres in the contrition and the other elements are mere outward signs of contrition. Accordingly, for him the matter of the sacrament is contrition in its outward manifestation; the form, on the other hand, is not the absolution — this is treated along with confession — but the grace which "informs" the contrition. In keeping with this, the sacrament of penance is defined as sorrow informed by grace manifested in outward signs (*dolor informatus gratia in signis exterioribus manifestatus, IV Sent.* d. 16 a. 1). Forgiveness of sins takes place when the attrition, along with the unformed acts of faith, fear and hope, is "informed" by grace and becomes contrition (a. 8). Inasmuch as the intention *(votum)* of confession and satisfaction must of necessity be included in sorrow, absolution is also a factor affecting the forgiveness of sins (d. 16 a. 3; d. 14 a. 3). Yet, seeing that in the actual bestowal of absolution sin is always already remitted through contrition, all that remains for it to effect is simply the remission of a part of the punishment.[23]

By way of contrast, Hugh of St. Cher († 1263), the first Dominican cardinal, attributes to absolution a real influence on the forgiveness of sins. He holds that baptism, and likewise confession, can produce contrition *(potens efficere contritionem.... Virtute enim confessionis et absolutionis vel datur, quod augmentatur dolor et detestatio peccati, et datur gratia, qua de attritione fit contritio).*[24] In contrast to William of Auvergne, Alexander and Bonaventure, what is meant here is a real sacramental effect *ex opere operato.* Hugh does not enter into details on the manner in which absolution produces the effect.

---

[23] D. 18 c. 7: *Dicendum, quod sacerdos non potest absolvere a culpa et poena aeterna, sed tantum absolvit relaxando partem poenae, nisi illo modo, quo supra dictum est, quod votum clavium est in contritione habendo vim quamdam ad remissionem totius peccati.*

[24] In IV *Sent.*: Cod. Vat. lat. 1098 fol. 151; Cod. Vat. lat. 1174 fol. 83ᵛ, cited by A. Landgraf, in *ZkTh* (1927) 190.

In St. Thomas Aquinas the scholastic doctrine of penance reaches its culminating point and, relatively speaking, its close. By the power of his systematic thought he united the personal and the ecclesiastical factors in penance to form an organic unitary principle, with the aim of thereby securing for absolution a causal significance in the remission of guilt. The instrument of his synthesis is the concept of a sacrament which he applied to penance also with a clarity and consistency not remotely approached before. This achievement is all the more remarkable as it is already present in the work of his youth, the *Commentary on the Sentences*. Personal penance, consisting in the three "parts", contrition, confession and satisfaction, is the matter of the sacrament of penance, and absolution is the form. The matter and the form do not produce their effect separately, but only in combination as a single cause — *una causa* — so that the personal acts of the penitent as well as the power of the keys are the cause of the forgiveness of sins (IV *Sent.* d. 22 q. 2 a. 1 sol. 1; cf. *S. th.* III q. 86 a. 6). In this operation the efficacy — *efficacia* — derives principally from the form, while the function of signifying — *significatio* — comes principally from the matter — *est ex parte materiae principaliter* (IV *Sent.* ibid. a. 2 sol. 2). The same principle holds good in penance as in baptism. The *Ego te absolvo* has the same effective power for the forgiveness of guilt as the baptismal formula (III q. 84 a. 3 ad 5; *Suppl.* q. 10 a. 1 and *passim*).

But Aquinas is not content with an external application of the concept of a sacrament of the sort which consists in forcibly pressing the component parts of penance into it; he seeks also to justify its unitary operation by an exposition of the intrinsic relation that exists between penance as a virtue and penance as a sacrament, or between contrition and the keys. The rest of his teaching both in content and method is confined to that of the school. In respect of justification, the sacramental theory of the *res et sacramentum,* interior penance, the distinction between contrition and attrition and other points he has merely taken over the teaching of his predecessors. The division of the material, which is not always a happy one owing to the frequent repetitions which it necessitates, was in substance imposed on him by the text which he had to explain; so too, for the most part, was the choice of the questions in the *Commentary on the Sentences.* This is the only work which deals with the doctrine of penance in its entirety, as the *Summa* breaks off after the first seven questions. Moreover, he felt himself obliged by piety occasionally to defend by means of limiting distinctions texts of which the sense intended by the Master is in opposition to his own opinion.[25] Given this encumbrance laid on him by the tradition of the school, it is not surprising if his teaching on penance, in spite of its firm attitude on the questions decided, presents on points of detail a rather complicated form, and is even affected by certain obscurities and inconsistencies. How indeed could he have examined and solved at the age of twenty-five, when he wrote down in the greatest haste the *Commentary on the Sentences,* all the complicated individual problems? Had he been permitted to complete the *Summa* he would undoubtedly have clarified a number of points.[26]

The question of the relation between absolution and the forgiveness of sins leads back to the concept of justification. As has already been mentioned,[27] according to St. Thomas justification exhibits three moments: the infusion of grace, the

---

[25] The most instructive example of this is *Suppl.* q. 18 a. 1 with the negative reply to the question *utrum potestas clavium se extendat ad remissionem culpae,* and the argument that the power of the keys is not the *causa principalis,* but only the *causa instrumentalis* of forgiveness.

[26] Of his other writings those of significance for the doctrine of penance are the *Summa Contra Gentiles* (written rather from an apologetic point of view), commentaries on relevant Scripture texts, some questions from the *De veritate* (q. 24 a. 14, 15; q. 27, 28); *De malo* (q. 2 a. 11, 12; q. 3 a. 14); *De virtutibus* (q. 2 a. 1—3); *De potentia* (q. 3), which treat individual questions in greater detail, and finally the *Opusculum de formula absolutionis* which is instructive for the history of penance.

[27] Above p. 165.

double movement of free will towards God and against sin, and the remission of sins. The three moments exercise reciprocal causality on each other. In the order of formal and efficient cause — *secundum ordinem causae formalis et efficientis* — grace makes possible the movement of the will towards God and away from sin, that is, faith and contrition; conversely, faith and contrition in the order of material cause — *secundum ordinem causae materialis* — are the indispensable subjective "disposition" for the reception of grace; finally, grace cannot enter before the elimination of sin, while the infusion of grace is in turn the formal and the efficient cause of the forgiveness of sins. Thus the three moments, according to the point of view from which they are considered, are, in relation to each other, either antecedent or consequent.[28] They are distinguishable from each other but not separable. Note particularly that no grace is conferred without the freely effected conversion of man, and in turn this conversion must already be the effect of grace. If then absolution is to have a causal significance for the infusion of grace and the forgiveness of sins, it must also of necessity cooperate as an instrumental cause — *causa instrumentalis* — in the production of the movement of free will, and so of contrition. St. Thomas expresses this with axiomatic clarity when, in line with traditional sacramental theology, he assigns interior penance — *paenitentia interior* — which in content is identical with contrition, as the *res et sacramentum* of penance. By way of explanation he says expressly that it is the *res* of exterior penance, in the sense that it is simply signified by the acts of the penitent, but that it is signified and caused by the same acts in conjunction with the absolution of the minister — *ut significata tantum per actus paenitentis, ut significata autem et causata per actus eosdem adiuncta absolutione ministri.*[29] It is this, not as an act of virtue — *actus*

---

[28] IV *Sent.* d. 17 q. 1 a. 4 sol. 1 and especially sol. 2; *De ver.* q. 28 a. 7 and 8; *S. th.* I II q. 113 a. 8.
[29] IV *Sent.* d. 22 q. 2 a. 1 sol. 2; in less detail *S. th.* III q. 84 a. 1 ad 3. The progress as compared with the conception of the Lombard is worthy of notice. Cf. above 163.

virtutis — which is not the effect, but rather the cause of exterior penance; but as an act operating for the healing of sin — *actus operans ad sanationem peccati ;* and it is only as such that it belongs to the sacrament of penance. In its function as an act remissive of sin it does in fact receive its efficacy of operation — *efficacia operandi* — from the exterior penance and in particular from the absolution.[30]

Yet how can absolution produce contrition, seeing that this, being the matter of the sacrament, is already necessary for its existence, and consequently for the effectiveness of absolution? Faced with this problem St. Thomas considers two possibilities: either the remission of sins takes place before absolution because of contrition, or coincides with it. The first of these alternatives is in keeping with the conception which was dominant up till that time, and is also the normal one for Aquinas; so much so that occasionally like earlier theologians he simply presupposes a state of grace for confession.[31] More often, however, he says that forgiveness can still take place at absolution and in fact does take place.[32] Taking now the normal case where the remission of sins precedes absolution, he safeguards its sacramental efficacy by his teaching on its antecedent operation in the contrition. Going beyond the doctrine, which was general from the time of Abelard, that the will to submit to the tribunal of ecclesiastical penance is an indispensable element of true contrition, he claims that contrition derives its power of obtaining for-

---

[30] IV *Sent.* ibid. ad 1; cf. d. 14 q. 1 a. 1 sol. 2 ad 3.

[31] Thus in the *Expos. orationis dominicae* (fifth petition) where the forgiveness of guilt is attributed to contrition and the remission of temporal punishment to confession (including absolution). Similarly IV *Sent.* d. 17 q. 3 a. 2 sol. 1 and 2; *Commentary on Mt* 8: 2—4 and on *Ps* 31: 5.

[32] *C. gent.* IV 72 (end): *Nihil prohibet, quin aliquando virtute clavium alicui confesso in ipsa absolutione gratia conferatur, per quam ei culpa remittitur.* IV *Sent.* d. 22 q. 2 a. 1 sol. 3: *(remissio peccatorum)* ... *aliquando tempore praecedit sacramentum exterius, aliquando autem in ipso sacramento efficitur.* Cf. *De form. absol.* 2, 7; *Suppl.* q. 10 a. 1; q. 18 a. 1; *Quodl.* 4 a. 10; *In Jo.* c. 11 lect. 6, 6. The passages from the *C. gent.* and the *De form. absol.* show that even in the later works St. Thomas still held to the view which has been expounded.

giveness of sin from the absolution subsequently bestowed. The reason is that only through absolution is the fruit of the passion of Christ communicated to the penitent as he co-operates with grace in the destruction of sin — *ad destructionem peccati* (*S. th.* III q. 84 a. 5). He is not thinking here merely of some kind of substitute for the sacrament by a desire of it which is efficacious *ex opere operantis* in the sense of later theology, but of a second mode of true sacramental operation. The sacrament operates not only in act, but also in the intention of receiving it *(proposito)*. *Sacramentum in proposito (voto) existens,* so runs the constantly recurring expression.[33] The theory is not the exclusive property of Aquinas. In its elements it was already proposed by his teacher, Albert (IV *Sent.* d. 17 a. 1 ad 6; d. 18 a. 1 ad 1; a. 7 *resp.*). Alexander, on the other hand, and St. Bonaventure reject it.[34] In fact it is untenable. It is quite intelligible that God in communicating grace should take account of man's intention, but the notion that a sacrament not yet in existence should exercise instrumental causality is impracticable.

In the second, rare case, where the forgiveness of sins coincides with the administration of the sacrament, St. Thomas likewise remains absolutely faithful to his basic teaching on justification, which affirms as indispensable the co-operation of grace with the movement of free will. Nowhere, however, does he embark on a discussion of the mode, his only positive remark being that one who has attrition, but not yet fully contrition, will obtain grace and forgiveness in confession and absolution if he does not interpose an obstacle — *si obicem non ponat* (IV

[33] IV *Sent. d.* 22 q. 2 a. 1 sol. 3; *Suppl.* q. 10 a. 1; *De ver.* q. 28 a. 8 ad 2; *C. gent.* IV 72 and *passim*. The question is treated ex professo in *Quodl.* 4 [q. 7] a. 10. That St. Thomas held the theory of antecedent efficacy to the end is shown by *S. th.* III q. 90 a. 2 and q. 86 a. 6.

[34] Alex., IV *Sent.* q. 14 m. 2 a. 1; Bon., IV *Sent.* d. 18 p. 1 a. 1 q. 2: *iste modus, licet videatur probabilis, tamen habet in superficie phantasiam.* Cf. P. Schmoll, 149, 133. On St. Thomas, see especially J. Göttler 45—55; against him R. Schultes, *Reue und Bußsakr.* 164—178, who holds that the explanation of an antecedent operation of the sacrament is unsuccessful.

Sent. d. 22 q. 2 a. 1 sol. 3). But it would be to misunderstand him completely if the opinion which was later prevalent were attributed to him, according to which in the confession of an *attritus* the effect of absolution compensates for the lack of contrition.[35] Against this there is not only the constantly repeated demand, often exclusively formulated, of the movement of free will which includes contrition (cf. *De ver.* q. 28 a. 3 and 8; IV *Sent.* d. 17 q. 1 a. 3 sol. 2; *S. th.* I II q. 113 a. 3; III q. 86 a. 6 ad 2) but also the fact that St. Thomas states quite plainly that a priest may not absolve a penitent in whom he does not see signs of contrition — *in quo signa contritionis non videt*.[36] The case of a forgiveness of sins in absolution is on this view only a practical one when someone thinks in good faith that he is contrite, although he only has attrition. For although contrition and attrition are essentially different — the one being "formed" by grace, the other not — yet psychologically they are closely connected. Attrition is the normal beginning of contrition (IV *Sent.* d. 17 q. 2 a. 2 sol. 6), leads to it and is a remote disposition for grace (ibid. q. 1 a. 3 sol. 3 ad 2).[37] It is therefore possible, as justification takes place in an instant, that the grace of the sacrament at the moment of absolution raises a remote disposition to a proximate one, which of necessity has information by grace, and therewith contrition, as its result. As the attrite person thus becomes contrite, he fulfils the condition for justification. The grace of the sacrament always enters if no obstacle *(obex)* is interposed through the withholding of co-operation, or, as St. Thomas usually says, if a man does not

---

[35] This view has been revived by J. Périnelle as against M. Buchberger, J. Göttler, R. Schultes and others. He has been conclusively answered by P. de Vooght.

[36] *De forma absol.* 2, 7 and 3, 8; similarly in *Quodl.* 4 (q. 7), written towards the end of his life.

[37] From this point of view St. Thomas can include it in contrition in a wider, improper sense of the word. But it is by no means true, although generally so claimed, that he used the word *contritio* simply as a generic concept for both kinds of sorrow. In reality he everywhere draws a sharp line between them. On this see P. de Vooght (1928) 248 ff.

receive the sacrament *ficte,* that is if he does not falsely simulate the requisite disposition. The *fictio,* however, consists in nothing else than the lack of contrition.[38] An efficacious absolution without contrition is unthinkable for St. Thomas, because there is no justification without conversion, and a true conversion is not possible without a turning to God. That is something essentially different from the later teaching that attrition is sufficient for the sacramental forgiveness of sins.[39] Yet with the same energy with which he defends the strict principle of the teaching on justification he insists on the principle of the authoritative power of the Church to forgive sins. His categorical demand for the indicative form of the absolution formula is striking evidence of this. In the *Opusculum de forma absolutionis,* which was expressly devoted to this question, not only does he hold with the greatest emphasis the necessity of the indicative form, but he also claims — against history — that it was always in existence.[40]

Recognition of the consistency with which St. Thomas understands how to do justice to both aspects of penance does not, however, permit us to gloss over the difficulties with which his

---

[38] *Suppl.* q. 9 a. 1 says of one who confesses *non contritus : quamvis tunc non percipiat absolutionis fructum, tamen recedente fictione percipere incipiet.* Cf. *Comm. in Matt.* c. 16. For further instances of this meaning of *fictio,* see de Vooght, ibid. 243 and n. 101.

[39] From this point of view St. Thomas is certainly a "contritionist". But he is not one in the sense of later theology, because for the indispensable contrition he does not make those lofty demands which are almost out of reach for average Christians. He teaches that contrition must necessarily proceed from a motive of the love of God (I II q. 113 a. 7 ad 2; III q. 84 a. 10; q. 86 a. 3; *Suppl.* q. 1 a. 3), yet he refrains from a further determination of the motive of this love. For him love is present in true conversion to God *(motus in Deum)* provided only that it includes an act of will strong enough to overcome all obstacles. Displeasure at sin *propter peccati turpitudinem pertinet ad caritatem,* and not only displeasure *propter Dei offensam* (III q. 85 a. 5 ad 1). Similarly desire of eternal salvation is closely related to the love of God (II II q. 17 a. 8; q. 27 a. 3). As regards practice, St. Thomas warns against meticulous weighing of motives, *quia homo affectus suos non de facili mensurare potest* (IV *Sent.* d. 17 q. 2 a. 3 sol. 1 ad 4). It has therefore been correctly stated that for contrition he requires less than some contemporary theologians do for attrition (P. de Vooght [1928] 255f.; J. Göttler 39).

[40] In consequence the indicative form quickly prevailed. Cf. Jungmann 259f.

construction is burdened. One principal difficulty has already been mentioned. If the conception of the sacrament *in proposito* as a true sacrament is untenable, then the sacramental remission of sin becomes effective only quite exceptionally, indeed irregularly — only when the penitent is deluded about the quality of his sorrow. That is absolutely inconsistent with the meaning of the sacrament. In St. Thomas, too, as in Alexander and St. Bonaventure, all that in fact remains as the normal effect of the sacrament is the remission of a part of the punishment due to sin (IV *Sent.* d. 18 q. 1 a. 3 sol. 2 and ad 4 and *passim*), and in addition, as he likewise teaches, reconciliation with the Church.[41] No less a difficulty lies in the double rôle of contrition, which is both an indispensable disposition for grace and yet itself presupposes grace. The solution offered, with its appeal to different kinds of causality (above 169 f.), is difficult to understand, and seems to be invalidated from the outset by the fact that the disposition can only in a very limited sense be called a material cause. Consequently, the axiom which applies to natural substances: matter is the cause of form, and form is the cause of matter — *Materia est causa formae, forma est causa materiae* — cannot here be applied without any reservation. Moreover, surely the act (and not just the habit) of contrition produced through sancti-

---

[41] The scope of this second effect is clear from the arguments used in its support: Through sin a man is cut off from the Church, at least *merito*, if not *numero* (d. 16 q. 1 a. 2 sol. 5), and juridically the separation continues until it is formally removed by absolution. There is no title to the sacraments of the Church before absolution. One who is justified simply by reason of contrition has no more right of access to them than a person who is baptised only by *baptismus flaminis* (d. 17 q. 3 a. 3 sol. 2 ad 3). In this juridical consideration the ancient idea of the *pax ecclesiae* as the *pignus vitae* has dwindled away. When A. Landgraf (*ZkTh* 1927, 91) derives from the last-mentioned text that for St. Thomas too the absolved person is a partaker in the holiness of the Church he fails to see that in the *sanctificatio, quae ad hominem pervenit,* it is not the holiness of the Church itself that is meant, but the sanctification which she conveys sacramentally, just as baptism does in the case of one already justified by the baptism of the Spirit. If the ancient teaching in its full sense had still been known to Aquinas, his theory of the sacrament of penance would probably have had a different character and the difficulties in question would have been avoided.

fying grace must enter the consciousness of the penitent in confession? How does this square with experience? It is not surprising then if the theology of the ensuing period saw itself more or less forced to take another course in its efforts to find a solution to the problem. However, on the main issue, which was concerned with the sacramental causality of the forgiveness of sins, and with the conjoint causality of the sacrament and the virtue of penance, the new teaching of Aquinas finally prevailed.

In comparison with this major achievement the other points of his teaching on penance have only a subordinate interest. Here his importance lies in the clear and perhaps definitive synthesis of the scholastic tradition. To begin with confession, he teaches that it is presupposed for the exercise of the power of the keys (*Suppl.* q. 6; *C. gent.* IV 72); for one in mortal sin it is necessary for salvation (III q. 84 a. 5), while venial sins are forgiven also outside the sacrament (q. 87 a. 3). Moreover, all are bound by the obligation of annual confession in virtue of the decree of Innocent III (Denz. 473) which, however, only applies to those in mortal sin, while others satisfy the law if they report to the priest that they are not conscious of any grave sin (*Suppl.* q. 6 a. 3). The sole minister of confession is a priest, because only he has by the consecration of the eucharist ministerial power over the true body of Christ, and grace descends from the head to the members (IV *Sent.* d. 17 q. 3 a. 3 sol. 1). Besides the power of order he must also have jurisdiction over the penitent, so as to be able to "command" him to perform the acts which belong to the matter of the sacrament (*Suppl.* q. 8 a. 4). In necessity, however, a layman can take the place of a priest, just as in baptism. Indeed St. Thomas not only recommends confession to laymen, but in certain circumstances even makes it obligatory (*Suppl.* a. 2; cf. a. 4 ad 5; q. 9 a. 3 ad 5) — a doctrine which is only explicable by the conceptions of the time. It is difficult to harmonize it with his sacramental theology, and it was not adopted by later theology.[42] The same applies to

[42] A. Teetaert, *La confession aux laïques* 325—329.

the much discussed question of the *confessio informis,* or valid but fruitless confession. This supposes that confession is valid even without contrition, and that it becomes fruitful without a new confession — *recedente fictione* — that is, once the indisposition arising from the deficiency of contrition is removed. This thesis, which occurs only once in his earliest work (*Suppl.* q. 9 a. 1), was probably taken over by the youthful teacher from the tradition of the school (cf. Albert d. 17 a. 6) without his realizing the contradiction which it involved with the principles of his doctrine of penance.[43]

Satisfaction serves for the elimination of temporal punishment and as a remedy against sin (*Suppl.* q. 12 a. 3; q. 13 a. 1). As a part of the sacrament its effect is *ex opere operato,* and thus it has greater atoning power than belongs to the penitential work in itself (*Quodlib.* 3 a. 28). The state of grace is a condition for its efficacy, because only friendship with God makes acceptable the works of the sinner, which in themselves are always inadequate (*Suppl.* q. 13 a. 1; q. 14 a. 1). This doctrine puts the ethical side of satisfaction in sharp relief as against a merely juridical conception of compensation for guilt.[44] The amount of remission of punishment merited is dependent on the intensity of the satisfaction, because, in contrast to baptism, in penance a man only participates in the power of the passion of Christ according to the measure of his own acts — *secundum modum propriorum actuum* (III q. 86 a. 4 ad 3). The decisive factor is the degree of charity. It can be so great that the entire punishment is immediately remitted through contrition (*Suppl.* q. 5 a. 2; q. 18 ad 4).

Passing over other questions of less importance for the

---

[43] Further detail in J. Göttler 21 ff.

[44] Difficult, however, to reconcile with this is the notion that voluntary undertaking of penance on behalf of another should without reservation imply divine acceptance (q. 13 a. 2). St. Bonaventure adopted a contrary position; later theologians are divided on the subject. Cf. B. Poschmann, *Der Ablaß* 91 n. 425.

dogmatic development,[45] we will deal briefly with his attitude to the problem of the "return of sins" which had been a subject of lively discussion in the early scholastic period. The question had become an actual one ever since absolution was bestowed immediately after confession before the completion of satisfaction. Given that the will to make satisfaction is a presupposition for forgiveness, what happens, it was asked, when the man who had been freed from sin did not fulfil the obligation of making satisfaction which he had undertaken? The significance of the outward sacrament and scriptural texts such as Ez 18: 24 and 33 : 12 appeared to demand the annulment of the pardon; yet, on the other hand, such a revocation on the part of God was scarcely conceivable. The question, therefore, found very various solutions, with qualifications tending in greater or less degree towards one side or the other.[46] St. Bonaventure taught that according to the majority of modern teachers — *doctores moderni* — sins in no way returned in regard to their guilt — *quoad culpam* — but that they did in regard to their punishment — *quoad poenam* — in so far as this has not yet been expiated. St. Thomas, arguing from the objective power and efficacy of the sacrament, rejected with St. Albert (IV *Sent.* d. 22 a. 1) even any reviviscence in regard to punishment (IV *Sent.* d. 22 q. 1 a. 1 sol.; *S. th.* III q. 88 a. 1).

The great and epoch-making achievement of Aquinas' teaching on penance was the integration of the sacrament in the process of justification, and consequently the proof that it was an indispensable cause of the forgiveness of sins. The heritage thus bequeathed to theology was at the same time a task. That was because very considerable difficulties confronted the arguments on which he had based the unity of the sacrament and personal

---

[45] For example, the unlimited efficacy of the sacrament of penance in regard to all sins without exception, the remission of the *reliquiae peccati,* the restoration of virtues and the reviviscence of good works. On these points, see J. Göttler 66 f.; 86—101.

[46] A. Landgraf, "Die frühscholast. Streitfragen vom Wiederaufleben der Sünde" in *ZkTh* (1937) 509—594; J. Göttler 70 ff.

penance. The result was that some rejected his theory, others on the other hand sought to master the difficulties by making considerable modifications in it. The teaching on penance of his followers in the "Thomist school" which was before long in process of formation, does, therefore, in spite of its attachment in principle to his theory, take its problems a step further, and marks a real development.[47]

First there was a widely discussed question, with which others were more or less connected, concerning the efficacy of the sacrament of penance. The problem was that of the *res et sacramentum* of penance. In the *Commentary on the Sentences* and the *De veritate* (q. 27 a. 4 ad 3), and also in the later *Quaestio de potentia* (q. 3 a. 4 ad 8) St. Thomas, with Alexander and St. Albert, held the theory that sacraments do not produce grace itself, but only a disposition. Consequently, the *res et sacramentum* is the character or (in those sacraments without a character) some kind of adornment of the soul — *aliquis ornatus animae* — or, as he expresses himself in the same article, some effect in the soul such as the character or something of this kind — *aliquis effectus in ipsa anima, sicut est character vel aliquid huiusmodi* (IV *Sent.* d. 1 q. 1 a. 4 sol. 1). The dispositive efficacy — *dispositive operari* — holds good for absolution just as for baptism (*Suppl.* q. 18 a. 1). This disposition which it produces, and which itself is a cause of grace, is then the *res et sacramentum,* and, as has been already indicated, this is interior penance or contrition. Hence interior penance — *paenitentia interior* — is identical with the *ornatus* of the sacrament of penance.[48] But, how can interior penance, which is a subjective and moral act, nevertheless be the effect of the outward sign just like the character in baptism, which is an objective reality independent of subjective dispositions? This seems to be impossible, and yet it is assumed by

---

[47] There is a detailed account in the second part of Göttler's book. Cf. also A. Michel *DTC* XII 994—1022.

[48] St. Thomas uses the word *ornatus* only once. This is when he is treating of the sacraments in general, *loc. cit.,* where he makes no special reference to penance.

St. Thomas in connexion with the *confessio informis* already touched on, which though fruitless is valid and does not need to be repeated (*Suppl.* q. 9 a. 1). Naturally the settlement of this contradiction gave the commentators plenty to do. In the first period distinguished Thomists such as Bernard of Clermont (c. 1300), Herveus Natalis († 1323), Petrus Paludanus († 1342), sought a solution by separating the *ornatus* from the *paenitentia interior;* they regarded it as the objective effect of the outward sign, and as a physical disposition for the remission of sins, holding that it was produced in every case, even when the absence of the interior disposition, *i.e.,* contrition, placed an obstacle to actual remission.[49] Although it caused the greatest trouble to apply the distinction and to assign an appropriate function to each of the two factors postulated, the theory was dragged along throughout the fourteenth and fifteenth centuries. It was in vain that Durandus of S. Porciano († 1332) described the *ornatus* as a pure invention — *pura adinventio* (IV *Sent.* d. 1 q. 4). In the fifteenth century Capreolus, prince of Thomists, went to enormous pains on the point in lengthy dissertations, in which he tried to unite the *ornatus* with the sacramental grace.[50] Franciscus de Silvestris (Ferrariensis, † 1528) was the first to dispose of it, proving that St. Thomas knew nothing of any *ornatus* besides interior penance, and refuting the view of Capreolus.[51] Even more effective was Cardinal Cajetan's demonstration that St. Thomas himself, as is clear from the *Summa,* had later abandoned the theory of the dispositive causality of the sacraments in favour of the view that sacraments are direct causes of grace. Once the *dispositio praevia* is dropped, the *ornatus* goes too, in the sacraments generally, and in penance also. Here it is sufficient to regard interior penance as the *res et sacramentum.*[52] Cajetan's verdict on Aquinas' change of opinion in regard

---

[49] More detail in Göttler 130 ff. and 158 ff.
[50] IV *Sent.* d. 22 q. 1 a. 3. Göttler 189 ff.
[51] *Comm. in Summ. c. gent.* lib. IV c. 72. Göttler 226—234.
[52] *Comm.* in III q. 62 a. 1 and 2; q. 84 a. 1. Göttler 237 ff.

180

to the causality of the sacraments was accepted by the majority of theologians, and is in fact difficult to contest. However, as St. Thomas gave no intimations in the *Summa* on this point, particularly in connexion with penance, there are still today some who believe that he remained faithful to his original teaching of dispositive causality even in his later period.[53]

Connected with the disposition for grace is the question of the significance of attrition. On this point all the Thomists were at one with their master in requiring contrition for the forgiveness of sins, and they forbade a confessor to give absolution if the penitent confessed that he was not contrite. Only when the latter in good faith mistakenly thought he was contrite did they ascribe to absolution the effect of making contrite one who was attrite. To this extent they were all "contritionists".[54] Yet the doctrine that a person could still become contrite through the sacrament necessarily impelled them to go further than St. Thomas and determine the degree of attrition required for this effect. Consequently, nearly all of them from Petrus Paludanus onwards distinguished an attrition sufficient for this; it is a profound attrition, sufficient for a valid but fruitless confession — *confessio informis*. In addition they distinguished a lower kind of attrition which is ineffective even for this. With their first kind they came close to the Tridentine doctrine that attrition is a disposition for grace — *disponit ad gratiam*.

Cajetan above all others showed signs of progress. He did not shrink from designating the highest degree of attrition, that which had information by grace as its outcome, as *contritio informis,* which was a contradiction in terms according to the terminology hitherto received. This *contritio informis* was contrasted with *contritio formata,* or formed contrition, the infusion of which was exclusively the work of God. On the part of man it requires no act extending further than *contritio informis (Opusc.*

[53] Thus Göttler 26f.; P. de Vooght (1928) 226—256; (1930) 663—675.
[54] See the summary judgement in Göttler 272.

tom. 1 tr. 4 q. 1). The clear distinguishing mark of *contritio informis* is the motive of the love of God above all things; whereas in attrition the love of God does not extend above all things. By means of the concept of *contritio informis* Cajetan is the first to distinguish between the act and the habit of charity in connexion with contrition.[55] He thus also paves the way for the distinction of attrition and contrition as personal acts without reference to information by grace. Thereby one of the chief sources of the complications of the scholastic theology of penance, with its interdependent forms of causality, is stopped up. The change in terminology on this point is big with consequence. In essentials Cajetan remains true to the principles of St. Thomas. For him too there is no forgiveness without contrition, that is, sorrow deriving from the love of God. To this love belongs not only the infused habit; even more indispensable is the act of love, the movement towards God, the *motus in Deum* in the sense of the ancient scholastics. In this respect Cajetan is no less a contritionist than St. Thomas, but on the other hand he is no more so, inasmuch as he likewise teaches that a sorrow which is not yet sufficient for contrition can by the reception of the sacrament be raised to contrition (*Comm. in* III q. 84 a. 1 and 2). So, too, in his requirements for the quality of the love necessary for contrition — love of God beyond all that is lovable *(amor Dei super omne amabile)*, without any closer determination of the motive of the love of God, his position is apparently bounded by the mild outlook of Aquinas *(Opusc. loc. cit.)*.

The contemporary Spanish Thomists departed further than Cajetan from the principles of the master in the place they gave to attrition in the sacrament. Francis Vitoria († 1546) defended the efficacy of the absolution of a sinner who has mere attrition. This was because with Scotus he distinguished two remedies: penance and the keys — *paenitentia et claves* — although in this

[55] Göttler 243.

182

matter he was not consistent.[56] The same tendency is discernible in his pupils Melchior Cano and Dominicus Soto. Cano asserts that the sacrament is efficacious even in the case of conscious attrition, but requires for it, in contrast to Vitoria, an explicit act of love,[57] while Soto with Vitoria demands at least an attrition which is putative contrition — *attritio putata contritio*.[58] Both are at one in teaching the raising of attrition to contrition through absolution in such wise that it is produced simply through the habit of grace without a new act of the will.[59] Thus an essential part of the ancient teaching on justification is allowed to drop out along with the movement of free will. The later Spaniards also took up a divergent position on the question of the antecedent operation of the sacrament, just as they had done in the doctrine of contrition.[60] Down to the time of Cajetan the entire school had maintained firmly that, if not in the majority of cases, at least as often as in the reception of the sacrament itself, forgiveness of sins takes place antecedently by reason of the retroactive power inherent in the sacrament. Capreolus especially (IV *Sent.* d. 22 q. 1 a. 3) and Cajetan (*Opusc.* tom. 1 tr. 18 q. 5 ad 2) sought thus to defend the position of St. Thomas that even then there is a proper sacramental activity. For the Spanish theologians the makeshift theory which is irreconcilable with the strict concept of a sacrament is superfluous, because they, as has already been mentioned, saw in penance or contrition a second way of salvation alongside of the sacrament.[61]

---

[56] *Summa sacramentorum ecclesiae* (Ingolstadt 1580) 21—24.
[57] *Relect. de paen.* (Viennae 1754) VI 1056ff. and I 921f.
[58] IV *Sent.* d. 17 q. 1 a. 2; q. 2 a. 5 and passim.
[59] Cano VI 1056; Soto, *De nat. et grat.* lib. 2 c. 15.
[60] Above 171f.
[61] Soto, IV *Sent.* d. 15 q. 1 a. 6. In taking up his position in regard to the consequent operation of the sacrament in the case of a *confessio informis* Soto asserted that the teaching of the youthful Thomas was untenable. He maintained that in the solitary text in the *Commentary on the Sentences* St. Thomas had simply given the answer that was customary — *cum communi volgo* — and that in the *Summa* (III q. 69 a. 10) he had tacitly corrected himself.

XI. The Scotist Doctrine of Penance

It is remarkable that influential Thomists of the sixteenth century, in their efforts to find a solution of the difficulties which beset the doctrine on penance of their master, drew close in essential points to the conception of Duns Scotus. Therein lies strong evidence for the important points of truth which undoubtedly it possesses. The great opponent of the Angelic Doctor has in fact also manifested his acuteness and the power and independence of his thought in the doctrine of penance, and elaborated a system which for consistency is on a par with that of St. Thomas, and which has powerfully influenced later developments.[62]

In keeping with the whole turn of his mind the penitential doctrine of Scotus has a voluntaristic bias. That is already evident in the concept of sin as the object of penance. Habitual sin — *peccatum habituale* — is the state of soul after the commission of a sinful act; it is nothing more than a relation of reason — *relatio rationis, scilicet ordinatio ad poenam* — that is, ordination to punishment *(reatus)* (*Ox.* IV d. 14 q. 1 n. 7; d. 16 q. 2 n. 18 and *passim*). Consistently then the forgiveness of sins consists in the cancellation of the ordinance. This is also the starting-point for the definition of the concept of penance. God forgives sin in free love for the sake of the merits of Christ. Absolutely speaking, he could do so without the co-operation of the sinner. In fact, however, it is a law of justice deriving from his will that normally every fault is set right through punishment — *omnis culpa ordinatur per poenam* (*Report.* IV d. 14 q. 1 n. 8) — whether it be that punishment is carried out in full, as in the damned, or whether the sinner voluntarily takes punishment on himself in penance. Thus penance is essentially desire of punishment — *volitio poenae*. Here, however, the

---

[62] For what follows, see especially N. Krautwig, *Die Grundlagen der Bußlehre des Duns Skotus* (1938).

emphasis is put not on the exterior punishment, but on distress of mind or sadness — *tristitia* (*Ox*. d. 14 q. 1 n. 11). The essence of penance is expressed in the definition: *paenitere est detestari vel odire peccatum a se commissum vel displicentiam habere de hoc peccato* — penance is a detestation or hatred of sin which one has committed, or displeasure at this sin (ibid. n. 15 and n. 18). There can, therefore, be no question of an externalization of penance in spite of its juridical conception as desire of punishment — *volitio poenae*. Even in Scotus contrition is still the central point, and as the proper cause of interior sadness — *causa propria tristitiae interioris* — it is directly identified with penance (ibid. d. 16 q. 1 n. 6).

In his concept of contrition Scotus holds fast to the traditional idea that its distinguishing feature, as against attrition, is information by grace. But the act of sorrow itself, he teaches against St. Thomas, is the same in both in the natural and moral order of being — *in esse naturae et moris*. Hence the same movement which was previously attrition in the instant of the infusion of grace becomes contrition — *in illo instanti fit contritio* (d. 14 q. 2 n. 14). In these words an essentially higher valuation is formally put on attrition. Whereas before, even in St. Thomas, it is merely a preparation for penance, it now represents a true sorrow, which essentially — apart from information by grace — is the same as the movement of contrition of the earlier scholastics.[63] Even in a state of sin a man is able by his natural powers to make in attrition an act of moral perfection in which all the circumstances required for moral goodness are verified, including in particular the circumstance of finality — *circumstantia finis* — which directs the act to man's last end, so that it is elicited out of the love of God (*Ox*. IV d. 14 q. 1 n. 19; q. 2 n. 14). It is, therefore, wrong to regard the attrition of

---

[63] Cf. the *contritio informis* of Cajetan (above 181 f.). Already before Scotus his fellow Franciscan Richard of Mediavilla had taught the same (IV *Sent*. d. 17 a. 1 q. 3 ad 3). On this see J. Lechner, *Die Sakramentenlehre des Richard von Mediavilla* (1925) 258.

Scotus simply as "a fear sorrow".[64] In reality as compared with his predecessors he assigns a decidedly subordinate position to fear in his teaching on sorrow. It is not enough to fear God: he must also be loved (*Ox. & Report*. IV d. 20 q. un. n. 5). If fear is to have moral value it must not be without reference to God, and it must also in some way be determined by love. If it is sufficiently intense, attrition is a disposition for justification and at the same time merits it *de congruo*. It belongs to God to decide when it has attained this high degree, in order then to elevate it to contrition in the stricter sense through the infusion of grace (*Ox*. IV d. 14 q. 2 n. 14, 15). The acceptance of an "unformed" act of sorrow as a proximate disposition for justification is undeniably a substantial simplification as compared with the traditional scholastic view. But the doctrine of the merit of attrition is admittedly unacceptable, because by it Scotus has apparently in mind a purely natural sorrow unassisted by grace, and thus unconsciously he falls into Semipelagianism.[65]

If justification, then, is merited by sorrow, what significance remains to the sacrament of penance? In direct contrast to St. Thomas, who integrates contrition into the sacrament as an essential part of it, and thus proclaims the sacrament the only way to justification, Scotus announces two different ways of salvation each independent of the other. There is the extra-sacramental one in which attrition merits justification *de congruo,* and there is the sacramental one which produces justification *ex opere operato*. Not that the first way makes the reception of the

---

[64] Thus *e.g.* R. Seeberg, *Die Theologie des Joh. Duns Skotus* (1900) 322, 410.

[65] Further details in N. Krautwig 106—119. He takes up a position against the defence of Scotus by P. Minges, *Die Gnadenlehre des Duns Skotus auf ihren angeblichen Pelagianismus und Semipelagianismus geprüft* (1906). On the other hand J. Auer, *Die Entwicklung der Gnadenlehre in der Hochscholastik,* 1. Teil (1942) 255, 261 agrees with Minges. For a just appreciation of the position of the *Doctor subtilis* in this question it has to be remembered that the doctrine of actual grace and the problems connected with it had at that time received very little clarification, and the later form in which the problem was posed was far from his mind.

sacrament superfluous. For this depends on a positive divine law (*Ox*. IV d. 17 q. un. n. 11) in virtue of which the intention of confessing is an indispensable part of all sincere contrition. But it is not, as in St. Thomas, the sacrament which imparts to contrition power to remit sins through an antecedent operation which is effective even before the reception of the sacrament; on the contrary, the sorrow operates by its own power, which is truly extra-sacramental. Consequently, all that is left as the effect of the sacrament received subsequently is the augmentation of grace (*Ox*. IV d. 14 q. 4 n. 9). The provision of a "double way of justification" for the sinner is a sign of greater mercy than forcing him on to a single way (ibid. n. 6). The sacramental way is essentially easier, because it does not demand a high degree of attrition productive of merit *de congruo*. All that it requires, in addition to the intention of receiving the sacrament of the Church, is the absence of the obstacle — *obex* — of a grave sin. The place of the merit is taken by the power of the sacrament in virtue of a divine pact — *ex pacto Dei*. As no one can know whether he has sorrow sufficient for merit, the way of the sacrament is also more sure, and so every one is obliged to choose this easier and surer way. That is the reason why the Church has made confession a law binding all in spite of the existence of the other method of salvation which is available to the individual (d. 17 q. un. n. 14).

The idea of sorrow as a special means of salvation distinct from the sacrament is also worked out in his determination of the essence of the sacrament of penance. This is not, as in St. Thomas, a combination of personal penitential acts as the matter and of absolution as the form; instead, it consists of the absolution alone: *Paenitentia est absolutio, id est quaedam sententia definitiva absolvens reum* (d. 14 q. 4 n. 3). Sorrow, confession and satisfaction are indeed necessary as a disposition for the reception of the sacrament, but, as is expressly maintained against St. Thomas, in no way its parts — *nullo modo partes eius* (d. 16 q. 1 n. 7). Thus the sacrament and the *opus operatum* as opposed to the personal factor in penance, come into the foreground much more prominently even than in Aquinas. Striking confirmation of this is also seen in the sharp rejection of lay confession (d. 14 q. 4 n. 5). If the one and only sacramental reality is priestly absolution, then confession to one who is not entitled to give absolution cannot in any way be considered as a substitute. Scotus was the first not merely to repudiate all sacramental and obligatory character to lay confession, but also to raise doubts about its moral value in certain circumstances.[66]

In regard to the effect of the sacrament, Scotus sharply rejects the view of the Lombard, and maintains that it is a real cause of justification inasmuch as it confers grace and obtains the forgiveness of sin both as regards guilt and eternal punishment (d. 14 q. 4 n. 9—11). The causality is naturally only instrumental, and of such a kind that the sacrament is not, as in St. Thomas, itself the bearer of divine power, but rather an efficacious disposition necessary by a divine ordinance for the reception of grace: *dispositio efficax necessaria ex statuto divino ad gratiae susceptionem* (d. 19 q. un. n. 23). This does not mean that it produces a disposition in the soul in the sense of the interior penance of St. Thomas or of the *ornatus* of the later Thomists. Scotus rejects such an "intermediate efficiency" in principle (d. 1 q. 5 n. 4—7). The disposition is for him nothing else than the divine pact, in virtue of which God regularly brings about the production of grace on the occasion of the administration of the sacrament, in so far as no obstacle is put in the way. It is, therefore, a purely external disposition (d. 14 q. 4 n. 11; *Report.* IV d. 14 q. 4 n. 14).[67]

On account of the great emphasis placed on the facility of the sacramental way of penance Scotus has for long been accused of laxity both by Catholics and Protestants.[68] Yet a comprehen-

---

[66] Cf. A. Teetaert 429 f.   [67] Krautwig with good reason assimilates the conception to Billot's theory of the intentional causality of the sacraments.
[68] On this see G. Minges, "Die angebliche laxe Reuelehre des Duns Skotus" in *ZkTh* 25 (1901) 231 f.; 240—243; id., *Doctrina philosophica et theologica* (Quaracchi 1930) 636.

sive examination shows that the charge is unjustified. There are indeed resounding utterances such as that for sacramental forgiveness all that is necessary is the intention of receiving the sacrament and the elimination of any obstacle — *obex ;* and that even one with but slight attrition — *parum attritus* — who has some regret for his sin — *aliquam displicentiam de peccato* — receives the effect of the sacrament (d. 14 q. 4 n. 7, 19), and other similar expressions. Yet these occur without exception only when he is explaining the two ways of justification, and contrasting sorrow of high quality which attains to merit *de congruo* with a less perfect, but by no means contemptible, sorrow which is sufficient for the sacrament. The *obex* is simply the lack of attrition, and so the demand for its elimination is identical with a demand for attrition.[69] There is a mass of material in Scotus to prove that even this inferior grade of attrition is nevertheless a genuine and morally valuable sorrow.[70] His attrition should not, therefore, be equated with "imperfect sorrow" in the later meaning of the term, as if he required even less than this for the reception of the sacrament. However, he was in fact one of the first to teach, and to protect by his authority, the sufficiency of "imperfect sorrow" for the forgiveness of sins in the sacrament, although he used a different terminology, and as yet did not clearly delimit his concepts.[71]

It is in this teaching that the chief importance of the Scotist doctrine on penance consists. It gives to the sacrament, as the second way of justification, a field of activity which is its own. It is no longer only exceptionally, as in St. Thomas, but regularly that absolution exercises its full effect. With the clear separation of penance as a sacrament from penance as a virtue, no far-fetched constructions were necessary in order to show how the requirements of the one were verified in the other. In any case, the

---

[69] Thus d. 14 q. 4 n. 7; *Report.* IV d. 14 q. 4 n. 12; d. 19 q. un. n. 29. Cf. also the same conception in St. Thomas in reference to the *fictio* (above 174).
[70] N. Krautwig provides completely satisfactory proof 150—163.
[71] Henry of Ghent († 1293) had preceded him in this, *Quodl.* I q. 32.

penitential teaching of the *Doctor subtilis* commends itself by its simplicity. Admittedly the advantage is dearly bought by the abandonment of a uniform way of justification, and by the degradation of the sacrament to a means of salvation of an inferior kind; for it now becomes a substitute for the perfect contrition which the penitent has failed to provide.[72] Scotus need not have taken this surely very dubious way of justifying the existence of the sacrament if the early-Christian idea had still been alive in his mind that the immediate aim of the sacrament is peace with the Church — *pax ecclesiae*.

In basic questions the Scotist school held fast to the teaching of the master. His influence, however, spread far beyond the narrow bounds of the school. In this connexion mention may be made first of the important Dominican theologian Durandus of S. Porciano († 1334), whose position was likewise strongly opposed to that of St. Thomas. In his concept of sin, too, guilt and punishment coincide (IV *Sent.* d. 17 q. 7 n. 5, 10, 14). Forgiveness of sins is essentially non-liability to punishment (d. 14 q. 5 ad 2). Justification takes place in two simultaneous acts: the movement of free will — contrition — and the infusion of grace. Here contrition is again taken in the traditional sense as a disposition of the soul which begins with attrition and is perfected in contrition, which is prior in the order of nature — *ordine naturae* — to grace. Durandus here distinguishes with all clarity between attrition and contrition, not only by their relation to grace, but also by their motives of fear and love respectively (d. 17 q. 2 n. 5).[73] The importance of the sacrament of penance consists in the fact that in the case of mere attrition the inadequate sorrow is made "sufficient" (d. 18 q. 2 sol.). It is impossible to say whether this is to be taken in the sense of a subjective, actual intensification of sorrow (as in St. Thomas) or as an objective completion of equivalence (as in Scotus).[74]

---

[72] Cf. above 187.
[73] Cf. J. Göttler 141 f.
[74] Göttler, 145, against Morinus, holds that the latter is "... far more probable".

However, Durandus accepts with St. Thomas that normally justification occurs before the reception of the sacrament (d. 17 q. 2 n. 6; d. 18 q. 2 n. 6ff.), without, however, speaking of an antecedent operation of the sacrament. The sacrament of penance is constituted by the visible acts of the penitent (as the matter) and of the absolving priest (as the form). Contrition, not being visible, and satisfaction, which is only performed subsequently, do not belong to the essence of the sacrament (d. 16 q. 1). In the question of the causality of the sacrament Durandus again follows Scotus in teaching an efficacy by way of a pact — *per modum pactionis* (d. 18 q. 2). The sacrament is a mere condition for the bestowal of grace — *conditio sine qua non confertur gratia ;* all causal efficiency — *virtus causativa* — and consequently dispositive causality — *dispositive operari* — and the *ornatus* theory are rejected by him (d. 1 q. 4). All in all, his teaching on penance represents an achievement which, though related both to St. Thomas and Scotus, is thoroughly critical and independent, and it became a stimulating and fruitful source for the later developments.[75]

The teaching on penance of the Nominalists is also determined by that of Scotus. They pressed home the voluntaristic notion of the basic concepts of sin, penance and justification to its final consequences, even though they did not follow Scotus in all questions on the sacrament of penance. On God's side penance is not necessary for the forgiveness of sins according to his *potentia absoluta ;* but according to his *potentia ordinata* it is in fact required by him; and it consists in the *velle vindicare,* which comes to the same thing as detestation of sin as an offence against God. In proportion to its perfection detestation is either contrition or attrition. The latter is defined by Gabriel Biel († 1495) as sorrow for sin which is unformed and insufficient — *informis et insufficiens dolor pro peccato* (IV *Sent.* d. 23 q. 2 a. 1). Biel was the best and most influential exponent of the

---

[75] See Göttler 138—151. A. Michel, *DTC* XII, 1032—1035.

Nominalist system, but in essentials he reproduces the ideas of Ockham († 1349 or 1350) its real founder. The insufficiency of attrition consists either in the weakness of the sorrow or the lack of a really firm purpose of amendment, but especially in the lack of a right intention, inasmuch as the sorrow springs from self-love instead of from the love of God. Neither sorrow nor confession nor satisfaction belong to the essence of the sacrament; they are only necessary conditions for its efficacy. As in Scotus its real essence lies in absolution.[76] As, however, contrition, which is indispensable for justification, by itself already produces forgiveness of sins, absolution is left without any proper content, and so is the sacrament. By a reversion to the conception of the Lombard, it was taught that it remits neither guilt nor eternal punishment, but only indicates the remission which has already occurred, and that it does not confer grace but only increases it.[77] The power of the keys extends to the forgiveness of sin *in foro ecclesiae*.[78] The sacramental character of forgiveness is safeguarded by the desire of the sacrament.[79] Not all the Nominalists, however, hold this contritionism. John Gerson († 1429) for example teaches, in line with St. Thomas, that absolution remits sin even in the case of an *attritus,* inasmuch as by the coming of grace contrition is infused in absolution by the power of the sacrament — *per gratiam advenientem...in ipsa absolutione contritio virtute sacramenti infunditur*.[80] In conclusion we may say that in general the Nominalist teaching on penance kept within the bounds of ecclesiastical orthodoxy, as on the disputed points, including the effect of absolution, no decision of the magisterium was available. Nevertheless, the doctrine of the necessity of sorrow and of the power of the keys is already

---

[76] Ockham, IV *Sent*. d. 8 and 9 *passim;* Biel, IV *Sent*. d. 14 q. 1. 2; d. 18 q. 1. 2.
[77] Ockham, d. 9 Q and T; Biel, d. 14 q. 2; d. 18 q. 1; John Major († 1550), IV *Sent*. d. 16 q. 2; d. 18 q. 1. Moreover, that the Lombard's view was regarded at least as probable also outside the Nominalist school is clear from the later Pope Adrian VI († 1523), *Quodl.* 5 a. 3.
[78] Biel, d. 14 q. 2 concl. 5.   [79] Ockham, d. 9 Q; Biel, d. 18 q. 1 a. 2; q. 2 a. 2.
[80] *Notabile de forma absolvendi a peccatis.* Du Pin II 482. On the whole question see

manifestly endangered as a result of over-emphasis of the principle of the absolute freedom of God.

A general survey of the development since St. Thomas Aquinas justifies two conclusions: 1. The main proposition of Aquinas, that the sacrament as such effects the forgiveness of sins, has prevailed almost universally. Scotus and his followers stress the efficacy of the sacrament even more strongly than St. Thomas. 2. On the question of the relation of the sacrament to the ancient teaching on justification opinions are divided. The Thomists hold fast to the teaching of a single way of justification, as they consider that the sacrament is an indispensable element in the process of justification, and they go to great pains to justify their conception by means of complicated theories. Other theologians on the other hand distinguish two different ways, and regard the sacrament as important only inasmuch as it represents the easier way. At the same time attrition is given greater prominence, as it is considered a sufficient disposition for the easier way. Thus the manifest tendency of the development is to move away from St. Thomas, as is especially clear from the attitude of the leading Spanish Thomists in the sixteenth century. It is obvious that the tension surrounding these problems was likely to give a handle to the Reformers in their attack on the whole principle of the sacrament.

C. Feckes, *Die Rechtfertigungslehre des Gabriel Biel* (1925), especially 59—81, 107 ff.; 136 ff.; A. Michel, *DTC* 1035—1042.

Chapter Four

TRIDENTINE AND POST-TRIDENTINE

TEACHING ON PENANCE

LITERATURE: A.Michel, *DTC* XII 1050—1127. A.Beugnet, "Attrition" in *DTC* I 2235—2262. F. Cavallera, "Le décret du Concile de Trente sur la pénitence et l'extrême onction" in *BLE* (1932) 73—95, 114—140; (1938) 3—79. J. Périnelle (above 155). P. Galtier, "Amour de Dieu et attrition" in *Gr* 9 (1928) 373—416. H. Schauerte, *Die Bußlehre des Johannes Eck* (1919). A. Arndt, *Die unvollkommene Reue nach den Lehrbestimmungen des Trienter Konzils* (1912). M. Premm, *Das tridentinische "diligere incipiunt"* (Graz 1925). F. Diekamp, "Melchioris Cani de contritione et attritione doctrina" in *Xenia Thomistica* 3 (Rome 1925) 423—440. V. Heynck, "Die Stellung des Konzilstheologen Andreas de Vega O.F.M. zur Furchtreue" in *Franzisk. Studien* (1938) 301—330. Id., "Untersuchungen über die Reuelehre der tridentinischen Zeit" ibid. (1942) 25—44; (1943) 53—73. I.Döllinger and H. Reusch, *Geschichte der Moralstreitigkeiten in der röm.-kath. Kirche seit dem 16. Jahrh.* I (1889). V. Heynck, "Contritio vera. Zur Kontroverse über den Begriff der contritio vera auf der Bologneser Tagung des Trienter Konzils" in *Franzisk. Studien,* 33 (1951) 137—179. Id., "Zum Problem der unvollkommenen Reue auf dem Konzil von Trient" in G. Schreiber, *Das Weltkonzil von Trient,* I 231—280 (Freiburg im Br. 1951). L. Ceyssens, "L'origine du décret du Saint-Office concernant l'attrition" in *EThL* 25 (1949) 83—91. J. Etienne, "Ruard Tapper, interprète catholique de la pensée protestante sur le sacrement de pénitence" in *RHE* 49 (1954) 770—807. E. F. Latko, "Trent and Auricular Confession" in *Franciscan Studies* 14 (1954) 4—33. *Concilium Tridentinum,* ed. Societas Goerresiana, T. VI and VII (Freiburg im Br. 1950 and 1961). P. Anciaux, "Paenitentia est sacramentalis quia et in quantum est actus ecclesiae" in *Collect. Mechlin.* 27 (1957) 162—166. B. Poschmann, "Die innere Struktur des Bußsakramentes" in *MThZ* 1 (1950) 12—30. K. Rahner, *Kirche und Sakramente* (Freiburg im Br. 1961). F. Charrière, "Le pouvoir d'ordre et le pouvoir de juridiction dans le sacrement de pénitence" in *DTh* 23 (1945) 191—213. E. Lopez-Doriga, "Die Natur der Jurisdiction im Bußsakrament" in *ZkTh* 82 (1960) 385—427. K. Mörsdorf, "Der Rechtscharakter der iurisdictio fori interni" in *MThZ* 8 (1957) 168—173. J. Ternus, "Die sakramentale Lossprechung als richterlicher Akt" in *ZkTh* 71 (1949) 214—230. P. De Letter, "Two concepts of Attrition and Contrition" in *TS* 11 (1950) 4—33.

194

RIGHT from the beginning of the speculative treatment of the sacrament of penance sharply contrasting opinions had cropped up, but, generally speaking, up to the Council of Trent the teaching authority of the Church had allowed free rein to the development of theological doctrine and only intervened when dogmatic truths were at stake. One of the first cases of this kind was the condemnation of Abelard by the Synod of Sens (1140) on account of his denial of the power of the keys.[1] Much more destructive was the attitude of Wyclif in the fourteenth century who, along with his rejection in principle of external ecclesiastical authority, asserted that priestly absolution was an abuse and "all outward confession superfluous and useless" (Denz. 587). Hus was also accused of similar teaching (Denz. 670, 671). In 1478 Sixtus IV censured some propositions of the Spanish theologian Peter Martinez de Osma who, likewise ruling out the power of the keys, held that the guilt and punishment of mortal sins are forgiven by contrition alone, based confession only on ecclesiastical and not divine law, and averred that the sacrament of penance was simply a *sacramentum naturae* (Denz. 724 to 733).

A positive statement of the magisterium is found in the *Decretum pro Armenis* of Eugenius IV of the year 1439 (Denz. 699). The text concerning the sacrament of penance is taken almost verbally from the opusculum of St. Thomas *De fidei articulis et septem sacramentis*. Contrition, confession and satisfaction are the *quasi materia;* the words of absolution, the form; and the forgiveness of sins, the effect. With its decisions couched in general terms, leaving room for the conflicting opinions of the schools, the decree did not contribute to further dogmatic development. Its importance lay in its authoritative witness to

---

[1] See above 159.

the chief points of ecclesiastical teaching on penance in the century before the Reformation.

The Reformers were compelled by the inner logic of their system to reject the sacrament of penance. Given their concept of sin as a complete corruption of human nature and an annihilation of free will, their doctrine of justification by faith alone, and their basic rejection of all priestly power, no room was left either for "the virtue of penance" or for the sacrament of penance, for the personal or for the ecclesiastical factor. It was, therefore, not just chance that the Reformation had its historic starting-point in the attack on indulgences, which were part of the ecclesiastical institution of penance, and that a series of theses nailed up by Luther on 31 October, 1517, indirectly concerned the doctrine of penance. The first official condemnation by the Bull *Exsurge Domine* of Leo X in the year 1520 censured forty-one propositions taken from Luther's teaching, of which no fewer than ten were directly connected with penance (Denz. 745—754). In essentials these already contained the points with which the Council of Trent had later to deal. It was no longer merely a matter of questions debated in the schools, but of the substance of the doctrine of penance. Scholastic opinions did, however, continue to play a part to the extent that their mutual opposition provided welcome material for the polemic of the innovators; on the other hand, new light was thrown on their soundness or unsoundness by the denials of the heretics. Undoubtedly the Council saw itself confronted in penance by a task of the greatest moment, both as regards the dogmatic decisions which had to be taken and the attitude it was to adopt towards questions still open to discussion.

XIII. The Council of Trent

The Council was occupied with penance in its second period during the months of October and November, 1551. Among the outstanding theologians who took part in the deliberations

196

were Melchior Cano, the Jesuits Lainez and Salmeron, and the Netherlanders Tapper and Sonnius. The decrees, drawn up in nine chapters and fifteen canons, contained the definitive response to twelve articles compiled from the writings of the Reformers which had been submitted to the Council for examination.[2]

The first two chapters and the first three canons strongly emphasize the sacramental character of penance and its distinction from baptism. It is truly and properly a sacrament — *vere et proprie sacramentum* (can. 1). Jn 20:22f. is to be understood of the power of remitting and retaining sins in the sacrament of penance — *de potestate remittendi et retinendi peccata in sacramento paenitentiae,* and is not to be distorted to signify the authority of preaching the Gospel — *auctoritatem praedicandi evangelium* (can. 3). It was necessary to emphasize the distinction from baptism, because the Reformers maintained that baptism was itself properly penance, and in subsequent penance they saw only a return to baptism — *regressus ad baptismum* — consisting in a revival of faith. In regard to the matter and form and to the effect of penance (c. 3 and can. 4) the Council followed the *Decretum pro Armenis* with its essentially Thomist position. The Scotist view, represented principally by Tapper, was taken account of in connexion with the form by the insertion of the words: *forma, in qua praecipue ipsius (paenitentiae) vis sita est* — the form, in which the efficacy of penance principally consists — and again in connexion with the matter by the limiting term *quasi-materia,* and also by the assertion that contrition, confession and satisfaction are parts of penance in so far as "they are requisite for the integrity of the sacrament and for full and perfect remission of sins". The Council makes brief mention of reconciliation with God as the effect; this clearly coincides with the forgiveness of sin itself. The idea that absolution has a merely declarative significance is definitively repudiated. The question of the "inter-

---

[2] Printed by A. Theiner, *Acta genuina concilii Tridentini* (1874) I 531 f.

mediate effect" — the *res et sacramentum* — which with its involved theories had occupied theology for centuries no longer finds mention.

Among the most important points of doctrine on the sacrament of penance is contrition, which was treated in the fourth chapter. Here too it is the aim of the Council simply to establish the teaching of the Church against the heretics without entering into the controversies debated in the schools. Luther had rejected Catholic teaching on contrition on the grounds that it attributed the forgiveness of sins to personal merit instead of to the merits of Christ, and that fear of punishment on which contrition is based does not produce a real conversion from sin. It was this point of view which dictated his attack in particular against "the fictitious attrition of the Papists".[3] The Council, therefore, felt itself obliged to define in greater detail the nature of contrition and especially of attrition, and to defend them against misrepresentation. In doing this it uses the word *contritio* for sorrow in general, of which *attritio,* or *contritio imperfecta,* represents a particular kind. It is required by the nature of contrition, and therefore also of the imperfect kind, that it be sorrow of soul, and detestation of the sin which has been committed, and that it include not only cessation from sin and the purpose and beginning of a new life, but also hatred of the old one. "Sometimes", the decree continues, "contrition is made perfect by charity", and then it brings about reconciliation with God before the actual reception of the sacrament, in so far as it includes the *votum sacramenti.* Imperfect sorrow, on the other hand, has for its motive "the gravity, multitude and disgracefulness of sins, the loss of eternal happiness and the incurring of eternal damnation" (can. 5). Hope of the divine mercy is joined to fear, as also is "a beginning of the love of God", as is taught in the sixth chapter of the decree on justification (Denz. 798). So far then is the sorrow called attrition from "making a man a

[3] Cf. *De captiv. Babyl.,* Luthers Werke, Weimar edition VI, 544f.

hypocrite and more of a sinner" that it is "a gift of God and an impulse of the Holy Spirit", and although without the sacrament it cannot justify the sinner, yet "it disposes him for the reception of the grace of God in the sacrament" (c. 4).

This is the first time that the Church makes use of the theological term "attrition" in an official decision. The occasion was the teaching of Luther. The Council defines it as a true, though imperfect, sorrow *(non caritate perfecta)*. There is no longer mention of absence of information by grace as its distinctive characteristic. But it is also not said that love is entirely absent from it. The phrasing provided in the first draft of the chapter to the effect that attrition proceeds solely from shame or fear of hell *(timor servilis)*[4] was altered in the final version to read that this was ordinarily — *communiter* — the case. To what extent the requisite hatred of sin includes the love of God, and conversely in what the perfection of love consists which makes contrition perfect, was not decided. Similarly left open by the fathers of the Council after discussion was the disputed question whether attrition in conjunction with the sacrament is by itself sufficient, or whether contrition must first be produced through the grace of absolution. The words which stood in the first draft: *sufficere ad sacramenti huius constitutionem* were replaced by the more general assertions: *viam ad iustitiam parat* and *ad Dei gratiam disponit* respectively. These words could apply either to an immediate or to a remote disposition. In these circumstances it is waste of effort to claim the support of the Council which avoided a decision, either for the Thomist or the Scotist theory, for contritionism or attritionism, as has constantly happened. It is true, however, that by treating it as possessing equal authority with the Thomist opinion at a time when this possessed the authority of tradition, the Council did to this extent give a further impetus to the Scotist opinion, which commended itself by its greater clarity and simplicity. Now that it was free from dogmatic

4 Theiner I 584.

objections attritionism could prevail all the more victoriously against the complexity of the opposite view.[5]

Chapter five and canons 6—8 deal with confession against the Reformers. These did not reject it directly,[6] but by their denial of the priestly power of the keys deprived it of its real meaning. The necessity of confession and its divine institution are proved from the power of the keys which constitute the priests judges, because without knowledge of the case — *incognita causa* — they cannot exercise the office of judge. All mortal sins, including secret ones, are obligatory matter for confession, along with the circumstances which alter the species of a sin. Venial sins can be expiated by the use of other remedies, even though confession of them is also salutary. Special emphasis is laid on the justification and necessity of secret confession, which has been in use in the Church from the beginning, and was not first introduced by the fourth Lateran Council as some calumniously claimed. In contrast with the first draft which intended to assert plainly that secret confession too is of divine institution, the Council was content to repudiate the claim that the mode of confessing secretly to a priest alone is foreign to the institution and command of Christ — *modum secrete confitendi soli sacerdoti... alienum esse ab institutione et mandato Christi* (can. 6). Consequently it attributes the character of a divine law only to the fact of confession; the Church remains free to determine its

---

[5] It is only from this point of view that it is possible to agree with P. Galtier (*Gr* 9 [1928] 411) that the Council tacitly endorsed attritionism by refusing to define the necessity of a sorrow based on love. On the abortive attempt of J. Périnelle to prove that the Council required an *amor benevolentiae* for attrition see M. Premm 61 and Galtier, ibid. 398.

[6] Luther still recommended it in the *De captiv. Babyl.* (Werke VI 546) as a practice which "is necessary and ordered by God". However, under the pressure of polemic he found himself driven to an ever more intensive attack on ecclesiastical confessional procedure. Calvin retained it as a primitive and useful institution, which, however, is not of divine but of purely ecclesiastical institution and is not obligatory on anyone. Like Luther he reviled the obligatory confession of "the Papists" as mental torture (*Instit. rel. christ.* III c. 4).

form.[7] In this manner the dogma leaves room for the development of the procedure of penance, which was established by later research.

The sixth chapter, along with canons 9 and 10 is concerned with the minister of the sacrament and with absolution. In accordance with Mt 18:18 and Jn 20:23 only bishops and priests, and not all the faithful indiscriminately, are bearers of the power of the keys. Even priests in a state of mortal sin remain in possession of it by reason of ordination. Absolution is a judicial act, not a mere ministry of pronouncing and declaring that sins are remitted to one who confesses, provided he believes that he is absolved — *nudum ministerium pronuntiandi et declarandi, remissa esse peccata, modo tantum credat se esse absolutum* (can. 9). As judicial power only extends to one's subjects, ordinary or subdelegated jurisdiction is necessary for valid absolution. In the interest of ecclesiastical discipline the pope and bishops can reserve to themselves the absolution of particularly grave sins (c. 7). The denial of this right of reservation is condemned with an anathema. Fundamental to the teaching on satisfaction, which is contained in the last two chapters, 8 and 9, and in canons 12—15, is the assertion, already defined in Sess. VI c. 14 and can. 30, that the entire temporal punishment is not always remitted along with the guilt, as it is in baptism. Besides its retributory purpose satisfaction has at the same time an educative and a medicinal value. It does not injure faith in the power of the redemptive work of Christ because it derives all its power from him. Priests have the strict obligation of imposing a penance corresponding to the gravity of the sin because binding as well as loosing belongs to the power of the keys. In addition to penances voluntarily undertaken and those imposed by a priest, patient endurance of sufferings inflicted by God in this life is also reckoned as satisfaction, because in this way in particular one's love of God is manifested.

[7] Cf. the proceedings of the Council I 537 f. 562—580.

Summing up, we may conclude that the teaching on penance of the Council remains within the bounds of theology up to its time. The dogmatic decisions are the Catholic answer to the new attacks on the sacrament of penance which were made by the Reformers on the basis of their anti-ecclesiastical principles. The primary importance of the Council for the development of dogma consists in the fact that it sanctioned definitively the teaching which had been inaugurated by St. Thomas, and had soon become general, that the sacrament is the efficient cause of the forgiveness of sins. Moreover it swept away for ever the theory of the merely declarative character of absolution. Admittedly this does not mean that a complete solution had as yet been found of the chief problem at which theology had been labouring since the early scholastic period, that of the relation of the subjective and personal factor to the objective and ecclesiastical one in the production of the forgiveness of sins. The imminent outbreak of the controversy on contritionism and attritionism is evidence of this.

XIV. POST-TRIDENTINE THEOLOGY

THE TEACHING on penance of the theologians during the Reformation period was naturally directed for the most part towards the repulse of the attacks of the heretics. Among the defenders of the Catholic doctrine before and during the Council mention may be made of Cardinal Cajetan, Johannes Eck, John Fisher Bishop of Rochester, Melchior Cano, Ruard Tapper, Andreas Vega, Petrus Soto and Cardinal Hosius. The classical and normative exposition and justification of Catholic teaching was provided by St. Robert Bellarmine in his great work *Disputationes de controversiis christianae fidei adversus huius temporis haereticos* (3 vols. Ingolstadt 1586/93). As controversial theology had also to deal with the origin of ecclesiastical teaching and institutions it led to the historical treatment of the sacrament of penance. In this field the Oratorian Johannes Morinus was a pioneer with his standard work *Commentarius historicus de disciplina in administratione sacramenti paenitentiae tredecim primis saeculis observata* (Paris 1651). By reason of the new sources that it opened up, the mass of material exploited, and its astonishingly thorough historical criticism, the book is still indispensable for research on penance. To the creators of historical and positive dogmatic theology also belong the Oratorian Ludovicus Thomassinus (*Vetus et nova Ecclesiae disciplina*, 3 vols. Paris 1678/79) and the Jesuits Jacob Sirmond (*Historia paenitentiae publicae*, Paris 1651) and Dionysius Petavius (*De paenitentiae vetere in Ecclesia ratione*, 1622).

As compared with this fundamental historical research, the comprehensive treatises of speculative theology, which in the sixteenth century was flowering anew, are of less importance. Dogma had been settled at Trent, and as a result theological debate was confined to questions of secondary rank. In regard to the constitution of the sacrament, where the conciliar phrase *quasi-materia* in itself left room also for the Scotist view, the Thomist conception prevailed more and more. On the other hand the Thomist teaching on the *confessio informis*[8] was gradually allowed to lapse, although still supported by Cajetan, John of St. Thomas († 1644) and the Salmanticenses. In recent times too the attempt to revive it made by Cardinal Billot[9] as a consequence of his theory of the intentional causality of the sacraments has found small support.[10]

The main interest of the post-Tridentine theology of penance was centred on the doctrine of contrition. In dealing with this subject the Council had refrained from intervening in theological disputes by formulating its doctrine in general terms. The Thomists maintained, and still maintain to this day, that attrition is only a remote disposition for justification, and that this only takes place when true contrition is produced in the sinner through the grace of the sacrament. Some, however, such as Morinus

---

[8] Above 177 and 183 n. 61.
[9] *De ecclesiae sacramentis* II[3] (Rome 1901) Thes. 16.
[10] Cf. P. Galtier, *De paenitentia* (Rome 1956) 363.

(1. 8 c. 4) and the Augustinian Berti (*De theol. disciplinis* 1. 54 c. 6), went further, and required even for perfect contrition (*contritionem caritate perfectam,* Conc. Trid. sess. XIV c. 4, Denz. 898) a special degree of intensity if it is to bring about justification before the reception of the sacrament; it is to be a *contritio intensa,* and not *remissa.* Estius (IV *Sent.* d. 17, 2) would only admit an extra-sacramental justification in the case of one at the point of death. Conversely, others sought to extend the concept of perfect contrition which of itself produces justification beyond the limits of the strict motive of charity. They wished to attribute this effect to sorrow conceived from less high motives which included considerations of self-interest, in so far as they belonged to virtues which had God alone as the *terminus* of their acts. Such are the motives of justice, of gratitude, of the desire of the happiness which comes from the possession of God. This view was advocated especially by the Scotists; if not actually approved by Suarez (*De paen.* disp. 4 sect. 2 n. 6) and de Lugo (*De paen.* disp. 5 sect. 1 n. 4), it was at least recognized as not improbable. In more recent times H. Hurter among others (*Theologiae dogm. compendium* III [1878] n. 570) has argued in favour of it, and in our judgement it is also in harmony with the old scholastic position.[11]

The dispute about the quality of the imperfect contrition requisite for the sacrament raged more violently than that concerning the nature of the perfect contrition necessary for extra-sacramental forgiveness of sins. Baius and the Jansenists consistently with their principle of the twofold love, of charity and cupidity, flatly rejected sorrow motivated by fear as immoral, with the result that a succession of their propositions was condemned by the popes.[12] Their position was directly opposed to the Council of Trent (Denz. 898, 915). The theories of Catholic theologians divide naturally into two groups — allowing for shades of difference between individuals here and there — which

---

[11] Cf. above 174 n. 39. [12] Denz. 1038, 1297, 1304, 1305, 1394, 1411, 1412, 1523—1525.

in the seventeenth and eighteenth centuries were known as contritionists and attritionists. The former required in one form or another, even in the imperfect sorrow which sufficed for the sacrament, a beginning of the love of charity — *amor caritatis* — appealing to the Tridentine phrase *diligere incipiunt* (Sess. 6 c. 6, Denz. 798), while the latter were more or less radically opposed to this demand.[13]

The rigorist movement already mentioned, which included Morinus and Berti, belonged to the contritionists. In points of detail there was considerable divergence concerning the love which was postulated for imperfect sorrow. The Oratorian Juénin, whose work *Institutiones theologicae* was put on the Index by Clement XI in 1708, demanded a remiss or less intense charity — *caritas remissa* — which, however, had to be a love of God above all things (ibid. *De paen.* q. 3 c. 4 a. 2 n. 2). Palla-vicini[14] and after him Bossuet,[15] on the other hand, preferred to see the imperfect element not in any less intensity of the sorrow but in the fact that it was not a love of God above all things. This was an untenable view, because a sorrow which is not appreciatively supreme — *appreciative summa* — cannot be re-garded as sincere or as compatible with true love of God. In the eighteenth century the leading Thomist Billuart[16] sought another solution. For imperfect sorrow he does not require an act of charity in however weak a degree, but one of the love of benevo-lence — *amor Dei benevolus.* As contrasted with charity this act lacks the element of reciprocity of friendship, which, Billuart holds, is required to make contrition perfect. The distinction is impracticable and remains a purely verbal one. Every act of the love of benevolence on the part of a man necessarily introduces

---

[13] Cf. I. Döllinger and H. Reusch I 67 ff., 273 ff. Contritionism of this kind is there-fore to be distinguished from the pre-Tridentine contritionism in the sense of the Lombard for whom there was no question at all of imperfect contrition as a sacramental factor.

[14] *Assert. theolog.* lib. VII, *De sacr. paenit.* c. 12.

[15] *De doctrina concilii Tridentini circa dilectionem in paenitentiam requisitam* c. 6.

[16] *Tract. de sacr. paen.* diss. 4 a. 7.

the love of friendship as God's answer; indeed in reality God's love already precedes our love and makes it possible.[17] Even to-day Billuart's theory has still a following in Thomist circles. F. Diekamp, for example, is firmly in favour of it.[18] J. Périnelle has, unsuccessfully, attempted to find a new basis for it in St. Thomas and in the acts of the Council of Trent published by the Görres-Gesellschaft.[19]

We may now turn to the attritionists. In 1667 Alexander VII characterized the attrition which they taught by the fact that it is conceived from the fear of hell, excludes the will of sinning, includes the hope of pardon and does not require any act of the love of God — *concipitur ex metu gehennae, excludens voluntatem peccandi, cum spe veniae... aliquem actum dilectionis Dei... negantibus* (Denz. 1146). A large number of theologians accordingly abstained completely from mentioning love in defining the nature of attrition.[20] Others did not go so far, and while excluding the love of charity — *amor caritatis* — required for attrition a real movement towards God consisting in a love of concupiscence or hope — *amor concupiscentiae vel spei*. This act does not seek God for his own sake, yet it is in fact directed towards him.[21] The Tridentine requirement of "initial love" was regarded as fulfilled by this love which is found in hope.[22] The doctrine defended by the Salmanticenses[23] among others represents a kind of conciliation of this view with the one first mentioned. It likewise requires the love of hope, but holds that this is contained virtually or implicitly, without need of addition, in

---

[17] Cf. A. Beugnet, *DTC* I 2253.

[18] *Kath. Dogmatik* III[6] (1932) 267—275.

[19] *L'attrition d'après le concile de Trente* (1927). On this see P. Galtier, *Gr* 9 (1928) 373—416.

[20] Thus Suarez, *l. c.* disp. 20 sect. 1; de Lugo, *l. c.* disp. 5 sect. 9.

[21] Thus Tournely († 1729), *De Sacr. paen.* q. 5 a. 3, and the Wirceburgenses (1766—1771), *De sacr. paen.* disp. 2 c. 3 a. 3—4.

[22] Périnelle's efforts to interpret the *diligere incipiunt* in the sense of *amor benevolentiae* must be regarded as a failure. See P. Galtier, art. cit. 398 and especially M. Premm 60 ff.

[23] *Curs. theol.* X *De paen.* disp. 7 dub. 1 n. 39—57.

every act of attrition, so that it need not be elicited explicitly. At a later period Alphonsus Liguori[24] made himself the special champion of this opinion, and to-day it may be regarded as the common opinion — *sententia communis*.[25] The dispute concerning the doctrine of contrition came to a head about the middle of the seventeenth century, when it finally assumed forms which caused Pope Alexander VII by the decree of 5 May, 1667, (Denz. 1146) strictly to prohibit both parties from indulging in mutual defamation by theological censures or other offensive imputations until such time as some decision on the question should be given by the Holy See.

The decree is still in force to-day. If attritionism could already be described by Alexander as the more common opinion in his day — *sententia hodie communior* — it is now much more prevalent in theology and in the practice of the Church. Yet the contritionism of the small minority is not in any way opposed to the faith. In its favour it can claim the weight of tradition, which regards love, considered as a movement towards God, as an indispensable factor in justification. Against it the objection is raised that the initial love which it demands necessarily produces forgiveness before absolution, and thus it is a return to the old contritionism of the Lombard, in which the power of absolution to forgive sins practically never comes into operation.

---

[24] *Theologia moralis* lib. 6 n. 442.

[25] Cf. P. Galtier, art. cit. 376 and *De paenitentia* (1956) 354—359. Whatever position be adopted in regard to further points of detail, sincere attrition which is required for the sacrament must always be a real turning away from sin and a true conversion to God. Even attrition motivated by fear must be joined to a firm resolution of fulfilling all God's commandments including that of loving God. A "gallows-repentance", springing from purely servile fear — *timor serviliter servilis* — which only ceases from doing evil but not from interior attachment to it, is rejected by all theologians as immoral, as it is the repentance of the damned — *paenitentia damnatorum*. It is, therefore, an unjust and offensive imputation on A. von Harnack's part when he pillories Catholic teaching on attrition as a "withering up of morality" (*Dogmengesch.* III³ 426ff., Eng. tr. VI 251 n. 6). Cf. J. Mausbach, "Historisches und Apologetisches zur scholastischen Reuelehre" in *Katholik* (1897) I 56ff.

That being admitted, is it not, on the other hand, also difficult to accept, quite apart from tradition, that the sacrament was only instituted as an emergency substitute for the quality of contrition which is intrinsically necessary for justification, or as a compensation for the defective disposition, and that where there is perfect repentance it loses its essential significance?[26] Undoubtedly, both schools of thought have their difficulties, and discussion has arrived at a hopeless impasse, as is proved by its history over four centuries. The reason for this is its false starting-point. This goes back to the early middle ages, and consists in a misunderstanding of the immediate formal effect of the sacrament of penance. If St. Thomas, in line with the conception of the early Church had assigned reconciliation with the Church as the *res et sacramentum* of penance instead of *paenitentia interior,* the development of the doctrine of penance would have taken another road. If the *pax ecclesiae* is its immediate end, and the indispensable means for reconciliation with God, the sacrament would retain its irreplaceable significance even in the case of perfect contrition, and it would not have been necessary to have recourse to imperfect contrition in order to vindicate its right to existence. There would have been even less cause for exaggerating the requirements for the perfect contrition which produces justification extra-sacramentally. Such exaggeration is contrary to St. Thomas and the scholastics, and has made perfect contrition appear quite beyond the reach of ordinary Christian people. Moreover, a return to the ancient conception would have made possible a reconciliation between the parties to the dispute. This is even truer today when a stricter form of attritionism is prevalent, and the high qualities which it demands even of imperfect sorrow do not in reality fall below the minimum which Thomas consistently requires for contrition.[27]

The opposition that still exists in connexion with the doctrine

[26] Cf. P. de Vooght, *EThL* 7 (1930) 664f., 673.
[27] Cf. above 174 n. 39; de Vooght, art. cit. (1928) 255f., (1930) 674.

of contrition is the last offshoot of the problem which has dominated the entire history of the sacrament of penance. This problem is the determination of the rôles of the subjective and personal factor and the objective and ecclesiastical factor in penance.

Chapter Five

INDULGENCES

LITERATURE: R. Bellarmine, *De indulgentiis libri duo* (Op. omn. 7 [Paris 1873]). Eus. Amort, *De Origine, progressu, valore ac fructu indulgentiarum* (Aug. Vindel. 1735). P. Collet, *De Indulgentiis,* Migne, Theol. curs. compl. t. 18. A. M. Lépicier, *Les indulgences, leur origine, leur nature, leur développement,* 2 vols (Paris 1904). H. C. Lea, *Confession and Indulgences* III (Philadelphia 1896). Th. Brieger, *REPTh* IX (1897) 76—94. A. Boudinhon, "Sur l'histoire des indulgences" in *RHLR* 3 (1898) 435—455. M. Koeniger, *Ursprung des Ablasses,* Festg. f. A. Knöpfler (1909). J. Hilgers, *Die kath. Lehre von den Ablässen und deren geschichtl. Entwicklung* (1914). E. Göller, *Der Ausbruch der Reformation u. die spätmittelalterl. Ablaßpraxis* (1917). N. Paulus, *Geschichte des Ablasses im Mittelalter,* 3 vols. (1922/23). Et. Magnin, "Indulgences" in *DTC* VII 1594ff. B. Poschmann, *Der Ablaß im Licht der Buß-geschichte* (1948). F. Beringer - J. Hilgers - P. A. Steiner, *Die Ablässe, ihr Wesen und Gebrauch* (Paderborn 1921/22[15]). Seraphinus De Angelis, *De Indulgentiis, Tractatus quoad earum naturam et usum* (Città del Vaticano 1950[2]). K. Rahner, "Bemerkungen zur Theologie des Ablasses" in *ZkTh* 71 (1949) 481—490 = *Schriften zur Theologie* II (Einsiedeln 1955) 185—210. Id., "Ablaß" in *LThK*[2] I (1957) 46—53. F. Courtney, "New Explanations of Indulgences" in *CR* 44 (1959) 464—479. P. Galtier, "Les indulgences, origine et nature" in *Gr* 31 (1950) 258—274. Id., *De paenitentia,* (Rome 1956) 517—546. H. Karpp, "Buße u. Ablaß im Altertum und MA" in *ThR,* NF 21 (1953) 121—136. E. Campbell, *Indulgences* (Ottawa 1953). K. Frings, *Der Ablaß nach der Lehre des Alexanders von Hales und der Summa Halensis* in Miscell. Martin Grabmann (Munich 1959) 31—54.

XV. The Growth of Indulgences

ALTHOUGH not a component part of the sacrament of penance an indulgence stands in the closest connexion with it. In its narrower sense it is an authoritative remission of temporal

210

punishment, valid before God, which the Church grants outside the sacrament after the guilt of sin has already been forgiven (cf. CIC can. 911). The Latin word *indulgentia,* originally synonymous with *remissio, relaxatio, absolutio,* only became fixed as the specific term for an indulgence in the thirteenth century. In the narrower sense of the definition given an indulgence, unlike the sacrament, is not of divine institution, but an ecclesiastical usage which grew out of the penitential procedure in a later stage of its development. Historical research, for which we are chiefly indebted to the standard work of N. Paulus, has shown that indulgences first appeared in the eleventh century.

A preliminary condition for their rise was the early medieval tariff penance. The scale of the penances prescribed for individual offences was so high that it was difficult, and often indeed impossible, to complete them. Redemptions were first of all employed by way of relief.[1] In principle it was maintained that these were of equal value with the penitential works for which they were substituted. In fact, however, their effect was an alleviation of penance, although, admittedly, this only extended to ecclesiastical penitential requirements, as the Church did not guarantee that they had the same atoning power in the sight of God. Another way of easing for a sinner the payment of his debt of penance was the ancient one of the support of the Church, priests and people, through intercessory prayers and shared penance. Faith in the efficacy of such vicarious penance was especially manifested by the martyrs' privilege which was in operation here and there in the early Church. This meant that in consideration of the presumed efficacy of a martyr's intercession with God a sinner was excused part of his ecclesiastical penance.[2] In the assistance given a penitent by the entire

---

[1] Cf. above 127 f., 134, 150 ff.
[2] Above 75 ff. The practice was not an indulgence in the proper sense in spite of the striking resemblance to one, because it was not the authority of the Church which offered a guarantee of divine forgiveness but that of individual martyrs who pledged themselves to make intercession with God.

congregation lay the chief significance of public penance.[3] The transition to private penance in the early middle ages naturally made no difference to faith in the power of intercessory prayer and shared penance; the only alteration was that the assistance took on a more private character. Most abundant evidence for this is to be found not only in the penitentials and instructions for confession, but also in other religious literature. The time for rendering this assistance was before reconciliation while as yet this was only given after the completion of penance. When, however, about the year 1000 reconciliation came to be given immediately after confession, and the sinner had still to discharge the whole burden of satisfaction after the conclusion of the ecclesiastical procedure, the Church had obviously now to support him with her aid "outside the sacrament" in the same way as formerly she had done in the course of the procedure. This she did, apart from the forms of intercession which were in general use, in particular by the bestowal of "absolutions". In these we see the antecedents of indulgences.

Originally, as recurring linguistic usage attests from the time of Gregory I, an absolution signified an intercessory prayer for the remission of sins. It was one pronounced by a holder of the apostolic power of the keys, and consequently it was regarded as specially efficacious.[4] Popes and bishops made abundant use of them, either on request or spontaneously in the form of blessings both in private letters and official documents, in appeals for contributions to good causes (e.g. the building of churches and taking part in war against the enemies of the Church) and on other occasions. Absolutions were also often granted to those who were seriously ill. The special power of the prayer of the bishops was based on their official position as the possessors of the power of loosing. For this reason such prayer contained a certain objective guarantee of being heard

[3] Tertullian, De paen. 10, 5f.; Ambrose, De paen. 1, 15, 80; 2, 10, 92; Jerome, Dial. c. Lucif. 5; Augustine, Serm. 392, 2. Cf. B. Poschmann, Der Ablaß 7 ff.
[4] Copious instances in N. Paulus I 39—119; cf. Poschmann 15—36.

independent of the personal character of its author. This explains why gradually absolutions took on a more or less authoritative form,[5] and for the most part contained an express appeal to the power of binding and loosing. It made no essential difference whether they were formulated in deprecative or indicative terms.

Precisely however because of the authoritative form in which they were couched, absolutions were also incorporated into the reconciliation rite of the penitential liturgy from the tenth century onwards. Here they were at first supplementary to the ancient supplications, but gradually they ousted them. Reconciliation had originally signified restoration to communion with the Church, but understanding of this meaning had been progressively lost sight of, as indeed also of the judicial and sacramental character of the act. Consequently, the need was felt to combine the judicial function of the priest with his prayer for sinners, and for this purpose the absolution, which had formerly only been used extra-sacramentally, provided a suitable form.[6] Correspondingly, even the word "reconciliation" gradually dropped out of theological terminology from that time onwards, to be replaced by "absolution". As has been demonstrated earlier, clear ideas were lacking on the significance and effectiveness of the act, and the result was that the distinction between a sacramental and a non-sacramental absolution was endangered.[7] Nevertheless, whatever the ideas that were current on the efficacy of absolutions, it is clear from the formularies that "forgiveness of sins" was always attributed to them in the sense that they produced a certain remission in the sight of God of the punishment still outstanding for sin. In this effect they were equivalent to personal satisfaction, and were meant to be of assistance to a penitent in its performance. Nevertheless, they had nothing to

---

[5] Cf. in papal letters of the tenth and eleventh centuries such phrases as: *absolutos esse optamus — absolutos esse decernimus* etc. See N. Paulus I 62ff.
[6] Poschmann 18ff.; J. A. Jungmann, *Die lat. Bußriten* (1932) 252f.
[7] See above 149 and Poschmann 31f.

do with the remission of ecclesiastical penances; it was a mistake to regard them as indulgences, and indeed even as plenary indulgences, on the grounds that they simply speak of forgiveness of sins without any limitation.[8] However, even if they brought no alleviation of penance on earth, they were highly prized and sought after by the faithful, because the thought of punishment in the life to come, of which they held out the prospect of at least a partial remission, ultimately outweighed the burden of ecclesiastical satisfaction.[9]

Naturally a spirit of repentance in the recipient was a presupposition for the effectiveness of an absolution, and this was normally manifested by the performance of some good work. This could be mere participation in the solemnity on the occasion of which an absolution was bestowed; usually, however, an offering was also made to the church concerned. Frequently too popes and bishops appealed directly for contributions, "unto the remission of sins", on the occasion of pious undertakings such as the building of places of worship and the defence of the Church.[10] Precisely because they were recommended by the bearers of the power of the keys, such good works were in their turn regarded as particularly efficacious. In time the recommendations themselves gradually acquired an authoritative form, just as the absolution prayers had done. Correspondingly, the popes of the twelfth century made use of the stereotyped phrase: *in remissionem peccatorum iniungimus.*[11] Just as in the sacrament of penance "binding and loosing" go together,[12] so too here both functions of the power of the keys were in evidence. This procedure, therefore, is directed towards an extra-sacramental remission of temporal punishment in virtue of the power of the keys, and is consequently closely connected with an

---

[8] Thus M. Koeniger 187. On this see N. Paulus I 67.
[9] Cf. the enthusiastic account of an eyewitness of one of these absolutions granted by Alexander II, 1071, on the occasion of the consecration of the Church of Monte Cassino, cited in N. Paulus I 76 n. 1. [10] Instances in N. Paulus I 60 ff.
[11] N. Paulus 120—131. [12] Cf. above 146 f.

indulgence. Yet it does not represent a real indulgence. The reason is that neither in the absolutions nor in the good work prescribed for the forgiveness of sins is there question of a judicial act producing as a result a precisely determined remission of punishment. The power of the keys is merely a guarantee of the greater efficacy of the prayer or of the good work respectively. An indulgence is found only when an ecclesiastical superior remits the entire penance, or a definite part of it, on the understanding that God allows this gratuitous remission and cancels the corresponding amount of punishment due for sin.

The transition was effected in practice. It went unremarked and without any antecedent theory. It is, therefore, often difficult to decide whether documents of the eleventh and twelfth centuries are speaking of an indulgence or only of an absolution.[13] The essential novelty of the indulgence lay in the fact that the presumed effect of an absolution for the hereafter was taken into consideration in the assessment of the penance imposed by the church on earth, and this was correspondingly reduced. In this way the absolution, which was formerly a prayer, became a formal remission of a strictly determined amount of ecclesiastical penance, and thereby an act of jurisdiction. An indulgence was no longer merely an earnest for the time after death, but also an exceedingly welcome relief in life on earth. And it was this which secured for it such rapid diffusion.

The most ancient historically attested indulgences derive from bishops in southern France in the first half of the eleventh century — supposedly earlier records of indulgences have all been proved spurious. They were granted for visits to churches and for almsgiving. One form they took was that in consideration of the performance of the good work the penance imposed for a portion of the mortal sins confessed was remitted. Another was the reduction from two or three days, to one day a week, of

---

[13] Thus both in the past and in more recent times the grant of plenary indulgences on a large scale has been erroneously attributed to Gregory VII. See N. Paulus 77 ff.

fasts of a year's duration which had been imposed by way of penance. Others again were the remission of the first year in a penance of several years, and the remission of a fraction of the penance (a quarter, a third or a half).[14] Later it became the custom to determine the remission of penance exclusively by time, and to grant indulgences of so many days or of one or more years. A feature of the oldest documents containing grants of indulgences is that they add to the remission of penitential obligations defined by time an absolution from all sins for the case in which the penitent should die before the expiry of this time.[15] This is not to be regarded as some kind of plenary indulgence (such as an indulgence for the hour of death);[16] it is only a release from the penitential obligations which have been imposed but not yet completely discharged. This is evident from the formulae of absolution framed in very similar terms which are found in the penitential *ordines* of that period.[17] The dead man is to go before God free of all ecclesiastical bonds, and the Church prays that God also will absolve him. In this way, therefore, a clear distinction is made in the oldest records of indulgences between a precisely determined remission of penance on earth and an indefinite absolution of which the effect is left to God in the manner of the earlier absolutions. The distinction is also apparent in the formulation: in the former it is authoritative and categorical — *absolvimus* — in the latter,

---

[14] Thus, *e. g.,* the indulgences for the abbey church of S. Pedro de Portella in the diocese of Urgel 1035, and for the church of Notre Dame of Arles 1046. The spurious indulgence privilege of the abbey of Montmajour is instructive for the form of the oldest indulgences, because the forgery dates from early in the twelfth century and its amplitude gives a picture of contemporary practice. N. Paulus assembles and critically examines the oldest indulgences with details on their essential content I 132—194.

[15] Thus in the charter of Notre Dame of Arles (N. Paulus 143 n. 2), in the forged bull for the church of Correns, a monastery connected with Montmajour (ibid. 137 n. 2), and in an indulgence privilege for the monastery of Psalmody (supposedly 1029, ibid. 138).

[16] Thus N. Paulus 136, 138, 144, notwithstanding evident hesitations.

[17] See above 145. For more detailed proof see B. Poschmann, *Der Ablaß* 48 ff.

deprecative and containing a reference to the grounds of priestly power *ex nostra parte, quantum permissu (!) nostrum est* — and similarly. In any case the initial conjunction of an indulgence with an absolution in the old sense is instructive for its history.

In the eleventh century indulgences were still of rare occurrence. Episcopal grants of indulgences of which we have knowledge originate from southern France and northern Spain. A series of papal indulgences is said to be of the same or, in part, even of an earlier period, but the great majority of them have been proved to be forgeries.[18] It is certain that Pope Urban II (1088—1099), who came from France, granted alms indulgences on several occasions, quite apart from the great crusade indulgence. Even in the twelfth century concessions were kept within moderate bounds both in respect of their number and their size. The popes particularly observed restraint, generally being content with indulgences of twenty or forty days. The only exceptions were Calixtus II, who appears to have granted an indulgence of three years on one occasion, and Alexander III, who frequently made similar grants of one to three years.[19] The bishops were less discreet; we find that they often gave indulgences of one year, and occasionally of three to five years.[20] Already the Fourth Lateran Council felt itself obliged to make a stand against "indiscreet and superfluous indulgences". As yet, however, it only had in mind certain prelates who did not shrink from misusing their authority in the concession of indulgences.[21] Hence the reproach of over-extravagant use of indulgences motivated by covetousness must not be generalized or exaggerated, however much, unfortunately, consideration of their material yield contributed to their adoption and diffusion. It is also by no means true that, as has been claimed, up to the time of Innocent III indulgences were generally not given

[18] According to N. Paulus (151 f.) an indulgence of Nicolas II (1069), three years, and one of Alexander II (1070), eight days, are also to be considered as genuine.
[19] N. Paulus 160, 165 f.
[20] For a collection of them cf. ibid. 177—192. [21] Mansi XXII 1050.

without monetary contributions. There are numerous documents which make no mention of any such condition, and only require the devotional act of a pious visit to a church.[22]

In general a penitential work is necessary for the gaining of an indulgence, because of its nature it is not meant to be a substitute for the personal penitential effort of a sinner but an aid. In proportion as the prescribed work is relatively trifling the more the power of the ecclesiastical absolution is exerted; the weightier it is, the less the absolution has to accomplish. Ultimately a border-line case is reached when the prescribed work is equivalent to the penance that is due; strictly speaking here there is no longer question of an indulgence but of a redemption. To all intents and purposes we encounter the case in the crusade indulgences which are representative of a second and even better known type of the oldest indulgences. At all events the conditions laid on the crusaders could in respect of their arduousness be regarded as a substitute for the complete canonical penance with the same right as the pilgrimage to Rome and the other holy places. Accordingly, in the famous proclamation of Clermont (1095), which was to be the model for the later period, Urban II expressly says: *iter illud pro omni paenitentia reputetur*.[23] Consequently, in contrast to the oldest indulgences attached to churches and almsgiving, the remission granted to the crusaders usually had the character of a plenary indulgence. Strictly speaking, however, the distinction between the two kinds was only accidental. Similarly, in indulgences attached to churches and almsdeeds a commutation or substitution of penance took place; and conversely the crusade only acquired its validity as a substitute for penance through the proclamation of an indulgence or absolution by the pope.

---

[22] N. Paulus 194.
[23] Mansi XX 816. Similarly too beforehand Alexander II (1063), and later Paschal II (1101) in the indulgences which they granted to those who were fighting the Saracens in Spain. See B. Poschmann, 55 f.

For this reason in an historical explanation of indulgences the starting-point can either be redemptions or absolutions.[24]

XVI. THE THEOLOGY OF INDULGENCES

As so often in life, so also in indulgences practice went before theory. Men made use of them without being aware of the innovation which they represented, and regarded them from the point of view of redemptions or absolutions which were customary in the procedure of penance. As a result a long time elapsed before theology took notice of them and made them the object of critical judgement. We find the earliest response in Abelard's Ethics (*Scito te ipsum* c. 25), composed between 1125 and 1138, and it is one of sharp rejection. He says that it is shameless cupidity on the part of bishops which makes them so prodigal in the relaxation of penances at the dedication of churches and other solemnities, as they expect copious offerings from the concourse of people present on these occasions. They remit now a third now a quarter of the penance, and not merely to individual penitents, but indiscriminately — *indiscrete omnibus communiter* — that is, purely mechanically in consideration of the performance of some prescribed work and without reference to personal worth. Abelard regarded this as arbitrary conduct exceeding comprehension. Precisely because the bishops justified their procedure by appealing to their official power, he disputed their possession of the power of the keys, as has been shown above.[25] Even though in this he was at odds with tradition, yet he was

---

[24] Ibid. 58 n. 287. It is, on the other hand, incorrect to see with A. Gottlob (*Der Kreuzablaß und Almosenablaß* [1906] 3) the general manner of their distribution as the historically new element distinguishing indulgences from absolutions; or with M. Koeniger (op. cit. 180, 187f.) to locate it in the utilization of the works of penitents for the temporal interest of the Church. Neither the one nor the other can conceivably be necessary for an indulgence. N. Paulus (22ff.) believes that the earliest indulgences can actually be found in individual reductions of penance such as were granted to pilgrims to Rome from the ninth century onwards, a view with which candidly I cannot agree. [25] Above 159.

in the right in maintaining that the claim of the bishops to excuse sinners at their unfettered discretion from making satisfaction, at least in part, was something new and unheard of up to that time. In judging his protest one must not forget that a theological justification of the practice of indulgences was still only a desideratum for the future.[26]

Nothing is known of the attitude to the new procedure of other theologians contemporary with Abelard. Neither the Victorines nor Peter Lombard mention indulgences. It is not before the second half of the twelfth century that the early scholastics begin to deal with them. As it would take us too far to enter into the opinions of individual authors, a brief indication of the state of the problem may suffice.[27] Generally speaking, the same questions concerning the conditions and value of indulgences constantly recur, and the variety of the answers is proof of the obscurity and uncertainty that attended efforts to reconcile the new practice with the principles of the ancient theology of penance. An attitude for the most part sceptical, where it is not positively hostile (cf. Peter of Poitiers), is progressively overcome, chiefly by consideration of the authority of the Church granting indulgences. But all hold firmly that an absolute remission, without any corresponding penitential work, is inadmissible. Thus the idea of a redemption is the central point in the attempts at an explanation. Either some work equivalent to the penance remitted is required of the recipient of the indulgence, or compensation has to be provided by others. But the question was put: how can there be a fair estimate — *iusta aestimatio* — of an equivalent work where there is a general distribution of indulgences? In this case the same alms will weigh much heavier on a poor man than on a rich man. Again, who is responsible for providing the compensation? Some make the distributors of indulgences themselves liable for it (*e.g.* Praepositinus); on the

---

[26] B. Poschmann, *Der Ablaß* 63—68.
[27] There is a full account in N. Paulus 212—252, summarized in Poschmann 69 to 88.

whole, however, the tendency is to regard the Church as such as the guarantor. In the first place means for compensation are at hand in the suffrages of her living members, although, admittedly, a doubt arises concerning their sufficiency (William of Auxerre). Next there are those also of the saints in heaven, to the extent that they have a special relationship to the indulgenced work, as for example to the building of a church dedicated to them (William of Auvergne). Now and again it is emphasized that the indulgenced work possesses as such a higher satisfactory value by reason of the power of the keys of the distributor of the indulgence (William of Auvergne). Another question concerns the recipient of the indulgence. Some writers would have an indulgence valid only in the case when the performance of the penance which had been imposed is not possible, whether because of sickness or by reason of a person's occupation (Alan of Lille, Stephen Langton and others). Others make its validity dependent on the permission of the confessor, because there is question of the alteration of a penance imposed by him (Peter the Chanter, Stephen Langton). As regards the distributor of indulgences, the same reason is used to attribute power to grant indulgences not only to bishops but also to parish priests (Peter of Poitiers, Peter the Chanter, James of Vitry). By the canonists it is required that there must be jurisdiction over the recipients of indulgences (Huguccio). Although it is admitted on all sides that the remission of penance is a judicial act, yet all are unanimous that an indulgence is not a direct absolution from punishment in the hereafter, but that in this respect, to use a later expression, it operates *per modum suffragii.*

It is the merit of high scholasticism that it worked out a fairly consistent scheme from the welter of opinions, questions and doubts. Two contemporary factors contributed substantially to this result. First there was a change of view in regard to the effect of an indulgence; then in the doctrine of the *thesaurus ecclesiae* there was a new theory to explain its efficacy. In regard to the effect, it now began to be asserted that an indulgence is a direct remission of the pains of purgatory, instead of a remission of penance imposed, as had hitherto been maintained. An indulgence was now defined as a remission of condign punishment (whether it had been imposed or not) — *remissio a poena condigna (sive iniuncta sive non)*.[28] This is altogether intelligible, as the transcendent effect naturally imposes itself more forcibly. It does not in the least signify a dogmatic "transformation" of the concept of an indulgence, as if now for the first time an indulgence was extended to the pains of the hereafter.[29] It was indeed taken for granted from the beginning that the remission of penance had as a consequence a corresponding remission of punishment in the hereafter. Otherwise the use of indulgences would have been meaningless and, as St. Thomas proves (*Suppl.* q. 25 a. 1), would have done the recipient more harm than good. N. Paulus has brought exhaustive individual proofs of this conviction of the effect for the hereafter which existed from the earliest period. As a supplement to these it is enough now to refer to the historic connexion of indulgences with absolutions. Where they differed was precisely in this, that in an indulgence the effect of an absolution for the hereafter was now also credited to ecclesiastical penance. Therefore, the development did not proceed from the remission of ecclesiastical punishment to the remission of the pains of purgatory, but conversely. However, even if the transformation in the outlook on an indulgence did not affect its essence, yet it was of far-reaching importance for the theory of its mode of operation. From the time when punishment in the hereafter was regarded as the direct object of an indulgence, the judicial process, of which the Church had only availed herself for the remission of the strictly defined penances

---

[28] The earliest example occurs in the *Quaestiones diversae theologicae,* which date from after the Fourth Lateran Council; similarly Albert IV, *Sent.* d. 20 a. 18 ad q. 1, and Thomas, *Suppl.* q. 25 a. 1.

[29] Thus especially Th. Brieger, op. cit. IX 80 ff.; he is followed by A. v. Harnack, *Dogmengesch.* (1910) 602 n. 1; A. Hauck, *Kirchengesch. Deutschlands* IV³ (1913) 946. Against this view N. Paulus, esp. I 259 ff.; Fr. Gillmann, *Katholik* (1913) I 365 to 376; E. Göller, op. cit. 48 ff.

imposed by herself, was, so to speak, spontaneously extended to the remission of the punishment of purgatory. Thus it appeared as if she had control over the latter in the same way as over the former. Hitherto, however, remission in the hereafter had been besought from God, and its scope had been left to God. This impression was left less evidently in the case of partial indulgences, because they continued to be granted according to the scale of the old penitential ordinances as remissions of a definite number of days or years. But the question at once became a practical one in regard to plenary indulgences which signified the remission of all punishment.[30] Accordingly St. Thomas taught that the *indulgentia omnium peccatorum* granted by the pope refers to the *universitas poenarum* and that consequently one who dies after gaining the indulgence goes straight to heaven (*Quodlib.* II q. 8 a. 2).[31]

The theoretical justification of the retention of the judicial form in the concession of indulgences was provided by the doctrine of the "treasury of the Church". This did not originate with Alexander of Hales, as was held up till quite recently; it was proposed by Cardinal Hugh of St. Cher as early as 1230.[32] The doctrine maintains that in the blood of Christ, and also in the blood of the martyrs who were afflicted far beyond the measure of their sins, "every sin has been punished. This blood which has been shed is a treasure deposited in the shrine of the Church of which the Church holds the key. She can then open the shrine at her discretion and by the grant of indulgences impart a share of the treasure to whom she desires. And in this

---

[30] As early as the crusade bull of the Lateran Council of 1215 the earlier description "remission of penance imposed" is replaced by the phrase "full remission of sins" (Mansi XXII 1067).

[31] The view prevailed against a minority of theologians who wished to limit the effect for the hereafter of a plenary indulgence in proportion to the size of the entire penance remitted. Complete unanimity on this question has even yet not been reached. Cf. E. Göller 106 ff.; N. Paulus II 211 ff.

[32] A summary is given by the canonist Henry of Susa (Hostiensis † 1271), *Summa Aurea* lib. V *tit. de remissionibus*, 6.

way the sin does not stay unpunished, because it is punished in Christ and his martyrs." By this theory the difficulty concerning the sufficiency of compensation for penances remitted was removed at one stroke. The idea of making use of the help of the saints for this purpose was thoroughly in line with tradition. New, however, was the utilization of the commutation value of their merits, and the claim of the Church to a juridical control over them. The remission of punishment in the hereafter, which formerly had been besought through the intercession of the saints,[33] was now granted by means of an act of jurisdiction. What had been a matter of practice from the beginning in indulgences had now also acquired its basis in theory.

The great scholastic theologians sought to define the theory even more precisely. St. Thomas in particular carried its basic ideas to their final consequences. As against St. Albert and St. Bonaventure, who with earlier authors required a reasonable proportion — *iusta proportio* — between the indulgenced work and the size of the indulgence granted,[34] he derives the efficacy of the indulgence solely from the treasury of the Church; hence the indulgenced work no longer comes into consideration as an effective cause, but only as a reason — *causa motiva* — which moves the ecclesiastical superior to make use of his power over the treasury in favour of the individual. Its meaning is simply to safeguard the intention of the saints, who naturally desire their merits to be employed only for the honour of God and the general good of the Church. Any cause — *quaecumque causa* — tending to this end is a sufficient reason. The amount of the remission produced by an indulgence depends, therefore, absolutely on the decision of its distributor. Undoubtedly he sins if he grants an indulgence inordinately and practically for nothing — *inordinate et quasi pro nihilo* — nevertheless it will accrue to the recipient in its full extent (*Suppl.* q. 25 a. 2 and ad 1). With few

---

[33] On the question why the merits of the saints were called on besides the infinite merits of Christ, see B. Poschmann 84 ff.

[34] Albert IV, *Sent.* d. 20 a. 17; Bonaventure, IV *Sent.* d. 20 p. 2 a. 1 q. 6.

exceptions later theologians have not followed St. Thomas in this. For the validity of an indulgence they also require a proportionate cause — *causa proportionata*[35] — in order to make personal moral achievement more effective as a precondition for the replacement of penance by the use of the treasury. Thereby they come closer to the pre-Thomist conception that an indulgence is meant to provide not so much a replacement as a completion of personal penance. This means, admittedly, that the certainty of its effect is endangered.

The separation of indulgences from the penitential procedure also influenced the question of the distributor of indulgences. The reduction of a penance which had been imposed belonged in the first place to the confessor; hence in the beginning, as has already been noted, power to grant indulgences was also attributed to parish priests. Indeed the effect of any grant of indulgences was often made dependent on the permission of the confessor, although admittedly less in practice than in theory. That came to an end, when with the doctrine of the *thesaurus* power to grant indulgences was in principle differentiated from sacramental power in penance. Control over the *thesaurus* was now reserved to the pope and the bishops as a consequence of their jurisdiction. This was already taken for granted by the great scholastics. They expressly denied to simple priests power to grant indulgences; on the other hand they admitted that it was possessed by bishops not yet consecrated (Thomas, *Suppl.* q. 26 a. 1 and 2). In order to justify this reservation to bishops St. Bonaventure appeals to the Old Testament law of the Levirate, and makes the point that only the bishop is the spouse of the Church, and that as the representative of Christ the true spouse he has to beget children to the Church and to exercise control over the goods of the Church and over the education of her children. St. Thomas makes only subordinate use of these mysti-

---

[35] So also the indulgence bulls of Clement VI (Denz. 551) and of the Council of Constance (Denz. 676).

cal ideas with a view to proposing his own purely juridical explanation. The bishop, and he alone, as head of the Church can exercise control over her treasure in the same way as the head of a society over its common property (*Suppl.* q. 26 a. 1). He had then consistently to go even further, and assign the power of granting indulgences in his own right to the pope alone, because only he is the head of the whole Church to whom the treasury belongs. Hence, although he had to take account of ecclesiastical custom — *consuetudo ecclesiae* — and leave to the bishops power to grant indulgences, he derived this power from papal authorization.[36] In this he was in any case simply conforming to already existing practice, as Innocent III as early as the Fourth Lateran Council had limited episcopal indulgences to one year for the day of the dedication of a church, and to forty days for its anniversary and for certain other indulgences.[37]

The transformation in the manner of conceiving indulgences also made itself felt in the question of the recipient of indulgences. So long as an indulgence was considered predominantly as a substitute for personal penance based on the work of others, striving after it was regarded more as an imperfection than a proof of special piety, as it seemed to be a mark of unwillingness to do penance. Hence some early scholastics desired that it should only be valid for the case when the sinner himself was no longer able to fulfil his penance. For religious in particular it was not deemed expedient. Even Albert (d. 20 a. 18) and Bonaventure (d. 20 p. 2 a. 1 q. 4) wished to allow it only to worldly-minded religious and not to the fervent. Thomas on the

---

[36] *Suppl.* a. 3: *et ideo potestas faciendi indulgentias plene residet in papa ... Sed in episcopis est taxata secundum ordinationem papae. Et ideo possunt facere secundum quod eis est taxatum, et non amplius.* Bonaventure *(loc. cit.)* is content with the assertion that all bishops and especially the Summus Pontifex possess the power of granting indulgences.

[37] Mansi XXII 1050. Ecclesiastical law today decrees that besides the pope *ii tantum possunt potestate ordinaria indulgentias elargiri, quibus id expresse a iure concessum est* (CIC can. 912).

other hand expressly rejected this view, teaching the contrary on the ground that pious religious by reason of unavoidable daily sins are no less capable of being helped by the merits of others than seculars (*Suppl.* q. 27 a. 2). Clearly any hesitations would be bound to disappear in proportion as an indulgence ceased to be thought of as a shifting of penance on to the shoulders of other men still living, and instead was regarded primarily as an act of grace by which the Church made good use of the heavenly treasure which was at her disposal for the benefit of all her children. Accordingly, for the gaining of an indulgence all that was generally required with St. Thomas (q. 27 a. 1 & 3) was a state of grace and the performance of the indulgenced work.

However, as against the common opinion, Cajetan (*Opusc.* t. I tr. 10 q. 1), Tournely (*Praelect. theol. de sacr. paenit.*, q. ultima de indulgentiis a. 7) and in more recent times H. Oswald (*Sakramentenlehre* II⁵ 277 f.) revived an opinion, already mentioned, of some early scholastics, and required in addition a firm will of making satisfaction oneself as far as possible, on the ground that an indulgence is only a supplementary help for satisfaction — *subsidium et supplementum satisfactionis.*

Indulgences for the dead call for special treatment. Naturally they could only arise when an indulgence was no longer considered as a remission of penance, but as a direct remission of the pains of purgatory. Here too practice preceded theory. From the middle of the thirteenth century there is abundant evidence that the faithful on their own initiative, or often at the invitation of preachers, made over to the souls in purgatory the indulgences which they had gained. This chiefly applied to the crusade indulgence, but also included others.[38] Thus the theologians were obliged to deal with the question; and all the more so as they often failed to perceive that the proclamations of mercenary-minded preachers of the crusade were spurious. Hugh of St.Cher, who was the first to treat of indulgences for the dead, rejected

[38] Instances in N. Paulus II 167 ff.

them out of hand, on the ground that the power of the keys did not extend to the dead, and so did Henry of Susa (Hostiensis). In contrast, Raymund of Peñafort held that they were efficacious, provided that provision for their application to the dead is made in the concession of the indulgence.[39] So too the attitude of the most important scholastics was altogether in their favour. However, the question of the mode of their application received different answers. St. Albert *(loc.cit.)* maintained that it was primarily based on the power of the keys; St. Bonaventure *(loc.cit.* q. 5) held that it was only possible *per modum deprecationis.* St. Thomas does not express any detailed opinion on the question. However, given the explicitly juridical character of his doctrine on indulgences, there can hardly be any doubt that he was in favour of the former view.[40] In principle, however, the question whether indulgences for the dead are possible, still remained open for the future. About the middle of the fifteenth century Antoninus of Florence concluded that the majority of theologians were in favour of them; yet even towards the end of the century there were preachers who asserted that indulgences for the dead were useless.[41]

The first historically attested papal indulgences for the dead originated with Callistus III (the crusade indulgence against the Moors, 1457, and an indulgence in favour of the cathedral church of Tarragona).[42] The numerous documents containing similar grants from an earlier period are all forgeries. However, a much greater stir was caused by an indulgence granted in 1476 by Sixtus IV in favour of the cathedral church of Saintes. This was propagated with all means in his power by Raymond Perraudi, the dean of the cathedral, who had been named commissary of the indulgence. Perraudi asserted that the formula employed in the bull, *per modum suffragii,* did not mean "after the manner of an intercession", but "after the manner of a help"

---

[39] Instances ibid. 171 ff. [40] Cf. N. Paulus I 300; II 173.
[41] Ibid. III 375. [42] Ibid. 380 f.

through substitution, and that the indulgence granted "by way of a help" benefited the dead absolutely infallibly and in its full scope. In addition to this he also taught, like others before him, that indulgences for the dead could be gained even in a state of mortal sin, and that nothing more was required beyond the prescribed monetary contribution. It is therefore intelligible that popular preachers of indulgences provided grounds by the content of their proclamations for the satirical verse: "when in the box the coin does ring the soul from out the fire will spring"; and that others claimed that the pope could, if he desired, empty purgatory.[43] Naturally such extreme statements also met with sharp contradiction. The Sorbonne on a number of occasions censured them as dangerous and scandalous. Among the theologians who rejected them mention must be made of Cajetan. He made the application of the indulgence dependent on God's gracious acceptance, and also on a state of grace in the person applying it.[44] However, conflicting conceptions survived, and even to-day are not resolved, although in recent times the great majority of theologians have disassociated themselves very emphatically from those extreme views.[45] Naturally from the time when the popes made authoritative grants of indulgences for the dead opposition to them on theoretical grounds was no longer heard. The contrary teaching of Peter de Osma and Luther that indulgences for the dead are of no value was condemned by Sixtus IV and Leo X (Denz. 729 and 762).

Turning to the later history of the doctrine of indulgences, we note that in general theology has remained faithful to the theory worked out in the high scholastic period, especially by St. Thomas, although on points of detail there has been divergence

[43] On Perraudi's theoretical and practical position in the question of indulgences, ibid. 382—389.
[44] Ibid. 89 f.
[45] Among those in favour of an infallible effect are Soto, Suarez, de Lugo, and in more recent times Chr. Pesch, F. Beringer, J. Hilgers; those who admit that a state of grace is not always required where the indulgence is applied to the dead include Suarez and Pesch, *Prael. dogm.* VII[5] (1920) 250.

of opinions. In the Jubilee bull of the year 1343 (Denz. 550—552) Clement VI gave authoritative expression to the view which based indulgences on the treasury of the Church, even if the bull has not the significance of an official doctrinal statement, still less that of *ex cathedra* decision.[46] The Council of Constance rejected the calling in question by Wyclif and Hus of the power of granting indulgences (Denz. 622 and 676), and Sixtus IV repudiated similar teaching on the part of Peter de Osma (Denz. 729). In the decretal *Per praesentes* addressed to Cardinal Cajetan, 9 November 1518, Leo X insisted against Luther on the power of the Church to grant indulgences by reason of the treasury of merits (Denz. 740a), and in the bull *Exsurge Domine* (1520) condemned the denial of this doctrine and other attacks on indulgences (Denz. 757—762). Similarly later Pius VI in 1794 defended the treasury against the Synod of Pistoia (Denz. 1542).

The Council of Trent did not go into any greater detail on the content of the doctrine of indulgences; it contented itself with affirming two points as doctrine of faith. These are that the Church has received from Christ power to confer indulgences, and that the use of them is most salutary to Christian people (Denz. 989 and 998). These two statements are, therefore, all that is to be held as strict dogma with the certainty of faith. This assertion does not mean, however, that the doctrine of the treasury of merits is just a theory which is not binding. On the contrary by reason of the theses condemned by the Church it is to be regarded as "theologically certain"; and moreover the Code of Canon Law (can. 911) has incorporated it into the definition of an indulgence. On the other hand, in addition to others, the very important question whether for the validity of an indulgence a *causa proportionata* is necessary has remained open to this day.

The results of recent historical research make possible a positive advance in the doctrine of indulgences. In its origins an

[46] Cf. N. Paulus II 203.

indulgence is a combination of the early-medieval absolution, which had the efficacy of a prayer, and an act of jurisdiction remitting ecclesiastical penance. Its sense was that the presumed efficacy for the hereafter of the absolution was credited to the penance of the Church on earth. This being so, it is clear that the efficacy of an indulgence rests primarily on the prayer of the Church which makes the remission of penance possible in the first place. Even so an indulgence is an act of jurisdiction and remains one. As such, admittedly, it only extends to the remission of satisfaction imposed by the Church. This was originally real; later it was a legal fiction. In contrast, remission of the pains of purgatory is besought from God, and depends on his gracious acceptation. Under this aspect an indulgence always operates *per modum suffragii* — and not only indulgences for the dead. Nevertheless, it is not after the manner of an ordinary, but, so to speak, of an authorized prayer to which the official character of the one who offers it gives a guarantee of the desired result. Those who grant indulgences pray in the name of the Church; they can, especially by reason of the communion of saints, call on the intercession and merits of the Church triumphant, on whose readiness to assist penitents they can count. That is the real meaning of the treasury of merits and of the control of the Church over it extracted from its metaphorical covering. If an indulgence is in this way primarily considered under the aspect of a prayer, and its jurisdictional effect restricted to the realm of the Church on earth, then the moral and religious scruples which are raised against its one-sided juridical formulation at once fall to the ground. These object that the sinner's debt in the sight of God is balanced by concrete services from the other side just like a material debit account. In its essential core, then, an indulgence is clearly in line with the whole of Christian tradition. From this we know that the Church has from the very beginning considered assistance of penitents to make satisfaction one of her most urgent concerns. An indulgence is the immediate sequel of the general absolutions. The specific form of a remission of ecclesiastical penance which characterizes it is only of secondary importance. This owes its origin to the juridically ordered arrangement of penance at the time when it came into existence. To this day it clearly bears the stamp of it in the manner in which the amount of the remission of punishment is defined.[47]

For reasons of space we must refrain from entering on the history of the practice of indulgences. The growing frequency of indulgences, their concession in ever greater dimensions, their various kinds (jubilee indulgences, indulgences for the dying etc.), the increasing facility of their conditions, the beneficial results of their use, the scandalous and disastrous abuses connected with them, and the decrees against these abuses promulgated by the Council of Trent, the ecclesiastical authority over indulgences and present-day forms of the grant of indulgences — to describe all these belongs either to general church history and the history of culture or to the history of Christian piety. For the pre-Reformation period N. Paulus provides in the second and third volumes of his work abundant material from every angle. The dogmatic foundation of indulgences has remained unaffected by the development in practice.

[47] A first attempt to utilize the new historical knowledge in this sense is to be found in B. Poschmann, *Der Ablaß im Licht der Bußgeschichte* (1948) 99—122. On this see Karl Rahner, *ZkTh* 71 (1949) 481—490; F. Courtney, *CR* 44 (1959) 464—479.

The Anointing of the Sick

LITERATURE: J. Launoy, *De sacramento unctionis infirmorum liber* (Paris 1673). de Sainte-Beuve, *De sacramento unctionis infirmorum extremae* (1686), Migne, Curs. Theol. XXIV 9—132. F. Kattenbusch, *REPTh* XIV³ 304—311; F. W. Puller, *The Anointing of the Sick in Scripture and Tradition* (London 1904). M. Boudinhon, "La théologie de l'extrême onction" in *RCE* 1905 t. 2 p. 385 ff. J. Kern, *De sacr. extremae unctionis tractatus dogmaticus* (1906). F. J. Dölger, *Der Exorzismus im altchristl. Taufritual* (1909) 137—157. M. Meinertz, "Die Krankensalbung Jak." 5, 14 f., *BZ* 20 (1932) 23 ff. Poschmann I 52—63. F. Lehr, *Die sakramentale Krankenölung im ausgehenden Altertum u. im Frühmittelalter* (Diss. 1934). K. Lübeck, "Die hl. Ölung in der abendländ. Kirche des Mittelalters" in *ZkTh* (1931), 515—561. H. Weisweiler, "Das Sakr. der letzten Ölung in den system. Werken der ersten Frühscholastik" in *Sch* 7 (1932) 321—353, 526—560. C. Ruch u. L. Godefroy, *DTC* V (1913) 1897—1985 u. 1985—2022. A. Chavasse, *Etude sur l'onction des infirmes dans l'Eglise Latine du IIIe au XIe siècle. Tome I : Du IIIe siècle à la Réforme Carolingienne* (Lyon 1942). J. Chaine, *L'Epître de saint Jacques* (Etudes bibliques, Paris 1927). R. Leconte, *L'Epître de saint Jacques* (Bible de Jérusalem, Paris 1953). J. Michl, *Der Jakobusbrief* (Das N. T. Bd. 8, Regensburg 1953). L. Lercher, *Institutiones theologiae dogmaticae³* IV/2 (Innsbruck 1949). A. d'Alès, "Extrême-Onction" in *DBS* III (1938) 262—272. H. Friesenhahn, "Die Lehre des Duns Skotus über die Wirkung des Sakraments der Krankenölung" in *Franzisk. Studien* (1938) 93—97. Th. Spáčil, *Doctrina Theologiae Orientis Separati de Sacra Infirmorum Unctione* (Orientalia Christiana XXIV/2 (Rome 1931). A. Verhamme, *Collationes Brugenses* 45—47 (1949—51) [A systematic treatise in Latin on Extreme Unction in thirteen articles. Tr.] S. J. Brzana, *Remains of Sin and Extreme Unction according to Theologians after Trent* (Rome 1953). E. Doronzo, *Tractatus Dogmaticus de Extrema Unctione,* 2 v. (Milwaukee 1954—55). H. B. Porter, *The Origin of the Medieval Rite for Anointing the Sick, JTS* N. S. VII (1956) 211—225. P. F. Palmer, *Sacraments and Forgiveness* (Westminster [Md.] 1959, London 1960) 273—320. Id., "The Purpose of Anointing the Sick. A Reappraisal" in *TS* 19 (1958) 309—344. Z. Alzeghy, "L'effetto corporale dell'Estrema Unzione" in *Gr* 38 (1957) 385—405. E. Marcotte, "L'extrême-onction et la mort d'après saint Thomas d'Aquin" in *Rev. Univ. Ottawa* 30 (1960) 65*—88*.

XVII. THE ANOINTING OF THE SICK IN SCRIPTURE
AND IN THE EARLY CHURCH

THE last anointing is closely related to penance. According to the Council of Trent, which in the fourteenth session dealt with both sacraments together, it is the completion of penance — *consummativum* (Denz. 907) — yet it is an independent "true and proper sacrament instituted by Christ", suggested — *insinuatum* — by Mark and promulgated by James (Denz. 908, 926).

Mark 6:13 relates that the Twelve who had been sent out to preach penance "cast out many devils, and anointed with oil many that were sick, and healed them". It is a question of a charismatic healing. In the civilization of that age the use of oil for the healing of the sick was common both among the Jews and pagans.[1] Jesus, therefore, has adopted the usage and simply enhanced the effect of the apostolic anointing charismatically. Many theologians, including St. Thomas, St. Bonaventure, Scotus, Maldonatus and Sainte-Beuve, have erroneously regarded the sacrament as already present in this anointing. Quite apart from its charismatic character, there is no mention of a spiritual effect of grace in connexion with it. However, inasmuch as it is evidence of his solicitude for the sick, it at least suggests that Jesus will also have thought of a corresponding institution for the benefit of the sick in the time to come. This suggestion is verified in Jas 5:14—16.

James is giving directions for the conduct of a believer who is seriously ill.[2] He should "bring in the priests of the Church, and let them pray over him, anointing him with oil in the name of the Lord". Office-bearers, therefore, and not charismatics have

---

[1] See H. Schlier in *ThW* I 230; F. J. Dölger 154ff. who shows that anointing was used especially in the case of the possessed.

[2] That in contrast with Mk 6:13 there is question of a serious illness is clear from the expression ὁ κάμνων (cf. W. Bauer, *Wörterb.* 668) and even more so from the fact that the sick man summons the presbyters instead of going to them.

to perform the action, as is generally admitted today,[3] and indeed by the charge and in the power of the Lord. The same phrase is used in 5:10 in reference to the Old Testament prophets. The text states the effect of the rite: "And the prayer of faith shall save the sick man; and the Lord shall raise him up; and if he be in sins, they shall be forgiven him." Both verbs σώζειν and ἐγείρειν can in themselves signify bodily or spiritual healing. Actually both are meant here, for, as Jesus shows (cf. Mt 8:1ff.; Lk 17:11ff.; Mt 9:2 and *passim*), bodily and spiritual recovery are closely connected. The "prayer of faith" will bring "salvation" to all; that is, what is salutary for each one here and now, whether it be recovery or death in a state of grace.[4] Even apart from the context, which is concerned with a sick man, bodily healing cannot be ruled out, for there is an anointing with oil, and this is expressly mentioned as a remedy in Mk 6:13. On the other hand James cannot possibly have promised recovery unreservedly to all sick believers who obey his directions, as in the long run this would be an assurance of immortality. The suggestion that he wanted to keep all the sick alive till the *Parousia* is groundless,[5] and quite inconsistent with the ideas of primitive Christianity.[6] The Apostle does not specify in detail the meaning of the clause ἐγερεῖ αὐτὸν ὁ κύριος. Besides recovery, in the event of that taking place, it includes the thought of a strengthening of confidence in God. Moreover, spiritual healing through forgiveness is strongly emphasized in the case of a sick man who has committed sins. Here the text gives no grounds for the claim that only venial sins are in question. Judging from the concluding words: "confess therefore your sins one to another; and pray for one another that you may be

---

[3] Cf. H. Schlier, ibid. 232.
[4] Cf. C. Ruch 1903; similarly, O. Bardenhewer, J. Chaine, F. Hauck, Th. Zahn, H. Schlier; M. Dibelius, H. A. W. Meyer, O. Holtzmann, L. Fendt, A. Oepke restrict it to bodily healing; H. v. Soden, F. S. Frenkle and M. Meinertz refer the text solely to eternal salvation. Fuller details in Poschmann I 55.
[5] Thus among others L. Fendt, *RGG* IV ed. 2 641.
[6] See M. Meinertz 30.

saved", James seems to have required a confession of sins by the sick man before the presbyters and the faithful who were present, as a preliminary condition for the prayer which procures forgiveness. For this reason some would like to see in the rite for the sick here depicted evidence not only for the last anointing but also for the sacrament of penance.[7] However, be that as it may, it is certain that James attributes to the prayer of the presbyters and to the anointing administered by them a power which is productive of grace and of the forgiveness of sins; in other words, he regards the rite as a sacrament in the later sense of the term.[8]

Naturally this clear directive, given "in the name of the Lord" could not have gone unheeded. True, in ancient Christian literature it has left very little trace, with the result that in the opinion of Protestants the anointing of the sick in the sense of the present-day sacrament was unknown in the early Church and owed its origin solely to medieval theology.[9] Yet such a conclusion is not justified, as the silence of the sources is at bottom not surprising. Without prejudice to its sacramental character, unction as compared with baptism, the eucharist and penance, which are institutions necessary for salvation, is only of subordinate importance and a remedy for a particular situation. Antecedently one must not expect that it would have been made the object of special discussion,[10] seeing that it was a usage which was not called in question in any quarter. Similarly even today it is seldom mentioned in sermons and writings on religious practice. The earliest commentary on the epistle of James that has come down to us is that of Bede († 735), and this provides clear evidence for the sacrament. But it is not true,

---

[7] Thus F. F. Dölger, *ThR* (1907) 552, and especially C. Ruch 1909 ff.; on this see Poschmann I 61.
[8] Cf. Schlier (232): "The oil has here in fact the character of sacramental matter." On other Protestant interpretations cf. Ruch 1917 ff.
[9] Instances in Kern 4f.; Ruch 1928.
[10] The usual but questionable appeal to the *disciplina arcani* (cf. Kern 20f.; Ruch 1928) is here quite unnecessary.

however, that in the early Church all references to its use are lacking. Still they are wanting in unequivocal clarity; they do not sufficiently distinguish sacramental from private anointing of the sick or they unite the rite for the sick with penance. All this is intelligible if it is remembered that as yet there was no clear concept of a sacrament clearly differentiating individual sacraments from each other and from non-sacramental actions.

Important evidence is found in the first place in ancient rituals which contain formularies of prayer for the blessing of the oil of the sick, and which, therefore, presuppose that it is in general use. In all probability this applies to the *Didache,* if the hitherto unknown Coptic fragment (10, 3b—12, 2a) published in 1924 formed part of the original form of that document.[11] The fragment contains the following text, later incorporated almost verbally into the *Apostolic Constitutions* (VII 27): "But for the word of the oil thus shall ye give thanks saying: We thank Thee, Father, for the oil which Thou hast made known to us through, Jesus thy servant. Thine is the glory for ever" (C. Schmidt 94). The question still remains, which oil is meant. Schmidt holds that it cannot be decided whether it is a baptismal prayer or one for the anointing of the sick. O. Casel thinks that the primary reference is to baptism and confirmation (*JLW* 5 [1925] 235). E. Riebartsch, on the other hand, has argued very persuasively in favour of connecting it with the anointing of the sick.[12] For one thing the *Didache* assigns the prayer to the same place after the eucharistic prayers where, as we know from other early-Christian evidence, the consecration of the oil of the sick had its place. Also in favour of this view is the phrase that God has made known, that is, revealed the oil to us through Jesus, which is

[11] In favour of this are E. Hennecke, *Neutest. Apokryphen*[2] (1923) 560, and K. Bihlmeyer, *Die Apostol. Väter* I (1924) XX, while C. Schmidt, *ZNW* 24 precisely because of the unction prayer which is so remarkable for so early a period thinks that it is an addition inserted not earlier than 200. F. Lehr, *loc. cit.* 2, rightly observes that in view of the text of James this argument is invalid.

[12] *LZ* 1 (1929) 201—206. Lehr expresses full agreement, 1—3; F. Diekamp, *Kath. Dogmatik* III (1932) 319 holds that it is at least a probable opinion.

only explicable by Jas 5:14. In later rituals the destination of the consecrated oil for the healing of the sick is clearly expressed. The *Apostolic Tradition* of Hippolytus contains the petition "that this oil . . . may give strength to all that taste of it and health to all that use it".[13] Here and in the *Apostolic Constitutions* (VIII 29), and also in the *Euchologion* of Serapion of Thmuis († after 362) n. 5 and 17, the emphasis is on bodily healing. In the same formulary of prayer provision is also made for the blessing of bread and water. However, the second prayer of the *Euchologion* also stresses the spiritual effect. The oil is to be conducive to "good grace and the remission of sins" as well as to "perfect health and strength of soul and body". The formulary is clearly influenced by the epistle of James; yet, seeing that it was also employed for the blessing of bread and water, one cannot conclude that the oil blessed by its use served exclusively for "sacramental" application.[14] In fact the early Church had no hesitation in also attributing the beneficial effects taught by James to personal use of the oil blessed by the bishop. The action specially reserved to priests did not on that account lose its significance.

First explicit mention of the epistle of James is made by Origen, *In Lev.* hom. 2, 4, when he is enumerating the various possibilities of forgiveness at the disposal of Christians (baptism martyrdom, almsgiving etc.). Here ecclesiastical penance is mentioned last: *Est adhuc et septima, licet dura et laboriosa per paenitentiam remissio peccatorum. . . . In quo et impletur et illud, quod Jacobus apostolus dicit : si quis autem infirmatur, vocet presbyteros ecclesiae et imponant ei manus ungentes eum oleo in nomine Domini et oratio fidei. . . .* The Alexandrian's words must not, however, be taken as evidence for extreme unction, as they usually are by Catholics. It is penance that he is elucidating by the use of the text. The

---

[13] *The Apostolic Tradition of St. Hippolytus of Rome,* ed. and tr. G. Dix (London, SPCK, 1939) 10. Cf. Th. Schermann, *Die allg. Kirchenordnung* I (1914) 45f.
[14] Thus apparently F. X. Funk, *Didasc.* II 191, and J. Kern 169 n. 2. For the opposite view cf. Lehr 5 who appeals to A. Franz, *Die kirchl. Benediktionen im Mittelalter* (1909) I 337f.

infirmitas is the sickness of sin, which has to be healed by the priests. This explains the connecting phrase *in quo impletur* and the alteration he has made in the text cited, where, instead of *orent super eum,* we have *imponent ei manus,* for the imposition of hands is a more characteristic mark of penance than prayer by itself.[15] This does not mean in the least that anointing is to be taken here in a purely symbolical sense. It is quite conceivable that an anointing was combined with the imposition of hands in penance. Later on the practice is expressly attested for a number of regions of the Orient. It is mentioned by the "Persian sage" Aphraates, *Abh.* 23, 3 (written between 336 and 345); it is also found in Maruta of Maipherkat (c. 400) can. 25; the *Test. D. N. J. Christi* (of the second half of the fifth century) I 24; the *Synod* of the Katholikos Joseph, 554 can. 19. Chrysostom too, who like Origen appeals in the *De sacerdotio* 3, 6 to Jas 5:14 for the forgiveness of sins in penance, probably assumed that there was an anointing of penitents.[16] But this does not rule out the proper anointing of the sick. This is clear from the passage of Aphraates already mentioned in which he mentions both rites together: *ungit infirmos et per arcanum suum sacramentum paenitentes reducit.*[17]

For the West the first clear and informative evidence is provided by Pope Innocent I († 417) in chapter eight of his letter to Bishop Decentius. This contains an authoritative explanation of how to carry out in practice the prescriptions of Jas 5:14. It appears to have been occasioned by excessive claims on the

---

[15] Thus F. L. Dölger 148; C. Ruch 1935; F. Lehr 3; Poschmann I 337f.

[16] Further details on the witnesses cited in Dölger, ibid. 148f. and *ThR* 6 (1907) 552f. In the conception of sin as ethical sickness D. sees a transition from the anointing of the sick to the anointing with oil in baptismal exorcism. Sin is ethical possession and consequently has to be treated in the same way as bodily possession. For the cure of this an anointing was combined with the exorcism, and similarly from the first half of the third century (the *Acts of Thomas*) there is evidence of anointing in the exorcism before baptism (*Der Exorcismus* 137 ff. 148 ff.).

[17] For other testimonies for the anointing of the sick adduced with more or less justification (from Irenaeus, Tertullian, Hippolytus, Eusebius, Ephraem and others) see Kern and Ruch.

part of priests as against the bishop[18] in regard to control over penance. As the text of James only made mention of priests, it was alleged in support of the claim of the priests for independence in the administration of penance. Against this the Pope sets forth the true sense of the scriptural text: *Quod non est dubium de fidelibus aegrotantibus accipi et intelligi debere,*[19] *qui sancto oleo chrismatis perungi possunt, quod ab episcopo confectum non solum sacerdotibus, sed et omnibus christianis licet in sua aut in suorum necessitate ungendum.* If then anointing is not specially reserved to priests as against the laity, there can be no doubt that bishops have a prior right to do what is permitted to priests. The reason why only priests are mentioned by James is that bishops cannot visit all the sick in person. Obviously a bishop, who alone is entitled to consecrate chrism, is permitted to visit a sick person whenever he pleases, in order "to bless him and anoint him with oil". The text of James is not applicable to penitents for the reason that consecrated oil *genus est sacramenti,* and consequently may not be allowed to penitents any more than the other sacraments. The decretal became a basic document for the late Roman and early medieval period. It was incorporated in the most important canonical collections, and so became the starting-point for theological discussion of the sacrament. Its content is in substantial agreement with the oriental evidence which has been adduced. The anointing of the sick is an established usage; the consecration of the oil is recognized as the prerogative of the bishop. It is admitted that the consecrated oil serves not only for sacramental application by priests but also for personal use by the faithful. Priestly anointing, on the other hand, is a usage that is taken for granted, seeing that it is justified by the observation that the bishop by reason of his other obligations cannot visit all the sick in person. Private anointing, therefore, was not put on the same footing as that performed by priests. The applica-

---

[18] See Poschmann II 216f. and n. 3.
[19] The meaning is then *non de paenitentibus.*

tion of the text of James to penance is rejected. Moreover, the granting of the anointing of the sick to penitents is stated to be unlawful, in the same way as admission to other sacraments. Here the reference is primarily to the eucharist and then to ordination to the clerical state.[20] This association of anointing with the "rest of the sacraments" — *reliqua sacramenta* — even though it occurs at a time when the word sacrament had not yet the narrower fixed sense that it later acquired, does, however, clearly express the high regard in which priestly anointing of the sick was held. In regard to its effect nothing is added to what is said in the epistle of James. Moreover, it is impossible to tell from the letter whether its reception was obligatory or whether it was only a matter of counsel.

Indirect evidence for priestly anointing is found, correctly it would seem, in Augustine who cites the words of James concerning the sick along with other scriptural directives for the conduct of a Christian life (*Speculum, PL* 34 1036). Of him his biographer Possidius reports: *Si forte ab aegrotantibus peteretur, ut pro eis in praesenti Dominum rogaret eisque manus imponeret, sine mora pergebat* (*Vita Augustini* 27). Even more frequent, however, are accounts and recommendations of private anointings with oil blessed by the bishop. Sulpicius Severus (*Dial.* 2, 3) relates of St. Martin of Tours that the people had him bless oil *ad diversas morborum causas necessarium*. St. Caesarius of Arles warns the faithful against having recourse to pagan superstitious practices in times of sickness: "How much more right and salutary it would be if they made haste to the church... and piously anointed themselves and their family with holy oil; and in accordance with the words of the Apostle James received not only

---

[20] Cf. above 105. Whether anointing was given to sick penitents after reconciliation, as Lehr (11) assumes, appears to me already very doubtful in view of the unrestricted mode of formulation *(paenitentibus istud infundi non potest)*. Besides, the Pope's argument only makes sense if the function of the priests mentioned in Jas 5:14 does not come into question at all in the case of sick penitents. Cf. also can. 13 of Nicaea which says that a sick penitent despite the reception of *viaticum* remains subject to the laws of public penance (above 101).

health of body but also pardon of their sins."[21] This passage shows that James' instruction was also considered to be carried out by private anointing. Intelligibly enough, most people were content with this more convenient form of a domestic religious remedy. Priests were only summoned, if at all, in cases of grave sickness. As, however, from the fourth century onwards penance also was for the most part only received in time of sickness,[22] and anointing was refused to penitents in accordance with the decretal of Innocent I, priests will have had few opportunities of administering it.[23]

XVIII. Medieval Practice

IN STRIKING contrast to the silence of the preceding period, from the eighth, and especially from the ninth century onwards we are confronted with an abundance of clear and certain evidence for the sacrament. Mention has already been made of Bede as the earliest commentator on the epistle of James. He does, it is true, also allow the laity the use of consecrated oil, appealing to the authority of Pope Innocent, but he unambiguously makes the forgiveness of sins dependent on confession to a priest.[24] The Carolingian reform laid very great emphasis on the administration of the sacrament. It is mentioned in the capitularies of Charlemagne (769), and also by Theodulf of Orleans (789), Herard of Tours (858), Hincmar of Rheims (852), and the Synods of Chalon (813), Aachen (836), Mainz (847), Pavia (850), and Worms (868).[25] The *Statuta Bonifatii,* probably taken from a

---

[21] *Serm.* 279, 5, *PL* 39, 2273; cf. *Serm.* 265, 3 (2238). Similarly the work attributed to Giles of Noyon *De rectitudine cath. conversationis* 4, *PL* 40, 1172.
[22] See above 108.
[23] Some of the examples for the actual administration of the sacrament at that time taken by J. Kern 38 ff. from the *Acta Sanctorum* are open to critical doubts in respect of the reliability of the lives of the saints which are difficult to date. See on this P. Browe 517, who declares that it is "very unlikely" that at that time many of the faithful received the sacrament.
[24] *PL* 93, 39; cf. also *Expos. in Marc. Evang.* II, *PL* 92, 188.
[25] See Browe 518 f.; Lehr 15 f.

Burgundian synod of the years 800 to 840, require that priests on journeys should always have the holy oil with them as well as the eucharist. Particularly remarkable, in view of the earlier approved practice, is their prohibition under pain of deposition of delivering blessed oil to non-priests for use as a remedy or for any other purpose. The reason given is that it is *genus sacramenti* (*PL* 89, 821, 823). In similar fashion certain ordinances of this period forbid under grave penalties the sending of viaticum to the sick by means of laymen.[26] The sacramental character of anointing could not be better declared than by this putting of it on the same level as the eucharist.

Yet, however much the obligation of administering the sacrament was urged on priests and its reception on the faithful, practice lagged far behind the injunctions of the Church. Like Caesarius three hundred years earlier, Jonas of Orleans complained in his *Institutio laicalis* (3, 14), composed before 829, that in sickness the people hastened to sorcerers instead of receiving the holy oil from the Church as a remedy not only for the body but also for the soul. As a result of this, he adds, the administration of this sacrament has fallen into complete disuse. Throughout the entire middle ages bishops and synods felt they had cause to insist on the use of the sacrament,[27] and this presupposes a widespread contrary custom. It is true that in general no direct obligation of receiving it was imposed. Indeed, particular decrees expressly left it to the choice of the sick.[28] This is also evident from a number of biographies of saints.[29] Thus the widespread neglect of the sacrament is explicable. Laziness and indifference often kept priests from

---

[26] Hincmar, *Capit. presbyteris data* 10; *PL* 125, 779; Rather of Verona, *Synodica* 7; *PL* 136, 560.
[27] Instances in Browe 524 ff.
[28] Thus the synodal *Statuta* of Sonnatius of Rheims († 630) c. 15, *PL* 80, 443, which date from a later period, and the so-called *Canones Edgardi* (10th cent.) c. 65, *PL* 138, 504.
[29] See Browe 521.

visiting the sick and the faithful from troubling about the sacrament. Matters were made worse by the custom which soon developed of remunerating the priest for his services, and what was at first a free-will offering became in a very short time a considerable burden for poorer people.[30] Significant of this state of affairs is the admonition frequently addressed to priests that they should require not only the rich but also the poor to receive anointing. A further reason which deterred many from its reception was a mistaken notion that it carried with it certain obligations for the conduct of the rest of one's life. This misunderstanding is traceable to a confusion of unction with the sacrament of penance.

In contrast with the practice of antiquity, from the early middle ages anointing always appears along with confession and viaticum as a regular element in the provisions for the sick. The reason for this may well be sought in the introduction into the West of the oriental custom, already considered, of anointing even ordinary penitents. First employed in Spain and Gaul for the reception of heretics, the rite also gained admission into the general *Penitential of Halitgar* (829/30), whence we may deduce that it became customary in certain other places.[31] As anointing itself thus became an element in penance, the law prohibiting its concession to sick penitents was rendered ineffective. In their case penitential anointing and anointing of the sick coincided as remedies for spiritual and bodily healing. Hence in the *ordines* for the penance of the sick anointing was simply incorporated

---

[30] On the misunderstandings arising from the introduction of stole-fees see Browe 526—534. The anointing of the sick offered special opportunities for the avarice of the clergy. Thus in the thirteenth century many parish priests claimed the linen sheets on which the sick man was anointed, others the candles which were lit during the anointing (ibid. 530f.). According to an anonymous writer from Passau (1260) some declared that the presence of several priests and twelve candles was necessary for unction, and that no one should ask for it to be administered who was not worth at least two cows.

[31] Fuller detail in J. A. Jungmann, *Die lateinischen Bußriten* 60f. 146f. 150f.

into the rite of penance.[32] The order of the three sacraments, however, showed some variation. According to Theodulf of Orleans and the sacramentaries of St. Denis (of the mid-ninth century) and Fulda (of the tenth century) the place of the anointing was between the acts of the reception of penance and reconciliation.[33] This placing of it before reconciliation should not surprise us, in view of the still unclear conceptions of sacraments and of their effects. However, the Synod of Pavia (850), with a reference to the decretal of Innocent I, protested against the practice, and forbade the administration of anointing to a sick public penitent before he had become worthy of holy communion by the reception of reconciliation. Up to the twelfth century and beyond by far the most usual order was therefore: penance inclusive of reconciliation, anointing, viaticum.[34] This arrangement brought out the meaning of anointing as the completion of penance. Here and there, however, even at that time the eucharist was given before the anointing and from approximately the twelfth and thirteenth centuries this order has been usual and has maintained its position until the present day. [In the United States of America anointing has regained its earlier place prior to viaticum in the new *Collectio Rituum* of 1954. Tr.'s note.]

This conception of anointing as a specific element of the penance of the sick may well have been the principal reason for the reluctance of the faithful to receive it. It should be recalled that in antiquity penance of the sick was regarded as public penance, and where there was a recovery it entailed certain obligations in regard to the conduct of life, apparel and sexual

---

[32] Halitgar's *ordo* for confession, inclusive of anointing, was significantly incorporated into the Romano-German pontifical in the 10th century as an *ordo paenitentis ad mortem* (Jungmann 151). The *Life of St. Tresanus* (6th cent.) which dates from a later period speaks of the *oleum reconciliationis* which the saint received before his death after making his confession (Browe 517 n. 7).
[33] Instances in Jungmann 114f.; Lehr 33f.
[34] Instances in Browe 550f.; Lehr 18.

abstinence, in similar fashion to the *conversio ad vitam paenitentium*.[35] This judgement persisted into the middle ages. It found external expression in the provision made in a number of *ordines* for a penitential garment *(cilicium)* for the sick at the reception of penance.[36] Men of the early middle ages often had themselves clothed in a religious habit shortly before death, as they were desirous of dying as penitents, and this carried with it the obligation of the vows and customs of the order.[37] This practice explains a conception which was widespread throughout the middle ages, especially from the eleventh century to the fifteenth, which the Church had constantly to combat.[38] It was thought that anointing, which was a characteristic feature of penance of the sick, and which also was associated with the ancient solemn rite of penance, carried with it the obligations mentioned above, and that those who received it had to renounce marital intercourse and the eating of flesh meat in addition to other consequences.[39] This idea was naturally a deterrent to the use of the sacrament, and as a result, even if it was not altogether refused, it was put off until the last moment. This is the reason why it was called "extreme unction" *(extrema unctio)*, a designation which is first attested in the tenth or the eleventh century, and was much used from the end of the twelfth.[40] In this way anointing became more and more a sacrament of the dying, although this corresponded neither to its nature as a remedy against sickness nor to the directives of the Church, which even in the early middle ages required a serious but by no means a hopeless sickness as a condition for its administration. These pronouncements certainly emphasized spiritual healing, yet bodily healing was by no means excluded; in fact often it

---

[35] Above 105 ff. and Poschmann II 150 289 ff.
[36] Lehr 32f.
[37] L. Gougaud, *Dévotions et pratiques ascétiques du moyen-âge* (1925) 129—142.
[38] Instances in Browe 557f.
[39] It is therefore not just a question of "a senseless superstition" and "comical opinions" as J. Kern (*ZkTh* 1906, 611) describes it.
[40] Browe 557 n. 4

was expressly given prominence.[41] When the Greeks, therefore, from Symeon of Thessalonica (1430) onwards reproach the Latin Church with corrupting the faith on the grounds that it has transformed the sacrament of the healing of the sick into a sacrament of the dying, their complaint is unwarranted. The objection is valid against an undeniable abuse, but not against the teaching of the Church and the practice approved by her.[42]

The rite of the administration of the sacrament, and not just of the ceremonial surrounding it, continued to be very various right into the high middle ages. In general all that was required was the anointing by priests with oil blessed by the bishop accompanied by prayer. This was in accordance with the practice of the early Church. It is clear from the Gelasian and Gregorian sacramentaries that in the Roman Church the blessing of the oil took place on Maundy Thursday. In regions where other liturgies were in use it was not connected with any particular solemnity but was performed before the administration of the sacrament. The oil of the sick, which was also that distributed for private use by the faithful, was at first probably the same as the oil of catechumens. Theodulf, and also Amalarius of Metz († 850) only distinguish between it and chrism, while Radulfus of Bourges († 869) makes express mention of it in addition to the oil of catechumens.[43] The anointing was made in the form of a cross on the most various parts of the body. The *Capitulare* of Theodulf provides for no fewer than fifteen anointings, but remarks that the Apostles only employed three, and that the Greeks in imitation of the Apostles observed the same practice, while others even exceeded fifteen and went up to twenty or more (*PL* 105, 221). Menard's edition of the *Gregorianum* names as parts to be anointed: the neck, the throat, the region between the shoulders, the breast, and the parts which are particularly painful; but observes that many anointed

---

[41] Instances in Browe 835.
[42] On this see J. Kern, *ZkTh* (1906) 597—624.
[43] See F. Lehr 30f.

in addition the five senses (*PL* 78, 235).[44] The same variety characterized the sacramental formulae which were in use; some of them were indicative, some deprecative, some mixed.[45] Some *ordines* have a special prayer for every part anointed, while others have the same formula for all, except that the particular part to be anointed is indicated. The form in use today is found already almost word for word in *Ordo Romanus* X, the papal pontifical of the thirteenth and fourteenth centuries.[46] An interesting feature of a whole series of *ordines* from the ninth to the twelfth century, beginning with the *Capitulare* of Theodulf is that the anointing is prescribed for seven successive days. At that time, when the concept of a sacrament was still unclarified, this repetition is not more astonishing than the repetition of absolutions. What men saw in these, and also in the anointing of the sick, was essentially a particularly efficacious prayer of the Church, the power of which could only be enhanced by repetition. Considerations of this kind led men to seek both absolution and anointing at the hands of several priests or bishops. An example of this appears in Bishop Hildebold of Soissons who petitioned both Hincmar of Rheims and the bishops assembled with him for absolution.[47]

The *Rituale* of Theodulf directs that the anointing be administered in church. This is in line with the frequently attested custom of laying the dying in front of the altar.[48] Obviously this regulation could not be generally observed, and is enough by itself to show that the reception of the sacrament was only expected to be of rare occurrence. The Carolingian capitularies of the ninth century also made provision for the administration in the sick man's dwelling in the same solemn form as in the church.

---

[44] Fuller detail in Lehr 38 f.; Ruch 1982 f.
[45] Examples in Kern, *De sacr. extrem. unct.* 146 f.
[46] See Lehr 42 ff.
[47] See Poschmann III 221 ff. This disposes of the artificial explanation with which J. Kern (338—345) attempts at great length to account for the administration of anointing for seven days. Cf. on this Ruch 1980 f.
[48] Browe 544.

Strictly speaking, that required the presence of several priests,[49] in accordance with the tenor of the text of St. James. However, the Carolingian capitularies laid the obligation of administering the sacrament only on the parish priest, without mention of participation by other priests. Nevertheless, this was regarded as more appropriate and correct right into the high middle ages.[50] In any case the expense connected with such a solemn form was an obstacle to the reception of the sacrament by ordinary folk.

XIX. THE THEOLOGY OF THE ANOINTING OF THE SICK

As IN other sacraments, so too here it was the scholastics who first set about the task of a systematic elaboration of the material which had been handed down in the regulations and rites of the Church and in the pronouncements of the Fathers and of theologians. The first point to be considered was its character as a sacrament. With Hugh of St. Victor (*De sacr.* II 15, 1) and Peter Lombard (IV *Sent.* d. 23 c. 1) the early scholastics at first distinguished three kinds of ecclesiastical anointings: those of baptism, confirmation and of the sick. Later, private anointing of the sick, administered also by laymen, was added to form a fourth kind; this, however, was not held to be a sacrament but charismatical in character, and was said to be no longer in use.[51] Accordingly, from the time when the septenary number was first attested only the *unctio solemnis infirmorum* appears in the list of sacraments properly so called. This is the designation employed by the unknown author of the *Sententiae divinitatis,* the first witness to the septenary number.[52]

In the twelfth century the institution of the sacrament is almost unanimously ascribed to the Apostles. Alexander of

---

[49] Thus Theodulf, Menard's *Gregorianum* and the *Fulda Sacramentary* (10th cent.).
[50] Thus St. Thomas, *C. gent.* IV 73.
[51] Thus Peter the Chanter and Robert Courçon. MSS texts in Weisweiler, *Sch* (1932) 327 f.
[52] See L. Godefroy, *DTC* V 1988.

Hales and St. Bonaventure (IV *Sent.* d. 23 a. 1 q. 1) also express this view. St. Thomas, on the other hand, holds that it is more probable that Christ instituted all the sacraments *per seipsum,* but that he only promulgated some of them personally, leaving the others, such as confirmation and anointing, to be promulgated by the Apostles (*Suppl.* q. 29 a. 3). St. Albert holds the same opinion (IV *Sent.* d. 23 a. 13), while Scotus takes a step further and asserts that the institution of all the sacraments by Christ is not only the more probable opinion, but that it is to be held as certain — *pro certo supponendum* (*Report.* IV d. 23 n. 9). However, the difference is one of terminology rather than of fact. Frequently the "promulgation" of the sacrament was also described as its "institution", even though the attachment of divine power to the outward sign, and consequently "institution" in the proper sense, was attributed to Christ. The Council of Trent in stating the dogma has expressly distinguished between *instituere* and *promulgare,* and left room for a closer determination of the concept of institution.[53]

In view of the unanimous tradition of the Church no doubt could exist concerning the matter of the sacrament. St. Thomas explained the appropriateness of oil, more particularly of olive oil to which in his opinion the term "oil" primarily applies (*Suppl.* q. 29 a. 4). Following the Lombard (d. 23 n. 3), it was unanimously required for the validity of the sacrament that the oil should be consecrated by a bishop. St. Thomas teaches that sacramental power is first given to the oil through its consecration (*Suppl.* q. 29 a. 6). Clearly the decisive reason for this view was tradition, as St. Bonaventure says: *sic enim institutum est fieri* (d. 23 a. 1 q. 3 ad 4). Similarly the Council of Trent declares that the Church has thus understood tradition (Denz. 908). The opinion of some later theologians (Sainte-Beuve, Juénin), that the Council has only prescribed

---

[53] Fuller details on the whole question in Franz Scholz, *Die Lehre von der Einsetzung der Sakramente bei Alexander von Hales* (1940).

episcopal consecration of the oil as a regulation, and not as necessary for validity, has been rejected in two decisions of the Holy Office, in 1611 and 1842, as *temeraria et errori proxima* (Denz. 1628, 1629). On the other hand, the position of Suarez and Estius, that consecration of the oil by a bishop is so indispensable that not even the pope can delegate a simple priest to perform it, is also untenable. Against it is the fact that the Church recognizes the rite of the uniate Greeks in which priests consecrated the oil of the sick. On the question concerning the parts of the body to be anointed St. Albert (d. 23 a. 2) and St. Thomas (q. 32 a. 6) declare that the anointing of the five senses which is universally observed follows *quasi de necessitate sacramenti*. St. Bonaventure and Scotus mention in addition the anointing of the loins and the feet, without, however, expressing any opinion on its necessity, and were followed in this by the *Decretum pro Armenis* (Denz. 700). Account being taken of the quite different earlier practice in which the anointing of the senses was often quite unknown, St. Thomas' opinion is untenable and has been abandoned by post-Tridentine theologians. According to canon 947 of the Code of Canon Law, "in case of necessity a single anointing on one sense, or more correctly on the forehead, is sufficient".

In connexion with the form of the sacrament, the varieties of which were not unknown to the scholastics, the chief problem considered was whether an indicative form was also sufficient for the valid administration of the sacrament. By that time the present-day formula expressed in deprecative terms was already in fairly general use. The great masters of the high scholastic period declared that the deprecative form was necessary, appealing to Jas 5:14. They believed that they could solve the difficulty of rituals with indicative forms by the suggestion that these were followed by another prayer which was to be regarded as the proper form of the sacrament.[54] This opinion appeared

---

[54] Albert, d. 23 a. 4; Thomas, *Suppl.* q. 29 a. 8 ad 3.

to be confirmed by the *Decretum pro Armenis* which simply laid down that the formula *Per istam sanctam unctionem* ... is the form of extreme unction. Other distinguished scholastics, however, such as Richard of Mediavilla, Paludanus and Aureolus, maintained that indicative formulae were also valid. Their view later received very impressive support, when, from the seventeenth century onwards, great scholarly publications uncovered indicative formulae in an abundance hitherto unsuspected. At that time the controversy revived and still exists today. A solution is either sought with Suarez to the effect that the indicative formula always virtually includes a prayer, or, following the lead of Tournely, recourse is had to a broader statement of the concept of "institution", and it is taught that Christ did not himself determine the formula of unction, but left its determination to the Church.[55]

The most difficult question which the anointing of the sick has raised for speculative theology concerns its effect. According to James and the whole of tradition it consists in a remission of sins and in healing of sickness. However, as Hugh of St. Victor informs us, some were hesitant in regarding bodily healing as the fruit of the sacrament, and wished to consider it solely as the effect of the "prayer of faith". Hugh himself maintained that both effects are produced by the sacrament. The healing of the soul is the primary effect; bodily healing is conditional on whether it is really beneficial for the sick man (*De sacr.* II 15, 3).[56] In general the early scholastics agreed with this view, and were divided only on the closer determination of the spiritual effect. The remission of sins was limited by individual theologians to certain sins — *quaedam peccata* (Roland), or to "the greater part of the sins" (*Epitome Theologiae Christianae*), or to venial sins (Peter Comestor). Others spoke in positive fashion of "spiritual

---

[55] See L. Godefroy 2010f.; J. Kern 152—166.
[56] To preclude misunderstandings, H. Weisweiler 338ff. points out the distinction made at the time between the reality conferred (*res*) and the effect (*efficacia*). The *res* was restricted to the interior effects in the soul.

recovery" (Hugh, Peter Lombard, Alan of Lille), of an "increase of grace" (Robert Courçon), of a special grace of the Holy Ghost which imparts a "specific splendour" to the body in the life to come (Roland), of a "preparation for the vision of God" etc.[57] The great scholastics were only taking over these ideas when they attributed to unction the elimination of all obstacles to entrance to heavenly glory, and saw in it the consummation of the efforts of the Church for the salvation of the soul. This was the teaching of St. Thomas (*C. gent.* IV c. 73), St. Bonaventure (*Brevil.* VI c. 11), Scotus, Durandus and of all theologians of note of the fourteenth and fifteenth centuries.[58] Theology, however, was still in search of a fuller answer to the problem of the principal effect of the sacrament: that on account of which it was instituted, and from which the other effects flow for the perfection of the soul.

St. Bonaventure (d. 23 a. 1 q. 1) and Scotus and his school after him saw the principal effect in the remission of venial sins which weigh on the soul of the dying man and prevent his complete abandonment to God. St. Thomas rejected this opinion on the grounds that contrition suffices for the pardon of venial sins. For him the primary end of anointing is the elimination of the *reliquiae peccati.* These are the result of original sin as well as of personal sins, and consist of weakness and unfitness *(debilitas et ineptitudo)* and of lack of strength and vigour *(ut non habeat perfectum vigorem ad actus vitae, gratiae vel gloriae).* The sacramental strengthening is, however, the work of grace, and because grace is incompatible with sin it also forgives *ex consequenti* sins which still remain, provided the sick man does not interpose an obstacle to this effect by an unrepentant frame of mind. The forgiveness extends not only to venial but also to mortal sins. On this view remission of sins is an effect of grace which occurs only in certain circumstances, and is not the primary effect towards which the sacrament tends; the sacra-

[57] Weisweiler 336—350.
[58] Instances in Kern 89—98.

mental grace — *gratia sacramentalis* — is the healing of the infirmity of sin — *infirmitas peccati* (*Suppl.* q. 30 a. 1). The diversity of views persisted through the centuries. The Thomist view also gave rise to further, fresh disputes which concerned the nature of the *reliquiae peccati*. Benedict XIV declared that the question of the primary effect of unction was an idle and unprofitable one.[59]

According to the general teaching of the early scholastics only one who is seriously sick is the subject of anointing. Disputed questions were: whether it should be given at the beginning of the sickness, or only in immediate danger of death; whether it should be given to unconscious persons, to the irresponsible and to children, or whether it should only be given at the request of the sick man.[60] In the high scholastic period attempts to find answers to these questions were based on the primary effect of the sacrament. St. Thomas taught that, as it is the final remedy which produces the immediate disposition for glory (*ultimum remedium quasi immediate disponens ad gloriam*), it should only be given to those about to depart this life (*in statu exeuntium*, [*Suppl.* q. 32 a. 2]). St. Bonaventure goes even further and says that administration is only lawful when it is "presumed" that death is imminent (d. 23 a. 1 q. 1). Scotus states the ultimate reason for this: if the principal effect of anointing is the remission of venial sins, in order that the dying man may be sent forth into eternity free from all sin, the sacrament can only exhibit its complete effect where the sick man is no longer capable of sinning (*qui non potest amplius peccare*, Ox. IV d. 23 n. 3). On this view anointing must be ruled out as a remedy for sickness. This extreme doctrine which would deny the grace of the sacrament to a great part of the dying found no favour outside the Scotist school. The *Decretum pro Armenis* says in general: *Hoc sacramentum nisi infirmo, de cuius morte timetur, dari non debet*

---

[59] Cf. Kern 168—241; F. Diekamp, *Kath. Dogmatik* III[6] (1932) 324f.
[60] See H. Weisweiler 542—554. Peter the Chanter and his pupil Robert Courçon in particular discussed the questions in detail.

(Denz. 700), the Council of Trent uses similar words (Denz. 910), and the Code of Canon Law, can. 940, § 1, speaks of danger of death through sickness or old age.

If the essential purpose of anointing is the overcoming of spiritual weakness arising from sin, only those are qualified to receive it who are capable of fighting against this weakness in a responsible way. Hence the scholastics are unanimous in teaching that it may not be given to infants who are incapable of sinning (St. Thomas, q. 32 a. 4). There was, however, considerable variation in the age proposed for lawful reception. Exceptionally, seven to nine years of age is mentioned, usually, however, it is deferred until the age of fourteen, and occasionally of eighteen. After the Council of Trent it was often stated that those who were admitted to communion were also capable of receiving extreme unction. In practice this also came to fourteen years of age. The present-day practice of administering it at the age when a child is able to go to confession began in the seventeenth century.[61]

The principle governing the administration of the sacrament to infants applies also to the mentally deranged. The scholastics teach that it is to be refused to them too, unless they have lucid intervals in which they can receive it with devotion. By this St. Thomas means actual devotion, not just habitual devotion. In the latter case the sacrament could be efficacious by reason of a previous act of devotion consciously elicited. In contrast with baptism, which is a remedy for original sin, he expressly requires for anointing a movement of free will — *motus liberi arbitrii* (q. 32 a. 3 ad 2).[62] Later theology and particularly ecclesiastical practice has abandoned the view of the *Doctor communis* on this matter which logically rules out the administration of the sacrament to the unconscious. If an intention of receiving

---

[61] Instances in Browe 539 f.
[62] On the *motus liberi arbitrii* cf. above 164 f and 169 f.
[63] Cf. *Rituale Romanum* tit. V c. 1 n. 6.

the sacrament and the requisite dispositions can be presumed, it may be conferred.[63]

How often may the last anointing be received? This question was hotly disputed especially in the early scholastic period. In certain quarters it was administered once only, and repetition was excluded on principle.[64] In a letter which he wrote to Master Simon, Ivo touches on the question and probably gives the correct explanation of this attitude when he says: "the anointing of the sick is the sacrament of public penance, and Augustine and Ambrose testify that like baptism it cannot be repeated" (*PL* 157, 88).[65] However, the contrary usage of a repetition of the sacrament was far more prevalent both in practice and in the teaching of theologians. The principal reason adduced was the purpose of the last anointing *si morbus non revertitur, medicina non iteratur ; si autem morbus non potest cohiberi, quare deberet medicina prohiberi?*[66] ("if the disease does not return the medicine should not be repeated; but if it cannot be checked, why should the medicine be forbidden?") The practical question of when and how often repetition is permissible must be distinguished from the question of principle. Many held that a repetition of the sacrament during the same sickness, or in others which follow each other in quick succession, should be allowed only after the expiry of one year.[67] It was only gradually that more frequent repetition became customary. St. Thomas, however, taught quite clearly that in the event of a fresh illness a renewed application of the spiritual remedy is necessary, just as in a cure for the body, and that a repetition of the sacrament is only unlawful within the same danger of death (q. 33 a. 1—2). The Council of Trent endorsed this principle. So too by the

---

[64] This is attested by Godfrey of Vendôme († 1132), Ivo of Chartres († 1117), Master Simon (mid-twelfth cent.) and others. See H. Weisweiler 524f.; J. Kern 331 ff.
[65] A confirmation of our statement above 245.
[66] Hugh of St. Victor, *De sacr.* II 15, 3.
[67] Thus, *e. g.* Albert, d. 23 a. 21; William Durandus (1230—1296) finds the custom attested in certain rituals: *Rationale div. officiorum* (1286—91) I c. 8 n. 25.

sanction which it gave in general to the doctrines worked out by the scholastics it brought the development of the dogmatic teaching on the anointing of the sick to a close for the time being. The attitude of the post-Tridentine theologians to questions that remained open has already been indicated in the discussion of individual topics.

The assertions of the Council were directed against the Reformers who rejected the sacrament of anointing altogether. They interpreted the directions in the epistle of James, which they held to be unauthentic, in the sense of a miraculous charismatic healing of the sick, and they claimed that this had ceased with the extinction of charismata.[68] There is also a certain opposition on the part of the Greek Orthodox to the teaching of the Church on anointing. Their symbolical books clearly acknowledge the εὐχέλαιον as one of the seven sacraments instituted by Christ, but there are notable differences in regard to the matter and form as well as in the rite. These are, however, of an incidental character. Of dogmatic importance is an opposite conception of the principal effect of the sacrament. The Greeks have traditionally[69] held that this consists predominantly in bodily healing, and they only attribute minor importance to spiritual healing. Connected with this is the fact that among them anointing may often serve as a preparation for communion, being administered even to the healthy. This is the opposite extreme to the Scotist conception[70] indicated above.

---

[68] Luther, *De capt. Babyl.* n. 184—192; Calvin, *Institutio rel. christ.* IV 19 n. 18—29.
[69] See above 238.
[70] See on this K. Lübeck, op. cit. 318—341, and Th. Spáčil, *Doctrina Orientis separati de s. infirmorum Unctione* (Rome 1931).

Lucien Cerfaux

CHRIST IN THE THEOLOGY
OF ST. PAUL

This book is more concerned than most works of its kind in seeing the gradual evolution of St. Paul's thought on Christology. Where others have divided the subject into categories that they themselves have superimposed upon it, Msgr. Cerfaux divides it into three parts, following the chronological order of the Epistles (Thessalonians, Corinthians, Galatians, Romans, Captivity Epistles). Thus he obtains a truer picture of St. Paul's work and sees each part as a distinct attempt by St. Paul to form a synthesis.

Thessalonians: Christ as the agent of salvation through his Death, Resurrection and Parousia.

Corinthians — Galatians — Romans: Christ's Death and Resurrection as the present life of the Christian, the heavenly wisdom for Greeks and the heavenly justification for Jews.

Captivity Epistles: Christ as God's mystery of salvation now revealed.

The basic content of each part is the same. It is the faith of the primitive community with its foundation in the Old Testament and in Judaism. But each takes a different pattern according to its changing center of reference, so that the progress from one part to another affords a more and more complete synthesis of Christology, a deeper and deeper insight into the meaning of Christ.

"This book is a monumental study of Pauline Christology."
American Ecclesiastical Review

"Even veteran students of St. Paul will find this work excitingly thought-provoking." *Catholic Biblical Quarterly*

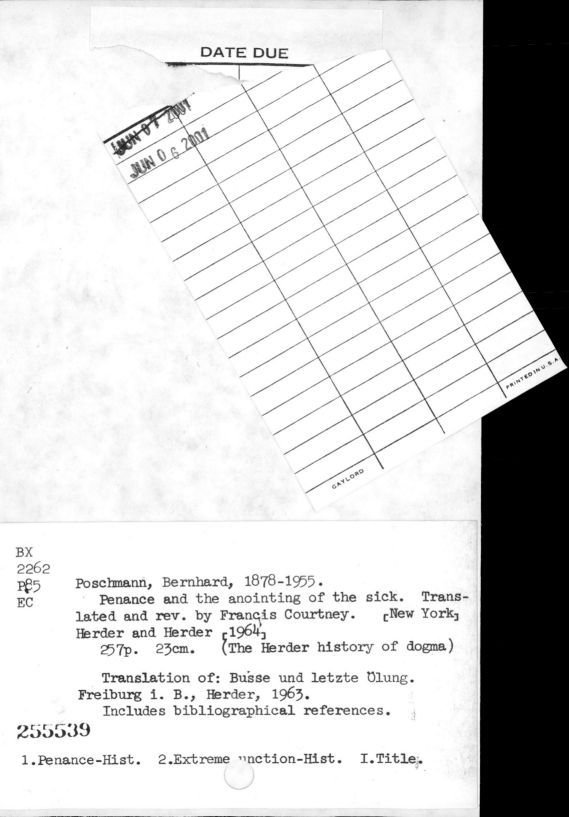